THE WAY
They
WERE

The WAY THEY WERE

DEALING WITH YOUR PARENTS' DIVORCE AFTER A LIFETIME OF MARRIAGE

BROOKE LEA FOSTER

with a foreword by Ian Birky, Ph.D.

THREE RIVERS PRESS
NEW YORK

Copyright © 2006 by Brooke Lea Foster
Foreword copyright © 2006 by Ian Birky, Ph.D.

Library of Congress Cataloging-in-Publication Data
Foster, Brooke Lea.
The way they were / Brooke Lea Foster.—1st ed.
Includes bibliographical references.
1. Divorce. 2. Adult children of divorced parents. I. Title.
HQ814.F779 2006
306.89—dc22   2005009423

ISBN-13: 978-1-4000-8210-0
ISBN-10: 1-4000-8210-2

Printed in the United States of America

Design by Namik Minter

10 9 8 7 6 5 4 3 2

First Edition

To my sisters, because we were in this together.

Acknowledgments

So many individuals took time out of their lives to share their stories with me, and I cannot thank you enough. While your identity is disguised in this book, I will not forget who you are. It takes courage to talk about your fears and insecurities, especially as adults, and each of you did it with grace. This book is my gift to you.

Thanks to Harmony and Three Rivers Press for believing in this project from the get-go. You are a wonderful family, and you treated me with a tenderness and care that I've been told has become an anomaly in publishing. My editor, Julie Will, supported this book wholeheartedly from the proposal onward, and it's because of her sharp eye and unfailing heart that you're holding these pages today.

Harmony wouldn't have even seen my idea if superagent Gail Ross didn't coach me through a proposal. Gail, your enthusiasm is inspiring. And thanks to Ian Birky for writing a wonderful foreword.

You get very few chances in life to thank all of the people who lifted you up along the way. Each one is just as important as the next. So I thank J. D. Salinger and Jane Austen for making me fall in love with words as a teenager, my zany high school English teacher, Mike Stegman, who told me I could write, and my college mentor, Georgia Sorenson, who offered vision, guidance, and, of course, leadership at a time when I was trying to figure out who the heck I was.

I'm not sure where I would have landed if the legendary Jack Limpert hadn't offered me a job at the *Washingtonian* in 1999. He's allowed me to grow in dozens of directions, all the while encouraging me to tackle lengthy narrative stories that few publications are willing to publish. Bill O'Sullivan, you're the editor every writer dreams of. You've improved my stories by leaps and bounds. To my office buddy, Cindy, your early readings of this book gave me the courage to turn it in. You are a true friend.

There are lots of others who offered love and support: Carol Guensburg, Robin Gerber, Stefanie Weiss, Carin and Laurie Daddino, Heather Hewitt, David Foster and all of the other Fosters, Carol Ann Guido, Patricia Simon, Ivan Sciupac, all of the editors at the *Washingtonian*, Joseph Lekuton, Nimfa and Donato Vargas, Sylvia Lang, and my grandmother, Marie Foster. I value my relationship with each of you.

Mom, without your talents as a writer I may not have had any of my own. As a child, you taught me to be curious about the world and the people in it, encouraging me to study daily life like an anthropologist. As an adult, I count you as a best friend.

Dad, you were able to make us laugh during times when we wanted to cry. I can't thank you enough for saying: "Let it all out, Brock."

Last, I wouldn't be who I am today if I hadn't met John Vargas ten years ago. You are yin to my yang, and your belief in love, our love, is what saw me through this.

Contents

Foreword by Ian Birky, Ph.D.   xi

Introduction   1

1 Ready, Set, Grieve   15

2 Who's the Parent, Who's the Child?   45

3 Caught in the Middle   83

4 Without Family   119

5 The Trouble with Stepfamilies   155

6 Truth, Lies, and Parents Who Cheat   193

7 Love Can Last   237

8 Going Home   269

Select Bibliography   291

Index   295

Foreword
Ian Birky, Ph.D.

A New Lens

During particular moments throughout my life, I have walked nature trails with a park ranger, gazed at the heavens with an astronomer, and toured art museums with a curator. I seldom pursue such assistance, however, because I generally hike, star gaze, and browse museums alone or with friends, and I do not forgo my more individualistic tendencies by asking others to show me how to do what I already spend much time doing. Nonetheless, when I've chosen to "sit at the feet of a teacher" who has committed to studying these areas professionally, I have had the profound experience of feeling as though my eyes were fitted with new lenses such that I could suddenly "see" added dimensions in objects that I previously thought I had seen in their entirety. I use the word *profound*, because with these new lenses I often felt I gained a better perspective of what I looked upon, a deeper appreciation of its uniqueness, and a greater understanding for how the pieces fitted together. I found myself amzed both by what I was seeing as well as what I had failed to see before. In a similar way, my experience conversing with Brooke and reading her book on adult children of divorce has left me aware of how much more there is to see. It is as though I have been given new lenses to see what I have been looking at for many years and now realize I had seen only in part.

As a psychotherapist working primarily with college and university students, I have encountered and heard the life stories of many young adults. I often listen to those stories within the context of particular frameworks of diagnoses or general life themes, whether as stories revealing depression or anxiety or about relationship conflict, disappointment, or loss. With professional colleagues, I have often reflected on questions about the essential features of psychotherapy and why counseling is curative. I have come to the partial conclusion that verbalizing one's life story in its imagistic detail, experiencing the emotions that either did occur or would have understandably occurred, and attaching some understanding, belief construct, or meaning to the experience is part of how we become, understand, and accept who we are. To tell and feel these stories is essential to being human. To do this in the presence of someone or a group of individuals committed to empathizing with and natured to cherish the experience, and the selves that emerge through the sharing of the stories, brings wholeness to our lives. This occurs because whether we admit to it or not, we are communal beings and our stories ultimately embody their deepest meaning within a shared social context.

In reading this book about the same-age persons with whom I spend time professionally, I was struck by how Brooke and her storytelling participants seem to understand how fundamentally important it is to tell and share the experienced stories of their lives. The author often uses her story and the telling of other's stories to capture the truth about the hurt and confusion of parental divorce. There is even an implicit recognition that most sharing of stories occurs in our daily interactions with friends, acquaintances, family members, and even strangers, and that for most people, these everyday storytelling occasions suffice such that we can honestly respond with the word *fine* when faced with the question "how are you?" But she also admits that for herself, and it is certainly the case for many of the young adults with whom I work, those everyday encounters of story-telling do not always suffice. They fail to do so because it is some-times too difficult to find compassionate and empathic listeners who are comfortable with, or accepting of, the full range of variance in the human experience. They are also insufficient because we and our friends tend to believe the myth fostered in our culture that only young children are affected enough by divorce to warrant automatic recommendations to see a therapist, thus perpetrating the notion that only the "stories" of young children are profoundly influenced by divorce. Like my clients, her storytellers and their listening friends grew up with the myth that an adult child should have no difficulty detaching and letting parents "work it out between themselves." They heard that they should be mature enough to avoid getting per-sonally involved or becoming deeply affected. Some relied on the myth to help them "suck it up" and move on with their lives.

Because the general population is sometimes prone to believe in and support such myths, it is no surprise that as a psychotherapist, some of my work with adult clients includes helping them to accept that it is normal and even expectable to want to talk about painful feelings, frightening thoughts, or yearned-for fantasies. But as evi-dence about the use of bibliotherapy and the self-help phenomenon in psychology has shown, this need not happen only in the thera-pist's office. What Brooke does so insightfully in her book is to pro-vide a lens that captures the multifaceted components of truth related to dealing with parental divorce. She artfully reveals in the stories told how important it is for adults to speak of their experi-ences, and in so doing, affirm the validity of the myriad thoughts and feelings sometimes suppressed, but always experienced, when reacting to the reality that their parents have divorced and that the parameters of home and personal identity defined within the con-text of family has changed. Her book offers a lens that allows the reader to become personally or more consciously aware of the uniqueness of this group of young adults struggling to make sense of their experience of parental divorce. It provides a lens to frame the experience of what happened and to reveal there is an oftentimes shared similarity in undergoing the experience. Her words and bulleted recommendations at the end of each chapter helped me better understand and empathize with the isolation and aloneness a number of my student clients have spoken of, when admitting, almost with some embarrassment, the multitude feelings of shame, hurt, abandonment, anger, lost identity, confusion, homelessness, and fear they experienced upon learning of their parents' termination of their marriage. With the gift of her lenses, I am more conscious that despite these students feeling devastated when hearing of their parents' divorce, they did not fully disclose their story because some of them bought into the myth that they should be thankful that their parents waited to divorce until they were "grown up" and that only young children are deeply affected by it. For her readers, this book offers confirmation and affirmation of the legitimacy of their stories—and will perhaps give them permission to protest, as Augusten did in *Running with Scissors*: "It's not just between you because I'm here too."

Finally, I would share one other thought. As a psychotherapist working in a university, I frequent a list-serve comprised of a group of national and international peers given to cyberspace dialogue about salient issues and dynamics of matters related to the seventeen-to-fifty-year-old student clients we see (the range is actually broader than that, although most of the students I've seen fall within those parameters). Almost weekly, one of my colleagues asks the list-serve members whether anyone knows of books that could be helpful to a student dealing with issues such as an eating disorder, disability, loss of a pet, sexual assault, or about how to grieve or express anger. For an inquiry regarding an appropriate book for adults struggling with the divorce of their parents, I now have the ideal book to place on the recommendation list or to add to the self-help section of their website. This text by Brooke Lea Foster may well become a "must read" for those many persons struggling to identify and accept the numerous recognized and sometimes unnamed feelings and thoughts they experienced upon being told of the occasionally surprising and frequently long-dreaded divorce of their parents. It will be equally valued by those persons committed to listening with greater empathy and compassion to those who have that particular story to tell.

"He who wants to tear down a house must
be prepared to rebuild it."
—African proverb

THE WAY
They
WERE

Introduction

Losing Our Nests

These things are not glorified, just recorded. Tattooed on the heart; burned into the family's history. This piecing together of the life of your child; this homage, this attempt to put it all in order; and even though you will one day wish for the heartbreak to leave you, it never will.

—WHITNEY OTTO, *How to Make an American Quilt*

I WANT TO SCREAM, CRY, BANG MY HEAD AGAINST A WALL. Instead, I push the phone hard against my ear, cradling it under my chin, so I can answer an e-mail from my editor while I listen. Mom is on the other end. She's yelling—so loud I fear my coworkers in the next office can hear. There are no pauses when Mom gets mad. She vents the way a tidal wave unfurls. Every second she goes on, she gets angrier and angrier, ranting about things we've all done wrong, creating one big ball of tension headed straight toward me.

"Dad said he'd go," I interrupt her. "Why can't you just *try* couples therapy?"

I've said the wrong thing—again—which makes Mom launch into a tangent about how she's been alone in her marriage for years, even before she decided my father needed to move out six months ago. Even before she had her lawyer draw up the separation papers. Did I even know what my father was putting *her* through? Did I know that she had to change the locks on the house because my father was showing up when he felt like it and snooping through her things? Did I know that someone's been driving past the house late at night?

Head is spinning. Forehead's sweating. Heart is breaking. My editor pops into my office. I'm on the phone with one of my parents nearly every day at work. I can barely concentrate on my article. Has my editor noticed? I panic, thinking I'm going to get fired. I force a smile, hold up my pointer finger, and mouth, "One minute." When my editor disappears down the hall, I say, quietly, "You've been married to Dad for twenty-seven years, Mom. Why are you acting like he is some psychopath out to get you?"

Mom says I can see what I want. She knows the truth. She says I'm too blind to see how much my father has turned me against her. She says that I don't even know half of what's gone on between them—

"I don't want to know," I interject. I have to remind Mom of this constantly. *I don't want to be in the middle,* I told her the day after I found out my parents were separating. Yet, somehow, that's where I've landed. Being in the middle is a self-perpetuating cycle: Dad calls and reassures me he's OK, even though his voice quivers as if he were on the verge of a nervous breakdown. He'll casually mention what Mom said to him that week. Then I get upset and call Mom, ready to argue with her over whatever Dad told me. When she bad-mouths

Dad, any accusations she makes about him roll off my back. *Mom initiated this divorce,* I think. *She needs to live with the consequences.*

"Where is Dad going to spend his birthday?" I ask. I can't hide the irritation in my voice. Mom often says she can't believe how hard I'm taking *her* divorce. She likes to remind me that I'm older, that she waited to divorce my father until I was an adult so I'd handle it better.

"You're acting like a child," Mom says. I imagine Dad sitting alone in his cramped studio apartment on his fifty-third birthday. I tell Mom she needs to think about someone other than herself, and I hang up.

Nothing tested me more in my adult life than my parents' split. I can say that now without feeling embarrassed or weak. For a long time, that's all I felt. I was twenty-six years old at the time. I had moved out of my childhood home to attend college several years before. I was in a long-term relationship. I had a great job and a small circle of close friends. My parents weren't sick or dying. I had all of the things that should make you feel rooted. Yet, when my parents announced they were separating, I felt as if the world had collapsed in on me.

My age made everyone assume I'd be fine. Even I decided I was overreacting. I figured, *I'm an adult. I should be able to handle this.* So I felt guilty hurting so much, as if my grief were out of place or unwarranted. I'd curse myself if I lost control of my emotions. I figured I had no right to sit in my apartment bedroom with the door shut crying about my parents' divorce, mourning the way I did the time my dog ran away when I was seven years old—the kind of crying that takes away your breath like a bad case of the hiccups. I was bullying myself over my own tears.

My parents were separated several months before I told anyone with whom I was close. I feared friends would laugh at my grief.

When I did confide in them, some said, "Better now than if you were a kid." Then I regretted saying anything at all.

There is an assumption that parental divorce won't hurt an adult child, that twenty-six- or thirty-five-year-olds aren't as likely to be affected by their parents' breakup. That they'll understand. After interviewing more than seventy-five adults whose parents divorced later in life, I can confidently say I'm not the only one struggling. Ninety percent of those surveyed said their parents' divorce was a defining moment in their lives. Nearly everyone felt as if their relationships with their parents had changed—sometimes for the better, more often for the worse. Many lost financial support, such as money for college. Lawyers drained inheritances. Adult children said they lost their sense of belonging. Divorce shattered their family and their concept of "home." Something inside of them died.

I envy young children going through a divorce. Everyone worries about them. They're sent to psychologists. Thousands of studies analyze their development through life. Dozens of books square off on how divorce impacts them. Parents go out of their way to ensure that a young child's transition is smooth. They're expected to hurt.

Adult kids aren't so lucky. Says one thirty-one-year-old woman, "If I could go back and tell my younger self what to expect, I think I would say, 'Just because you're almost thirty, don't feel like [your parents' divorce] shouldn't hurt. It will hurt like hell. In a way, it's harder for you than for a little kid. You've had thirty years for your parents' relationship to become part of your identity.'"

Our grief isn't taken as seriously as a young child's. Our parents stayed together *because* we'd be more mature once we headed off to college, walked down the aisle, had our first baby. Parents expect us to shrug off their split, as if the breakup of our family should no longer concern us because pieces of our adult life are in place. My mother wasn't the only one who thought congratulations were in order. Parents take such a big step in separating, some expect their adult children to be proud. Therapists say parents are shocked when their grown children show distress.

Adult children struggle with divorce just as young children do, only we're old enough to understand what's going on. We can attach words to all of the changes. We take on caregiver roles, watching out for our parents in ways we're used to parents watching over us. We grow depressed trying to understand what the word *family* means now that ours is split apart. Our emotional development suspends. Finding lasting love can seem fruitless.

Yet adult children and young children experience our parents' divorces differently. No one covers the adult child's ears or lowers their voices if we walk into the room as family matters are discussed. Parents openly burden adult children with their problems, treating us like friends. On their own for the first time in twenty years or more, parents need guidance and support. We teach Dad how to do laundry and cook a red sauce. We counsel Mom on dating. Says one twenty-five-year-old woman of her divorcing parents, "I felt like we were all growing up together."

If Dad cheats or Mom takes off with Dad's savings, adult children are the first to know. Parents forget that just because we're in our twenties doesn't mean we feel any less like their son or daughter. Hearing details of their problems—learning how miserable they've been—tears us apart inside. We have a personal stake in the loss. It's painful to listen to. Yet, as an older son or daughter, we're somehow expected to.

Divorce means watching the two people we love most turn against each other and sometimes try to destroy the other—and because we are adults, we are privy to every excruciating detail. Mom and Dad hire expensive lawyers. Sometimes they hide assets and lie. They push us to take sides, manipulating us with angry phone calls and emotional e-mails. Instead of sitting us down and explaining what's happening, as they would with a young child, parents suck us into the middle. They want us to hear about every jab and knockout punch they've exchanged. We cannot sit back like docile spectators and watch the drama unfold. We're old enough to understand what our parents are putting each other through. So we try to make peace. But trying to make things better only escalates the war. Each parent claims we're taking the other parent's side.

We're too old for custody decisions, which most people assume makes the process easier on us. But in actuality, adult kids without such clearly defined boundaries must negotiate separate relationships with each parent, which makes it harder. Parents compete for our affection and our time. Adult children have to figure out whether Mom is going to flip if we spend an afternoon with Dad or whether Dad will think spending Thanksgiving with Mom means we're taking her side. Often, we realize that we were closer to one parent and didn't interact much with the other. "After the divorce, I thought, 'Oh crap. Now I have to deal directly with Dad,'" says one thirty-one-year-old woman.

Parents start new lives. They remarry, have additional children. Reminiscing about our childhoods becomes off-limits. Bringing up the past only hurts. Some parents don't want us to acknowledge their former spouse in front of them. Parts of our childhoods must be forgotten so our parents can start fresh.

Researchers say those in their early to midtwenties, the age of most individuals interviewed for this book, have an especially difficult time. The security of our childhood homes, with all of the images and smells we imagine there, vanishes. "Home is the place where," as Robert Frost famously said, "when you have to go there, / They have to take you in." The loss of "home" makes adult children feel unrooted, as if the foundation upon which we built our lives were crumbling. Many of us grow unsettled. Our futures suddenly seem unclear. Coming of age is disrupted. One psychologist interviewed said that young adults who have led an uneventful middle-class existence might take parental divorce particularly hard. "It could be the most traumatic thing to happen to you," he said.

In a 1988 study conducted by the University of North Carolina–Chapel Hill of undergraduates, researchers found that two-thirds of the adult children of divorce surveyed felt "their lives were abruptly and unwillingly altered by their parents' divorce. Insecurity about the future was another common response; over half of the group worried that because of the divorce their plans for college and their adult lives would not work out." One nineteen-year-old in the study said, "I'm not sure of anything anymore."

I used to believe I came from the perfect family. I grew up playing at the beach on Long Island Sound. I collected rocks. My parents read me a story each night and tucked me in. Dad whistled when I curtsied at ballet recitals. Mom beamed. We took Sunday drives, and sometimes we stopped for lunch at clam bars.

But my childhood had a dark side. Dad sometimes drank. Mom and Dad fought so much that Dad packed—and ultimately unpacked—his bags more than once. Mom struggled to make ends meet if Dad's painting business slowed in winter. One night, Dad got so mad at Mom, he punched a hole in a bedroom ceiling. Another time, I listened to Mom bang her fists against Dad's chest. It felt as if the world were collapsing in on me then, too. I'd duck my head under the water in the bathtub, take a walk to the beach, put headphones on and blast music into my ears.

My parents stayed together "for the kids." Fearing we'd never bounce back from their breakup, they waited until my sisters and I were grown to separate. They fell victim to the twenty-five-year itch, like every other couple who bides their time together, slogging through years of marital discontent out of fear that parting ways would do irreversible damage to their children. They wait for the youngest to leave home. Then they duck out and call the kids: "Your father and I haven't been happy for a long time." We're children of the empty nest, only after our parents divorce, we're left with no nest at all.

Most divorces occur after the first seven years of marriage. But the twenty-five-year itch is a growing trend among baby boomers. Rutgers University's National Marriage Project (NMP) says the growth of divorce in this age group has become an accepted fact. According to the National Center for Health Statistics, about 20 percent of today's divorces take place among individuals married more than fifteen years, and of all couples who divorced in 1989 and 1990, the last year recorded, 47 percent had children over the age of eighteen or no children at all. The percentage of Americans sixty-five or older who were divorced or separated jumped 34 percent from 1990 to 2000, says the U.S. Census Bureau. Older couples are splitting up at such high rates, the American Association of Retired Persons (AARP) commissioned a study of midlife divorce in 2004, tracking habits of men and women who divorced in their forties, fifties, or sixties. One surprise: researchers found that 66 percent of these divorces were initiated by women. Our mothers are opting out.

Divorce is increasing among older adults for myriad reasons. For one, boomers married young, and over time, they grew apart. Their ideas about divorce evolved, too. When our parents were children, divorce was considered taboo. These days, splitting up is an accepted fact of life.

Popular culture would like us to believe that separating is the easiest road to self-reinvention. I recently saw an advertisement in *New York* magazine that exemplifies this. A pretty blond woman in her late forties is sitting on a fluffy chair with her legs draped over the armrest and her dogs curled up next to her. She is smiling brightly. The ad reads: *He left me. Good riddance. He never picked up his socks. He thought I was his mother. He didn't make me laugh anymore. He's gone. Who cares? . . . All I wanted was the sofa and the dogs.* Divorce is a time to get what you want. Says feminist writer bell hooks in her 2003 book *Communion,* "Now mid-life and there after has become not only a time to reclaim power but also a time to know real love at last."

Cultural views of marriage have shifted, too. Baby boomers, who grew up believing that legal unions should be centered around family, are latching onto the definition of marriage with which younger generations were raised. When younger people marry, we aren't looking only to build a solid family. We're looking for someone to fill our emotional needs, says the National Marriage Project. If we don't feel as though our marriages are a spiritualized union of souls, says one 2001 NMP report, we look for a new partner who fills that role, regardless of our kids' ages. In other words, we want to feel butterflies. We're not marrying for practical reasons anymore. When Mom and Dad split up late in life, they're making the same choice. Forget discussing the more traditional reasons for staying together. They want to feel butterflies, too.

Most important, people are living longer. On average, men can expect to make it to their seventy-fifth year and women, their eightieth. Viagra reinvigorated their sex lives. If our parents are in their fifties, they have plenty of time to redefine themselves, including finding a new partner with whom to experience life. Books such as Abigail Trafford's *My Time* and Ken Dychtwald's *The Power Years* have helped define this indulgent second phase of life. Both inspire the boomer set to live as if they were immortal. *Don't simply wait for the grandchildren! Volunteer. Travel. Separate.*

———

I want this book to be about beginnings, even though our stories begin with an end. We embark on a journey when our parents announce their divorce. At first, we are innocents unaware of the heartache ahead. Many of us think divorce can be wrapped up as tidily as an episode of *Friends*. But then time takes its toll. Our hearts are wrung dry, and our emotions tailspin. Our families become war zones. One twenty-nine-year-old woman felt so battered, she says, "During the divorce, there were times when I could look in the mirror and not see my soul behind the eyes staring back at me. I saw the shattered pieces of my life all around me."

When we're finally ready to let go, maybe even heal, we realize how much our parents' divorces transformed us. We are like meat being stuffed through a sausage maker: ground into little pieces and jammed in a new casing, creating something made of the same parts but with an entirely different texture and taste. We no longer recognize ourselves, let alone our families.

About six months into my parents' divorce—after too many days crying at my office desk—I went to the bookstore. I searched for titles about adults experiencing parental divorce. Surely, I thought, someone has been through this and written about it. There was one book. It was out of print. So I started talking. I opened up to friends, strangers, coworkers. I shared the extent of my grief, and I was surprised when no one laughed. Many knew other adults going through their parents' divorce, so I felt less alone. I realized how many of us there are.

On a whim, I talked to my editor about writing an article on my experiences for the *Washingtonian*. I wasn't sure what I'd write, and I was scared to see so much of my family's history in print. But I was shocked at how little attention was being given to adult children experiencing parental divorce. We are an oversight, even though late-life divorce is on the rise. When the article came out, I got a particularly touching letter from a reader. "Your story is my story," she wrote.

As a child, I believed I'd write a book retelling my far-flung adventures in exotic locales. So when a few readers suggested I write a book about kids of late-life divorce, I shrugged off the idea. Divorce was hardly a topic I wanted to ponder every day. I worried that my parents would disown me for revealing family secrets so publicly. Writing the article was hard enough, but writing this book would be exploitive—it would have to recount my family's darkest days, exposing our wounds for all to see.

Yet I couldn't turn my back on this book. My story *was* like that of so many other adult children. There were patterns to our grief and a pulse in our sadness. Telling our collective story became an unexpected calling for me. This book would make adult children feel less alone. Our struggles would be recorded and given a name.

We are the lost-nest generation: adult kids who age out of the house only to see our parents decide they've grown apart. Childhood homes are sold in the divorce. We go home to new places where we cannot find the silverware. Our nests are dismantled, blown apart by an unexpected gale.

Hints of the lost nest are evident in popular media. In 2003's *Something's Gotta Give,* starring Jack Nicholson and Diane Keaton, Keaton's adult daughter is shown crying about her parents' divorce just as she's about to run an estate sale at a large auction house. One episode of *The Real World: New York* focuses on a young man who finds out his parents are splitting up during the show. Books such as Joanna Trollope's *Marrying the Mistress* and Helen Fielding's *Bridget Jones's Diary* showcase older adult characters dealing with their divorcing parents.

But the grief of the adult child remains unappreciated and misunderstood. Marriage and family therapists, many of whom have seen an increase of lost-nesters in their waiting rooms, describe only the surface of our pain. Of the numerous articles written on late-life divorce, few reflect on the grown children at the heart of almost every dissolved marriage. It is as though the trend toward late-life marital dissolution comes without consequence.

Researchers have largely ignored us. Only a handful of studies have been conducted on the topic of adult kids of late-life divorce, and nearly all their findings have been incorporated into this book. "For so long, I was the *only* one looking into this," says Teresa Cooney, a family sociologist at the University of Missouri. She authored most of the research on the impact of recent divorce on adult kids in the early to mid-1990s. But funding dried up, and so did Cooney's interest. Only a handful of studies have been done since. Cooney says her work is suddenly getting more attention. There is growing interest in understanding the struggle of the adult child. No doubt this is perpetuated by the increasing number of parents splitting late in life.

Since the research on this subject is sparse, this book was informed by interviews with academics, psychologists, and therapists. I read journal articles and combed statistics. But early on in my research process, I realized that the true experts of this book are the lost-nesters themselves. It is our stories that I've relied on to shape these eight chapters. I could hear echoes of myself in nearly every adult child I interviewed, and anyone going through late-life parental divorce will hear that same echo in themselves.

I knew writing this book would be cathartic. I didn't realize how much I'd learn about myself: who I am to my parents and who I am to me. I learned that I was good at listening and not so good at minding my own business. I was fair to a fault: I divided my visits home equally. If I went home for five days, I'd spend exactly two and a half with Mom and two and a half with Dad. More important, I realized how much I still leaned on my parents emotionally even though I was in my late twenties. I wasn't as independent as I thought.

Years went by before the shock of finding out about my parents' split turned into an acceptance of my mother's and father's new lives. I was reluctant to heal—I'd have to say good-bye to everything I loved. So I clung to the past, at times trying to will my parents back together, as so many of us do. There were fights and tears, power struggles and disappointments. Consider this book a road map through these mountains and molehills, the uneven terrain in which you may find yourself. These pages speak of farewells to existing families and initiations into new ones. This is a guide to rebuilding relationships and forging ahead. A place to feel reassured that your pain is real, that you're allowed to hurt.

My mom and dad are going to read this book, and I dread their reaction when they do. I imagine Mom rushing out to a bookstore and picking up a copy, opening it to the first page—or this page—and collapsing against her steering wheel after only a few paragraphs. I picture Dad putting the book down on his nightstand a couple of pages in, wiping the corners of his eyes, before shutting off the light and turning in for a restless night's sleep.

I feel the need to apologize to my family for what's written in this book, even though we've all moved on from the divorce as I type these words. Some passages will inevitably dredge up feelings we've tried to forget. Much of what I've written is embarrassing: I am at my worst in many of these chapters, and so are my parents.

Then again, I want to remind Mom and Dad that we have nothing to be ashamed of. We screamed and argued only because we loved one another so deeply. We are guilty only of being human. I want to tell them, if the truth sets you free, then we are ready to fly. All of this is behind us.

1

Ready, Set, Grieve

> She came back to the table and sat down, and after a
> moment Shukumar joined her. They wept together, for
> the things they now knew.
>
> —JHUMPA LAHIRI, "A Temporary Matter"

I WAS AT MY OFFICE THE DAY MY PARENTS SPLIT UP. I WAS
gearing up to go on vacation. My boyfriend, John, and I were
flying out to Washington state, where we were going to drive
north of Seattle and ferry over to a cluster of islands in the Puget
Sound and camp. It was June 2001.

Stacks of legal pads covered my desk. I had been reporting a
story on "mean girls" for several weeks. I was fiddling with the beginning of the article when Dad called. "Hiya, Brooke," he said. He
asked about my weekend. We talked about when I was coming
home.

Then Dad grew serious. "I want you to know what happened today," he said. His voice sounded more formal than usual and a bit shaky, which made my heart race the way it does when I stumble out of bed to answer the phone in the middle of the night. Dad rarely called me. Mom would call, and after we caught up, she'd pass the phone on to him. I didn't even think he knew my number. I feared he was going to tell me that he had cancer or that my mother was sick. *Did my sister get in a car accident?*

I asked Dad what was going on and looked outside my office's picture window at the stream of suits on the city street below. *Is this the last scene I'm going to see before Dad delivers news that changes my life forever?* I focused my eyes on the tightly coiled black telephone wire. I stuck my pointer finger inside the coil and twirled it around. I waited. Before he called, my mind was already racing in twenty different directions. My story was due the following day. I still hadn't gathered all my camping gear for the trip. My younger sister, Chelsea, was deciding whether she should go away to college; it made me consider canceling my trip and visiting home instead to help her decide.

"I'm staying out at Junie's for awhile," he said. Junie is my aunt, Dad's youngest sister, and she lives near the ocean. "Oh, like a vacation?" I asked. I let go of the black telephone wire, spinning around to face my orange iMac computer, and felt the tension slide out of my shoulders. I could go back to writing my story on teenage girls. *Things are fine*, I thought. Then Dad said, more softly this time, "No, not really a vacation, Brock." Dad always called me that nickname when he was explaining something important. "Mom and I are just taking time apart to clear our heads," he said.

Dad didn't say that he moved out. Or that he left. Or even, Mom kicked me out. He couldn't. Even Dad wasn't ready to admit how serious this situation was. He sounded embarrassed to have to tell me.

He said he had packed up some clothes that morning and brought them out to Junie's. It was temporary. He said not to worry. They were sorting things out.

I said, "Well, this is the farthest you've ever taken a fight, huh?" I quickly apologized; I didn't mean to sound petulant. Dad said I sounded fine. I jotted down my Aunt Junie's number on a yellow Post-it note and stuck it to my computer, next to another Post-it that read, "Order Dad's Father's Day gift."

I told Dad I loved him. *Poor Dad,* I thought, and I hung up the phone, feeling bad that my parents were fighting. Then I grew steely and rolled my eyes. This is how my parents were—immature. They were two children who couldn't admit that the one they teased and taunted most was the one they truly wanted. I was more annoyed than upset. Of course they'd take a "break" from each other the week before I was leaving for vacation.

I blocked it out. I went to lunch. I chatted about reality TV at the water cooler with friends. I didn't say a word about the conversation with Dad to anyone that afternoon—not even to my boyfriend.

Later that night, Mom called me at home. I turned defensive and cool when I heard her voice. Without waiting for an explanation, I instantly blamed her. *She* was the one who had never seemed happy with Dad. I always suspected he loved her more than she loved him. Mom was strong-minded and independent. She longed for the kind of lifestyle you see in the pages of a Pottery Barn catalog—a lifestyle my father's painting business couldn't afford her. "Where's Dad?" I asked abruptly.

She didn't hesitate. "I told Daddy to leave," she said. I imagined Dad packing his belongings, carrying his toiletry bag and stacks of crisp, white painter's pants outside to his truck. He might've pretended he was just leaving for a weekend. He'd pull out of the driveway only after he was sure my youngest sister wasn't home. Then she wouldn't have to watch his truck drive away or follow it as it disappeared down the street.

Mom was silent. She was waiting for me to say something, but I couldn't find the right words.

"You know it has been a long time coming," she said.

Did I?

Again, Mom waited for me to speak. She wanted me to break the tension between us. I was silent. "We'll all be happier this way," she said, before we hung up. "I promise."

A friend once told me that you should look forward to beginnings. To start something is to embark on a journey—and journeys are the only way to learn and evolve. As a culture, we love to mark and celebrate beginnings: the first day of school, the new millennium, the start of a friendship. Beginnings are meant to be cherished. Without them, we would have nothing to reflect on how far we've come.

In divorce, the beginning is the end—the last act in the theatrics of family, one final scene that steals away any reason for celebration. "The day that Mom and Dad split up" is analogous with any tragedy for which we weren't prepared, such as "the day Dad died in a car accident" or "the day Mom found a lump in her breast." It marks a moment that changed our lives for good. One with a finality so heartbreaking that our senses instinctively record where we were and how we felt. "The day that Mom and Dad split up" is often one of the last moments you'll endure with your two parents still living in the same house. Even decades later, adult children of divorce can often recall that day in vivid detail, offering the date, the place, and even what their parent was wearing.

The news of our parents' divorce imparts a harsh reality. Mom and Dad's breakup is a "situation," because we can't think of any other way to describe it, and we must drop whatever we're doing to deal with it. We have a lot on the line. It's the end of *our* story as we know it, too. We will never find our parents standing side by side on the porch stoop, waving as we pull in the drive. Holidays lose their sense of tradition—of everyone's coming together and immersing themselves in the safety of sameness. We are creatures of habit who rarely welcome change into our lives. Divorce thrusts change upon us, turning relationships we often consider the most stable upside down. It is a good-bye to the most familiar of things, including our own sense of self, the identities that we have created for ourselves as daughter or son, sister or brother.

Because our parents stayed together, happily or unhappily, for more than twenty years, many of us believed that our families would continue to outlast others. Many adult children of divorce watched our parents shimmy onto the dance floor and slow dance cheek to cheek at their own twenty-fifth- and thirtieth-anniversary parties. We were the ones in the audience who oohed and ahhed, and cheered when Dad toasted Mom. We held our hands over our hearts and thought enviously, "I can only hope I know love like that someday."

After our parents' divorce, remembering moments such as this hurts, mostly because they are less believable. Mom and Dad were "faking it." It's like watching a rerun TV movie with really bad actors. Stephanie, a twenty-six-year-old administrative assistant, says that the moment she found out her parents had divorced was like having "the wind knocked out of me. I could not get up and catch my breath." Her parents were together for thirty years. Stephanie had just given them a party. "Then, six months later, we found out that Dad had been cheating on Mom for the past few years."

When our parents tell us they're divorcing, we can hardly believe what we're hearing. Our thoughts spiral away from us as soon as the secret is dispelled:

This must be a joke. My parents didn't stay married for twenty-

seven years—go to ballet recitals, work extra jobs to pay college tuition bills, take family vacations, bring flowers home after arguments—only to suddenly call it quits.

Isn't there a statute of limitations on when parents can split up? Mom and Dad are in their fifties. They're close to retirement age. What will they do without the other? Who will cook chicken soup for Dad when he's running a fever or brew Mom tea when she has a sore throat? They need each other.

I thought they loved each other.

Wait, did Mom really just say Dad is leaving? Who is she to say Dad has to leave? I don't want my family to change. I will not just let my mother step into the middle and say it's over.

This is my family, too.

Grief envelops adult children of divorce like a blanket. It tucks us in—*you may as well get comfortable*—making us yearn for what was and what will never be. Often, we find we are grieving before we even know how much there is to grieve. Part of our grief comes from doubting our right to hurt. In your twenties and thirties, you're *supposed* to be well entrenched in adulthood, living a life separate from your parents. Sitting in your office and crying about Mommy and Daddy's marriage is not only embarrassing, it's culturally unacceptable. It can make you feel vulnerable and weak, like a little girl who never quite grew up. Ironically, we often react like young children after our parents split up. We fall into old reflexes, demanding explanations, pleading with parents to stay together, asking how they could do this and say they still love us. In the months after Mom told me she was leaving Dad, I figured I'd make a spectacle out of how much I disapproved. Then maybe she'd appease me and stay with Dad. She didn't.

Psychologists say adults coping with their parents' divorce undergo the same sense of loss felt by adults experiencing a parent's death—and researchers agree. A majority of adult kids of divorce surveyed by Teresa Cooney, a family sociologist at the University of Missouri, said their parents' split hurt them as much as the death of a close family member. Divorce brings similar feelings of loss. Just as with losing a loved one, the pain is immediate and deepens over time. University of Virginia psychologist Robert Emery thinks the comparison helps others understand why a divorce is so troubling for adult children. "Are we surprised if an adult child is upset when her parents die? Of course not," he says. "Then why shouldn't we expect her to feel hurt, grief, and pain when her parents divorce?"

In some ways, grieving a divorce is different than mourning a death. Obviously, our parents are still alive. But this only makes our loss more nuanced. Our parents go through the same motions— work on weekdays, sailing on Sundays for Dad and pottery class for Mom—but now they're doing it without the other. There are no excuses we can think of to exempt them from having caused the hardship. No "it was a freak accident," or "the cancer took them too young." Our parents are *choosing* not to occupy the same physical space. The absence is strange precisely because it *isn't* by way of sudden death. We don't lose one parent; we lose our entire base. We experience the death of a *set* of people, a family unit, that brought organization and framework to an otherwise lonely existence.

Grief, in turn, comes quickly and suddenly, turning a blue sky to black, like an afternoon thunderstorm splitting open on a humid August afternoon. You mourn the end of your parents' marriage like a death because there is an instant realization that home will never be the same. This loss is so great, it sometimes feels as if we were losing a piece of who we are. "I felt like someone was trying to saw off my arm," says Rhonda, a graduate student in Chicago, of her parents' divorce. Rhonda had always taken pride in how happy her family seemed. Her mother and father were married for thirty-six years. Her father was a professor. Her mother stayed home with the children. They never fought in front of their three daughters. Rhonda and her sisters grew up in the suburbs of Knoxville, where their house, with a huge yard full of blackberry bushes, was the one where friends loved to congregate. "I was attached to my family," she says. "Looking back, I may have been unhealthily attached to my family. But they were important to me, more important than I was to me. I took pride that my family was perfect and that my husband's family was messed up. Every time I'd hear some drama about them, I'd think, 'Thank goodness my family isn't like that.' "

Rhonda was on a fellowship in New Mexico in 2000 when her parents called her one evening after work. "There's this book *Men Are from Mars, Women Are from Venus*," her mother began. "Well, around page 154, it says, 'Have you ever seen a marriage where they seem really happy and then suddenly they get divorced?' " Rhonda sensed where the conversation was headed. "What are you saying?" Rhonda asked, angrily. Her father began to cry, which Rhonda had never heard before.

In the days after the phone call, Rhonda's shock turned into a crippling sadness. "All I wanted to do was talk about it over and over," she says. That semester, Rhonda was supposed to return to school and begin researching her dissertation. "I'd go to my office," she says. "I'd surf the Web, and I would cry. I wouldn't even pay any attention to what I was surfing. It took me seven years to finish a degree I should have completed in five."

Thinking about our parents' divorce forces us to face all of the impending "lasts" we must endure—a final holiday, an end to eating eggs together at the breakfast table. Notions of our future must also be forgotten. No more visions of doting grandparents. Dreams of Mom and Dad walking us down the aisle at our weddings are lost. The end of our family is about as easy to accept as a parent's disregard for our own future fiancé, circumstances that crush any ideas we're taught to believe about family: parents and kids stick together, no matter what. "We all have dreams and fantasies of the perfect family—the one we grew up in, the one we hope to create," says Emery. "Divorce is the loss of those dreams, as unrealistic as they may be. No one wants to let go of their dreams."

Or their pasts. The ancient Greeks used mythology to make sense of their lives. They told stories to convey values and to teach one another life lessons. Over time, the tales became embedded in their minds, bonding them, and making each story a piece of who they were and how they came to be. We share the same types of tales within our families, on a much smaller scale: Remember the time . . . our dog, Shadow, got hit by a car? Remember when . . . I cut off all my hair in the weeks before kindergarten? We often recount our favorite memories, laughing at how stupid we were, how clever, or even how triumphant. Stories of our childhood, adolescence, or early adulthood illustrate our shared past.

There is a part in the 2003 film *Under the Tuscan Sun* in which the lead character, writer Frances Mayes, calls her best friend, Patty, to tell her she just bought a villa in Tuscany. There is excitement in the air until Patty mentions Frances's ex-husband. Frances is deflated. "Why did you have to say his name?" she asks.

Thinking about the past, even happy times, is a downer after a divorce. To reminisce about your childhood often means telling a story that includes the one person your parent is trying to forget. Even decades after they split up, we grieve the loss. It is especially difficult when a parent wants to rewrite history. Wendy's mother told her adult children not to talk about their father in front of her after they split eleven years ago. One recent holiday, Wendy, a thirty-one-year-old public relations specialist, her younger brother, Brian, and her mother were sitting at the kitchen table reminiscing. Her mother chuckled as she told them about the time Brian was sent to play in the backyard under strict rules that he shouldn't go anywhere near a wasp nest that had fallen from a tree. Within a few minutes, he walked over to the nest and started to poke it with a stick. He got stung in the face several times and ran inside crying. When asked why he'd played with the nest, he denied he was anywhere near it. Wendy's mother wanted to give her son the benefit of the doubt, so she went to investigate. She found the wasp's nest split open and wasps flying everywhere.

Wendy and her brother sat listening to their mother's story, giggling at the right moments, but feeling stunned inside. Their *father* was the one who went out to find the wasp nest after Brian was stung. Their mother had stayed in the house, comforting Brian. Wendy's mother had erased her ex-husband from the story, thus completely reinventing one of Wendy's childhood memories. *You can't just undo the past because you don't like the present*, Wendy thought to herself. Yet that's exactly what a divorce is. While untangling themselves from a marriage, parents become less connected to what was and more focused on a fresh future. A new beginning. Parents don't want to remember the parts of their pasts that hurt, and adult kids are expected to be mature enough to let go *for their parents' sake*.

Oral history bonds a family, which is why losing these stories is troubling to us. Our parents' split is a tale that figures prominently in our lives. In a family's shared narrative, the "leaving story" becomes an important part of the grieving process. It is the central story we'll tell when someone asks how our parents are or why we seem so down. The story marks the beginning of an end. Often we reflect on the "leaving story" as we try to figure out, *How did this happen?*

Living through a divorce is like living through any traumatic experience; it makes people behave in strange ways. Sometimes parents self-destruct, creating a "leaving story" that's even more tragic—and harder to share with friends. They cause bigger problems and bring their families down with them. These endings are no harder to grieve than any other. They simply create a different variation on the same "leaving story," a personal myth, carrying an absolute, and very personal, theme. *My parents abandoned me.*

Sarah, thirty-four, always considered herself close to her mother and father. She confided in her mother. Her dad would stop by her apartment with bagels for an impromptu visit. She'd drop by her parents' house as well. The homey bungalow where she grew up was just around the corner from the tiny apartment she and her husband rented. One day, Sarah's mother ran to the mall to return something. When she got back, there was a note from Sarah's father that read, "I went for a walk."

He didn't come back. Her father didn't call Sarah or her mother and say where he was. Nine months pregnant, Sarah urged her mother to call the police, who started searching for him. Sarah was distraught. *Had he been murdered?* About a week after Sarah's father's disappearance, her mother began opening her husband's mail, looking for clues as to where he might be. She discovered that in the past year, he'd racked up $100,000 in debt, taking out cash advances to pay bills. He'd also spent down his retirement money. Twelve days after he "went for a walk," Sarah's father returned home. It turned out he was in Los Angeles, shopping around a screenplay he'd been working on for several years. He'd also checked out some apartments with realtors.

Four days after Sarah's son, Steven, was born, her father told her mother, "I can't stay here anymore." Before Sarah, then thirty, could blink an eye, her father had packed his things and moved across the country to live with his sister, without ever saying good-bye. Her mother was left with a high mortgage and little money in savings. Sarah was still healing from the delivery of her son when she began planning how she and her husband might buy her childhood home, so her mother wouldn't be evicted.

Adults whose parents divorce are often surprised by how quickly their initial shock turns to anger. The "leaving story" can sometimes be so infuriating, it becomes difficult for us to look beyond it. Sarah was livid with her father for leaving, but she was even angrier that he had left her mother without a dime. Sarah refused to speak to him, with the exception of occasional e-mails, for several months. "If you had said, 'You guys are grown. We're going to end things,' " Sarah told her mother, "it would have been different. The way it happened is what bothers me most."

Understanding the "leaving story" is the first step in healing after parents divorce. Adult children look for answers in a split. They want to know why it happened but, more important, why they find themselves so angry. If you analyze how you tell your own "leaving story," you'll sometimes see clues. Sarah says that what bothers her most is not that her father left, it's the set of circumstances under which he left. It fell to Sarah to clean up a mess she had no part in making.

So much of the anger that emerges after divorce comes from issues having nothing to do with the basic idea that Mom and Dad split up. Divorce exacerbates existing feelings, playing a game of Russian roulette with our emotions. You can never predict where the little silver ball is going to land. One day, it might slide into resentment, and the next, it can lodge into jealousy.

For me, knowing Mom and Dad were divorcing was devastating enough, but dealing with Mom, who expected me to be *happy for her* for leaving Dad, was even more emotionally draining. I already resented my mother, who could be selfish at times. Growing up, she'd insist we go to seafood restaurants, despite the fact that my sister and I didn't like them. She'd make us late for a party while she coiffed her hair. The divorce, I felt, made her even more self-absorbed. Sarah felt similarly about her father. She often wondered whether he expected her to speak to him again or whether he even cared, which brought abandonment issues she'd struggled with since she was young back up to the surface. Her father was starting a whole new life in Toronto—a life Sarah knew nothing about.

The "leaving" isn't always as immediate as in Sarah's example. Parents trying to say good-bye to twenty-six years of marriage are like an alcoholic trying to quit drinking overnight. Parents have gone to that "bottle" for years for comfort and support. It made them feel as if they belonged—and that was even more intoxicating. So parents sometimes split up and get back together only to split up again, which confuses their adult kids, who are trying to figure out if they really have to say good-bye.

In the first few weeks of my parents' separation, clear lines were drawn in the sand. Then Dad moved back in with Mom. I called home and found them watching a movie together and, on another occasion, having a few glasses of wine. Mom expected me not to ask what was going on. Dad said, "I don't know what we are. We're really just talking." Two months later, Mom asked Dad to leave—again. Hopes of reconciliation were dashed. The camps sprang back up, the lines were redrawn. Mom swore it was over. That Christmas Eve, Dad was drinking eggnog in our living room, handing out gifts, and climbing into bed alongside Mom. My sisters and I were confused. Were our parents together or not? I don't think even they knew.

Adult children say parents lose all sense of logic as their relationship unravels. Parents think they want to leave. Then one will feel lonesome and call the other for a crutch. Talking reminds parents why they want to end it, filling them with regret for picking up the phone in the first place. Their hearts circle round and round, and the adult children are forced to witness the slow end. The finality of the divorce is suspended—and so is the healing process. How simple it is to get stuck in a phase in which you spend hours talking yourself into and out of your parents' divorce. Instead of moving on to grief, a more melancholy and nostalgic state, our confusion turns to anger—and the anger festers. It is the mere beginning of a very slow end, serving as the centerpiece to our mourning.

I was at the funeral of an acquaintance recently. One of the deceased's sons delivered the eulogy. "At funerals, you never hear the bad stuff. Only the good," he said. "Well, I only have good things to say. My father was a man of character and principles. He was someone you could count on. . . ." After someone dies, we often idealize who the person was to us when they were alive. "He was such a good father." "She was always there when we needed her." Once something is lost to us, we realize how much there is to miss. Good memories resurface. And in our greatest grief, we'd willingly take back all the hardship for a chance to feel the glory all over again.

Families are rarely flawless, especially those with parents whose problems have been brewing for decades. Adult children of divorce know this, and yet they'll say their families were "perfect" and wax nostalgic after divorce even though they used to call their families dysfunctional. *I want us to go back to being that perfect little family*, we say. I'm guilty of this myself. I wrote a first-person account of my parents' divorce for the magazine for which I write. One of the first lines was, "I always believed I came from the perfect family."

Many of us idealized our parents' unions over the years, simply because they remained married for so long. Longevity of marriage is honored and, in our culture, is commemorated with elaborate anniversary parties at which couples kiss passionately and stuff cake into each other's mouths as if they were teenagers again. Couples who make it to their twentieth year and beyond are revered. To endure marriage for that long must mean those two people understand the secret to true and lasting love.

But the fact is, my Mom and Dad remained married for twenty-six years, and their marital problems were plentiful throughout: Dad sometimes drank too much. Mom demanded too much. They fought as regularly as the sun set. As a kid, I'd sometimes fantasize about escaping into another family. So why, when my parents split up, did I hold on to this image that I had been a part of something so solid that I believed it an insult to everyone involved to dismantle it?

Divorce is a concept adult children of divorce hardly thought we'd have to understand. Writes Anthony Walton in the short story "Divorce Education," "I never thought much about divorce before it happened to me. It was like a car crash, a lightning strike, the very earth splitting into halves." Adult children take for granted that their family will always sit around the dinner table together. Divorce was something that happened to other people. "I always assumed if my parents were still together when I graduated high school, they'd make it," says Mandy, a twenty-seven-year-old graphic designer living in San Francisco. "Then, when I went away to college, I figured if they didn't split up by the time I graduated four years later, they'd stay together forever." Mandy's parents separated when she was twenty-six. She had come to count on the idea that her parents would be one of the few to keep their promise of "till death do us part."

For many of us, divorce was so commonplace among our childhood classmates that families who stayed together were envied, fostering a subconscious sense of pride among us. Rhonda, a graduate student, believed her family was as flawless as the one portrayed in *The Partridge Family*. Her parents never fought. They were often affectionate. She loved that they weren't a "statistic," like many of her friends who had divorced parents. She never wanted her family to be recorded by the census as "broken"; her life was too special to be reduced to just another number.

Some of us pitied the young child of divorce. One of my best friends in elementary school had a bedroom at her mother's house and another at her father's. I told her I thought that was cool. "But I always leave stuff at Dad's and then Mom won't let me get it until next weekend because she hates him," she said, her eyes tearing up. I didn't understand divorce. I remember thinking my friend was crying because she wanted her clothes and toys stored together. I often felt sorry for her. I wished she knew what it was like to come from a happier family, like mine. Sure, my parents fought. But they loved each other enough to make it work, and that made me proud. These sentiments aren't uncommon among adult children of divorce. Says one twenty-eight-year-old woman whose parents' divorced a few years ago, "I'd invite kids over whose parents were divorced so they'd know what it was like to be a part of a real family. Looking back, it's ironic. I thought we were such a strong family."

Our parents' split humbles us. "When I think about how I would talk about my parents in my classes, my cheeks turn red now," says one twenty-five-year-old woman, reflecting on her undergraduate years. "If love or marriage came up, I'd say, 'Well my parents always did this,' or 'My parents say that.' I'm sure a lot of people must have rolled their eyes."

Idealizing who our parents were before they split makes the ungluing even harder. There's more to let go of. Mandy says she was distraught after her parents split up, despite the fact that their marital relationship was always fraught with troubles. Because Mandy was an only child, her parents were her central source of love and support. Losing them, she says, is all she thinks about lately.

"I was definitely good at grinning and bearing it in high school," Mandy says. "I'd be home with my parents arguing and throwing stuff. Then, as a cheerleader, I'd have to go to a game and cheer and put a smile on my face. You would never know what was going on at home. I started that at a young age." To cope, Mandy began painting a different portrait of her parents. Instead of remembering the time Mom threw a dish at Dad, Mandy would focus on them making up afterward. "As long as they can get through this argument," she'd think, "they'll stay together. I'd only remember them holding hands or kissing afterward. In my mind, they played tennis. They traveled together. I liked the idea of my parents making it."

It was an idea that Mandy would perpetuate to friends, even in later years living in San Francisco. To compensate for her parents' true life problems, Mandy created a lightly fictitious and happier life. She left some details out. Instead of telling friends about the brawl her parents just had, she'd tell them about a trip they had planned to the Cayman Islands. It was a reflex. "Friends didn't know anything other than what they saw and what I told them," she says. "I didn't want to break the facade. I loved that we were a small three-person family. I feared if I accepted that they weren't perfect, they might split up, that it would come true."

So do we create images of marital perfection to escape from the not-so-great reality? Or do we really believe our parents have a perfect marriage, despite the flaws? Do we assume that, because our parents stayed together, they had a solid, working marriage?

"The mother (or father) who cried wolf" is a tale told by many adult kids whose parents divorce. This is about the mother who, every time she and her husband got into an argument, pulled her children aside to tell them that she was leaving. "I'm telling you," she'd say, "because I want to prepare you. I want you to know everything is going to be OK." Mom would burst into my bedroom like clockwork after she and Dad had a serious argument. I could hear the yelling from my bedroom. Mom's eye makeup would be bleeding down her cheeks when she'd come in. "I'm going to get us out of here," she'd promise. "Just give me some time." I'd always think to myself, *But I don't want to go anywhere.*

The adult child sprung from an unhappy marriage is old enough to remember many such occasions. One forty-seven-year-old man interviewed says his earliest childhood memory is of his father knocking his mother's teeth out. I remember when Dad got so angry at Mom, he punched a hole in the ceiling of their bedroom. Both of us recall the following morning just as clearly. Dad looped his arms around Mom's waist and apologized while she did the dishes. Other times, I remember everyone getting in the car and going for a Sunday drive to get clams and lobsters, as if the previous night had never occurred.

Parents set the example in a home. If they sweep their problems under a rug, it's inevitable that their children will do the same. Mandy's parents gave her reason to believe they'd always have troubles, but they also showed her that they'd always make up. Mandy could believe they were happy, despite the unsteadiness of their marriage, because she assumed that that is what a long, enduring marriage was made of.

Once your parents tire of the "leaving and returning" phase, and they're ready to actually go through with the divorce, denial is often our first reaction. *Mom has said she's going to leave Dad for eons*, we'll think. *This is just a phase, another bad patch.* A "mother who cried wolf" breeds distrust among her children. The now grown children think, *We've heard it so many times before. Why believe anything our parents say unless they actually do it?* So grief is postponed or ignored until some sort of physical proof is presented. Phrases such as "I'm leaving" become meaningless. Our hearts drop only when we hear "I left."

A mother who cried wolf is going to feel great anger from her children when she finally leaves. They won't understand why she endured a marriage so long only to end it. Watching parents constantly fight and make up forces a child to equate "constant reconciliation" with "a marriage that works." A perfect marriage, for some adult children, is defined as a relationship created out of the parents' determination to make the best of an unhappy situation. We didn't know that growing up, of course. But in retrospect, it's easy to see that many of our parents haven't been happily married for a long time. They only *made* things work. We expect them to stay in the marriage because they *always* have. It's a precedent they set. "I didn't really expect them to ever fix their marriage—neither of them seemed to realize they had a problem," says Michael, twenty-three. "But I didn't expect them to ever just quit, either."

Our concept of perfection—a resilient family—disappears when parents split up, which is why we hold on to the sentiment so tightly. The same could be said for a family like Rhonda's, whose parents never fought in front of the children. As far as Rhonda knew, her parents were still madly in love. They held hands often. They liked to spend time together. When her parents announced they were divorcing, it was as though a curtain were opened on a stage where an entirely different reality had been taking place. There was the play-acting she saw on holidays and on visits home. Then there was the unseen drama, which the divorce unleashed upon her. She found out that her mother hadn't really loved her father for a long time—and her mother, who announced she was a lesbian, had secretly been seeing a woman for the past year.

Shattering the image of the "perfect family" is inevitable in a divorce. The divorce announces to your friends, neighbors, and family members that your parents have problems. It makes your most private relationships with your family painfully public. You're forced to face the truth of your parents' relationship—and nothing hurts more than the realization that your childhood may have been a farce.

In the initial weeks after splitting up, many parents tell their adult children that they stayed together "for the kids." From the parents' point of view, remaining unhappily married is a very selfless act. They endured years of unhappiness to give their children the gift of a two-parent family. Parents, often the mothers, want their children to see them as martyrs who kept the family together for as long as they could. But in telling you, they also burden you with their unhappiness, which garners exactly the opposite reaction from what they expected. When parents say, "I did it for you," their children respond defensively: "Is it our fault that you've been so miserable? Are we supposed to thank you for not walking away earlier?"

Connecting the dots is easy. If parents stayed together for the kids, then what did all those years together mean to them? Adult kids spend days pondering this question: is the happy past rendered meaningless when you find out your mother or father wasn't always happy?

Somehow, hearing about a parent's misery makes our most treasured memories feel stale and phony. But why? If Mom or Dad stayed in the marriage for us, wasn't it because we made her or him happy enough to stay? In that sense, our memories should be construed as genuine because the love we felt from our parents was true at each moment. Then again, we never doubted our parents' love for *us*. What bothers us more is knowing that Dad was unhappy in his marriage, which makes us think that Dad was unhappy in his family. The meaning of actions that adult children might have explained away, such as why Dad daydreamed so much or why he holed up in the basement working on model cars, now becomes clear. *Can anyone really like rebuilding model cars that much?*

Knowing your parents stayed together for the kids spoils the most innocent of childhood memories. It forces you to regard many moments with a critical eye. Marisa, who grew up in the Denver suburbs, found out her father was cheating on her mother five years ago. She was at college when they called. As time went on, Marisa's mother told her daughter that her father had had numerous indiscretions over the years. "The fact that Dad stayed because he felt like he had to and not because he wanted to . . . hurt," Marisa says, three years later. "I just suddenly felt like our family had been a lie." Marisa thought about moments she'd spent with her father over the years. Few seemed innocent. "One of the things my Dad and I used to do when I was little was ride bikes. It was our special time. I looked forward to it. We'd pull our bikes out of the garage and ride around the neighborhood. There were times he wouldn't take me, and I'd get so upset. He'd go alone and say that he needed private time," she says. Her mother brought this up around the time of the split. "I don't know if you know," she told Marisa, "but sometimes he didn't take you because he was biking over to his mistress's house." The fondness Marisa felt for these special bike rides became tainted.

I didn't talk to one adult child of divorce who wasn't shocked by their parents' split, even when the parents had fought for years. We grow accustomed to their problems and expect them to keep slapping Band-Aids on their relationship. Parents keep secrets from their kids, even after they've reached adulthood. We think we know everything about their marriage. We think we understand why parents are splitting up. And we grieve their mistakes and bad decisions, their insincere hand-holding and gift giving. We need to trust our parents, and yet adult children have a difficult time believing in parents who seem as though they've been lying about who they are for years. How can we believe that they're making the right decision to divorce when it goes against who they've been to us—the devoted wife or husband—for the past few decades?

To learn a committed parent was actually a reluctant one stacks guilt on top of our already broken hearts. A part of us grieves not just for how their split changed *our* lives but also for how it crippled theirs. In "staying together for the kids," our parents are telling us that we played a role, albeit a small one, in their unhappiness. Unlike young children, adults don't blame themselves for their parents' divorce. An adult child has a more mature understanding of relationships. Adult children comprehend and maybe even relate to the difficulties of romantic relationships, so we cringe when we think about our parents living in an unhappy marriage for so long. So many of us wonder whether we perpetuated their discontent just because we went along with it. Did we allow the marriage to drone on because, selfishly, we were happy with the way it served us? Why didn't we think about what would make our parents happier?

Even as I write this, a voice in my head is yelling at me: *But you didn't know. Mom and Dad acted as though they were happy!* And this is all true. My mother would say I'm being ridiculous. But the guilt associated with knowing your mother stayed *for you* isn't lessened.

There is no neat and tidy "plan" for tackling grief. To say there is would be a lie. Dismantling a family is hardly a linear process, and grieving isn't either.

A family oozes apart slowly. A parent gets angry. A sister stops speaking to you. Your grandmother takes your mother's side. You become estranged from your father. They are all steps on an emotional continuum that makes up the initial months and years after parents separate and divorce. Instead of moving from denial to anger and bargaining to despair, like someone grieving a death, adult children of divorce grieve in circles. Without a funeral to finalize the end and with the issue of blame at stake, we deal with an ongoing grief cycle. Tensions that dogged a family before often continue long after the papers are signed. Every time we think we've moved on, a new drama invokes the past, pushing us around to the beginning of our grief and bringing us back to our initial question: *Why did Mom and Dad do this to me?*

Two summers after my parents split up, I went home for a week. Mom and I took a drive out on the east end of Long Island, stopping at farm stands and antique shops along the way. We were having a nice day. A relative calm had settled on my family, helping to dissipate some of the anger I'd been harboring toward Mom. She seemed less tense as well. Dad had finally agreed to sign the divorce papers, which made her feel less trapped. As we walked around Greenport, a tiny fishing village, I remember feeling relieved that our relationship was returning to normal. On the drive home, we talked about Mom's recent forays into dating. "It must be strange to be out there again," I said. I'm not sure what I said wrong, but the comment turned a quiet conversation loud. Mom began yelling about how I was never on her side. She said Dad could do anything he wanted and she was persecuted for every decision she made. My blood started to boil. Mom had to spoil every moment, making it about the divorce and *her* pain. She never once asked me how *I* was doing. . . .

And so it goes. After thinking I'd finally reached a plateau of forgiveness, I was right back to where I started, as angry as I'd been time and again in the months before. I was stuck in the circle of grief, which, unlike a full moon, comes and goes unpredictably. One morning, you're feeling alone and abandoned, longing for a time when your parents were together. Then they refuse to sit together at your college graduation, which makes you so angry that you stop speaking to them. Grieving in circles keeps you from moving on. You might accept and forgive one aspect of your parents' divorce, but then some action, such as Dad's marrying the woman with whom he cheated, gives you an entirely new set of circumstances with which to deal. Your emotions are whipped around at sonic speed by whatever drama is playing out in your family that day.

Holidays are particularly tough, especially the last one you spend as a family. One friend says it's because "everything you do carries a deeper meaning. There is a finality to it. You'll never sip eggnog or decorate the tree as a family again."

Mandy's parents announced they were divorcing in the summer. They hired lawyers. They began leading separate lives, even though they continued to live in the same house. That Christmas, they told Mandy to come home. They'd spend one last holiday together. At the time, Mandy hoped they might reconcile, so she agreed to fly home. Everyone seemed off, she says. Her mother typically complained about cooking Christmas dinner. This year, she acted excited and took great care to make the dinner perfect. Her father asked Mandy if she'd go to a jewelry store with him. He wanted to pick something out for his soon-to-be ex-wife. He found a necklace and asked Mandy to bring her mother back to see whether she liked it. "It was like everyone was going through the motions of a normal Christmas," says Mandy, "but there was no real heart in it." It turned out to be the worst Christmas of Mandy's life. There was no warmth or love between her parents. They couldn't pretend they weren't getting divorced. Her father may have bought her mother an expensive necklace. "But it was just a necklace," she says. "There was no meaning in it. It wasn't a gift."

Grief manifests itself differently in everyone. Mourning the loss of something so important to us causes great stress, and our bodies are sometimes the first to notice. Charlene, twenty-two, compulsively picked out her eyelashes after her parents separated. She was eighteen, living at home, and taking classes at a local college. Charlene sat in front of the TV one afternoon, twisting out her eyelashes one by one with her fingers. Rhonda developed a twitch in her eye the week before her mother said she was moving out. A twenty-seven-year-old woman watched her twenty-something brother chug Pepto-Bismol to relieve the pain of an ulcer, developed after their parents' split. Another started to have regular panic attacks. "I was trying to take care of everybody," she says.

In a study published in the *Journal of Family Issues*, researchers reported that "young adults with recently divorced parents reported higher levels of depression in the 2 to 3 year period immediately following parental divorce, and greater need for professional help than age peers with married parents. However, these significant differences were only observed for females." Sons and daughters may take on an equal burden during a divorce, but daughters seem to have more trouble insulating themselves from the pain. The study offers several explanations: Daughters tend to be more in tune with family dynamics. They tend to remain closer with parents in early adulthood than sons. Daughters are often turned to for mediation. But divorce is a problem they can't fix, which leads to a sense of helplessness.

Nearly every adult child I interviewed experienced some level of depression. Sometimes it was minor: reports of an inability to focus well at work or short periods of despondency. More often, adult children talked about waves of depression, in which they experienced on and off textbook symptoms such as irritability, crying in the middle of a college class, frequent headaches, and trouble falling asleep. Sometimes the never-ending sadness brought on drug use. "In my quest for answers," says Bob, twenty-seven, whose parents split up as he was entering college, "I tried nearly every drug I could get my hands on. I was coping over the fallout. You know when you're stressed and you lie in bed and your mind races at night . . . it just helped me not worry for awhile."

Depression is sometimes rooted in feeling alone, and divorce often fosters loneliness among adult children. Typically, we don't know anyone else in our shoes. We don't talk about our parents' divorce out of a sort of embarrassed fear that we might sound childish or selfish. If we bring it up to our parents, they may tell us we're acting like babies. *I should be able to handle this,* a voice tells us. So we keep quiet. We grow isolated, guilty about our grief. We search the Internet for support groups or for the words of one person who might tell us that what we're feeling is OK.

I would sit at outdoor cafés, staring into space, hoping one person in the steady stream walking by might approach me and say, "You're allowed to hurt, no matter how old you are. It's OK." Of course, no one did, so I tried to block out my emotions and will myself not to care. *I'll get on fine without my parents together,* I told myself.

"You're afraid it's not a legitimate hurt," says Jean, whose father left her mother for another woman. One morning at the library where she worked, she and a coworker were in particularly bad moods. "Sorry," said the colleague, "I'm just dealing with the fact that my father just moved out after thirty years." Jean closed the door of their shared office. They talked for four hours, ignoring any books that needed to be reshelved. "Just finding someone else who was going through it was a powerful moment for me," says Jean, now thirty. "It was my turning point."

If nobody else is experiencing what we are, we pretend we aren't either, pushing our pain away. We lose ourselves in work or school. Anything is better than facing our loss. After Luke, thirty-seven, finished his first year at college, he was supposed to head home and help his mother sort through his parents' divorce. "I ran away," he says. Luke, who was nineteen at the time, moved to a beach town instead. He got a job lifeguarding, and he made friends with a slew of people who had no idea he was struggling. He didn't call home at all that summer. His family didn't know where he was. He only sent a postcard to tell them he was alive. "It was the first time I felt like I had grown since they split up," Luke says.

But escaping problems from home isn't easy, even when you live on the opposite side of the country. There are constant phone calls and e-mails to drag us into a battle of he said / she said. When our emotions are spread too thin, we're faced with feelings of desperation. We think, *How can I escape this?*

Liza, a twenty-seven-year-old publications director at a top university, was in her sophomore year of college when her parents split up. "I was two and a half hours away from my family, and after my Dad and Mom remarried, I felt like they all had 'new' families. I had felt this way for awhile, pretty much the whole time I was in college," she says. "It was like once I moved out, everything changed and there was no 'home' to go back to. Then, when I started drinking in college—most of my friends' only hobby was drinking—I aggravated my depression. . . ."

Liza always got As and Bs in school, so there was no clue to alert her parents to how often she was out drinking. "I was just very lonely," she says. One night, she became instant friends with another young woman drinking alone at a college bar. Liza told the girl about what was going on with her parents. It was the first time she'd talked about it to anyone in over a year. The girl handed her two pills. "They're uppers," she told Liza. Liza had been contemplating suicide for months; she liked the idea of taking pills to fall asleep for good.

"Right before I did it, I was thinking about how nice it was to talk to that girl at the bar, because I hadn't talked to anyone about my emotions for so long," says Liza. "I was thinking about how I didn't have anywhere to go. My mom's house was too small. My dad's house was unwelcoming, and my sister and I never really got along. I felt like they all moved on and got new families and I was the left-over."

It is a cliché to say that only time heals. But the expression is overused because it's *true*. The intensity of your discontent will wither in years to come just as it does with any trauma life deals us. Think of your grief as a circle with stops. There are only so many times you can ride the merry-go-round before you grow tired of seeing the same things over and over. At some point, you're going to get anxious to step off. It's the same with grief. You will grow tired of spinning in circles. *Enough is enough,* you'll think, often a few years after the initial split. *I'm ready to move on.*

Points to Remember

- Adult children shouldn't minimize their pain. Losing your family in divorce is traumatic, and children of any age are going to hurt.

- When our parents divorce, we must let go of the idea that we come from a perfect family. Just because your parents made it for twenty years doesn't mean they should stay together for twenty more. Be honest with yourself: will your parents be happier apart?

- How our parents leave each other figures prominently in our grief. Analyze your parents' "leaving story." You may realize what bothers you most about your parents' divorce, which can help you heal.

- Grieving a divorce is like mourning a death. You need to treat your grief seriously. Watch for signs of depression or anxiety. Put your mental health first. Seeing a therapist is one option that may help.

- When parents say they stayed together for the kids, they're not saying they were unhappy being around their children. They loved you for all of those years. Try not to let the conflict of the present taint your good memories of the past.

2

Who's the Parent, Who's the Child?

> You only get one life. I've just made a decision to change things a bit and spend what's left of mine looking after me for a change.
>
> —HELEN FIELDING, *Bridget Jones's Diary*

THREE WEEKS AFTER DAD MOVED OUT, I WENT HOME to visit my family on Long Island. "Home" is a tiny clapboard rancher in a neighborhood crammed with fifties-era cottages. In the summer, nearly everyone has geraniums and pansies spilling out along their walkways. Our house has always had its drawbacks—one bathroom, all three bedrooms the size of most of my friends' walk-in closets—but we were steps away from the beach, which gave us plenty of space to roam. I always wished the houses in my neighborhood were spaced farther apart: everyone on the block knew when my parents fought; you could hear them yelling from the street. I used to love it when another set of parents got in a heated argument. I'd sit on my bed with the windows open, listening to each word, happy that for once it wasn't my family's business being smeared around the neighborhood.

As I boarded the Amtrak from Washington that morning in July 2001, I wasn't as excited to go home as I usually am. I felt anxious while I searched for a seat. *Did the separation mean we'd have to sell my house?* I would rather have spent the weekend in my cramped, un–air-conditioned apartment than deal with the issues awaiting me on Long Island.

More dread overcame me several hours later when I saw Dad. He was bony and gaunt. He had shaved his beard off, giving his face a hollow look. He'd lost about fifteen pounds since I'd last seen him, only a month earlier. I met him at my aunt's house, and then we drove to the ocean in Montauk, the easternmost point on Long Island. Dad usually stared at the horizon at the beach. Today, he kept his head down and gazed mostly at the sand. Seagulls squawked overhead as we walked.

"I just love her so much," he said. My father had been living with Junie, her husband, Mario, and their two children for the past few weeks.

Dad isn't a complicated man. The best part of his day is a soak in a hot bath after work. He relaxes his exhausted muscles and scrubs the paint and spackle from his skin. Even after he dries off, he'll still smell of cotton and chalk and fumes from the materials with which he works. When I am in a room where someone is painting, I feel as if Dad were all around me and I'm overcome with a strong need to talk to him or hug him. I want to push my nose into his shoulder to take a big gulp of his soft white cotton T-shirts. When I was growing up, he was rarely confrontational. If he and Mom were fighting, there would come a point when he'd want to forget everything that had happened. He'd say a quick "sorry" and try to get Mom thinking about other things: what they should do that day, a bill that was overdue. He'd try to turn their problems off with a switch.

Dad couldn't turn off the separation. He wasn't taking it well, even though he had lived through his own parents' divorce thirty-two years earlier. Dad was nineteen when his father packed up a Chevy sedan, leaving my grandmother, my father, his two sisters, and their brother behind for another woman. Now Dad and I walked barefoot along the oceanfront. We stopped and sat beside a large piece of driftwood. I ran my fingertips along the smooth, light sur-face and looked at Dad's hands, which were wrinkled and callused. Weakened.

I wanted Dad to stop hurting. I wanted him to jump up and down and do a little dance, or run straight for the water and dive in headfirst before the cold rushed up from his toes—things he'd do to get us girls giggling as children. If Mom was the disciplinarian, Dad was the class clown. Growing up, I knew if Mom wasn't letting me do something, I could rely on Dad to cave in. "Aww, Diane," he'd say, "let her go."

Now his eyes were welling up with tears. I'd only seen him cry once before, at my mother's father's funeral. Watching him react this way turned my toes and fingertips numb. Dad was how I defined strength. How was *I* going to be strong for *him*?

"Mom just needs a break from you," I said. He adjusted his bronze-rimmed prescription sunglasses, then put his hand on my shoulder, which made me so nervous that I talked faster. "Maybe you'll be able to do all the things you always wanted to," I told him. "Maybe this is a good thing." He studied my eyes, which darted away. I didn't believe a word I was saying. Dad sighed and stood up.

He didn't ask me how I was feeling. The answer was, terrible. Trapped. Confused. Unsure of what to say. And I couldn't focus on my own heart—I was too busy watching Dad's crumble. I didn't know how to act without Mom around us. Neither did he. I felt alone—and embarrassed. I wanted Dad to hold my hand and convince me I'd imagined all of this, as he did when I'd awaken after a nightmare as a child. Back then, I never dreamed that I'd have to comfort him someday. But now, on this sunny afternoon at the beach, Dad and I were reversing roles: I became the parent and he, the child.

Before sunset, I reluctantly drove back to our home on Oak Lane, where my mother still lived. Mom barbecued chicken and made macaroni salad. Earlier in the summer, Mom planted torches in her garden next to the deck, and she lit them for us to eat by candlelight.

Mom could tell I was upset. Images of Dad's shriveled stature ran through my mind like a stock ticker. Mom was the one causing him pain, which made me want to scream at her, demand that she take him back.

"Dad looks horrible," I said. "He lost weight."

Mom's back stiffened. Her eyes went from soft to steel. The look said I was disloyal.

"That's not my problem," Mom said. "He has his family. He has you girls. I don't have that support. I'm not going to sit here and be made to feel sorry for him."

"He misses you," I whispered, quickly wiping a tear off my cheek. Mom looked toward the woods out back.

"Don't you care?" I asked. "I don't understand how you can suddenly not care."

I have a great mother. Growing up, she was always on my side. She would pull me into her arms before bedtime and tell me that I would do great things one day. "More than what most people dream of," she'd say.

Tonight all she did was smoke. Every exhalation taunted me in the same way Mrs. Robinson's smoky Os tortured Benjamin in *The Graduate*. Anger sizzled in the end of her burning cigarette, and the smoke lingered around us, holding in all we were holding back.

"I just need to know you still love him," I said. Mom's red-painted toenails flickered as she tapped her foot, teasing me with evidence of happier days, of someone to paint her toenails for. "I need to hear that you always will." Mom took a long drag of her cigarette. She looked back into the woods. She crossed and uncrossed her legs. Then she looked at me.

"I can't do that," she said.

My mother always said she had a sixth sense when it came to her three daughters. She'd be at work or doing the laundry, not thinking of anything in particular, and suddenly one of our faces would pop into her head and she'd be overcome with worry. Sometimes her gut feelings were off, but more often than not, she'd walk into my room and find me belly down on my bed, bawling.

Parents raise children to rely on their love. They rush to their children's side when life goes terribly wrong and care for their every need: A scrape on the knee is neatly dressed. A nagging cold is comforted with homemade chicken soup. A dog hit by a car is given a proper backyard funeral. Devotion and unconditional love are what defines the parent/child relationship. Children thrive on their parents' love and support, and parents, in turn, are equally fulfilled.

Just as parents are committed to their children, children are expected to be equally loyal to their mother and father. Parents have an unspoken understanding with their kids: they'll change our diapers and put up with our adolescent rebellion as long as we repay them with kindness later. Most parents expect their children to support them unconditionally. This unspoken contract follows us into adulthood. We might spend our days contributing to society and impressing our colleagues, but if we don't rush to our parents' side when they need us, they can knock the wind from us with one disapproving look. Their eyes narrow, their brows furrow. They don't have to speak a word for us to get the hint. *Who else loves you like me?*

The subconscious fear that our mother or father might walk away, leaving us all alone, is a tension that drives our relationships with them. *We know we need them.* Even as we grow into adulthood and break away from the nest, taking our first job and moving into a new apartment, we look to our parents for help. There is a deluge of decisions that must be made. We call home for advice on how to deal with a boss or how to register a car in a new state. We rely on the emotional backup our family gives us. *If I fail, I can always go home*, we'll say.

Years later, after we've settled into our own lives and mother- or fatherhood has given us an air of maturity, we continue to look to our parents, our homes, as a hub, a dependable stopping point on our way to somewhere else. Just because we're in our thirties doesn't mean we don't need to crawl into bed beside our mothers and enjoy a good cry. For every problem that arises in our adult life, we expect that our parents will continue to help us find a way to fix it.

The way we see our parents is changed after their divorce. An adult child's feelings are for the first time considered secondary to a parent's. Parents step out of their expected roles: Mom stops behaving like the nurturing caretaker she once was. Dad ceases to act like the strong, solid father on whom we've come to depend. They move out of the house—our reliable, rock-solid home base—around the same time we do and start a new life, while we're still beginning ours. They reinvent themselves and the roles they play in our lives. In doing so, they give us the sense that they're leaving us behind. Divorce can bring out the worst in people, exposing aspects of a parent's personality that were kept below the surface in better times. In watching the divorce play out, we see our parents fall from their pedestals.

In my house, Dad was the provider. His job was to give us financial support. Though Mom always worked, we looked to her for emotional support. When my parents split up, I figured we'd work through it as we did any crisis. Mom would rub my forehead and bring me tissues when I was upset. Dad would lose himself in work. He'd stop by the house to hug and comfort me, but I didn't expect him to sit at the foot of my bed for hours and help me figure out what I was feeling. Many of us rest our hearts on an assumption that our mother will always put her family first. But in a divorce, mothers put themselves first, which makes them unrecognizable to us. Says one young woman, "It's like this person who lives in my house isn't my mom anymore. She's making our lives miserable, and I'm not willing to get to know this person. I want the old her back." Fathers, while an essential part of our lives, are often not as emotionally available, which makes us depend on them less. Says one study on adult children of divorce, "Supportive and warm mothering may be more of a given in many families, whereas fathering may vary more dramatically." So while we may blame a father for breaking up our family when he initiates a divorce, we may forgive him more easily than a mother in the same situation. A mother isn't supposed to just walk away from family.

Paige's mother left her father a few summers ago, right after Paige's college graduation. Before the split, Paige, now twenty-seven, often confided in her mom. They'd talk about everything from boyfriends to college classes. "I always felt so close to my mother," she says. "I believed everything she said." Her mother's choice to divorce her father cast her in an unflattering light. She wasn't a woman who would make love work at any cost. She was a quitter. "For so long, I believed my mom was similar to me. She taught me that you never give up on people," Paige says. "It made me wonder. . . . How could she give up on Dad? I was like, 'Wow. We don't see eye to eye as much as I thought.' "

Parents disappoint. All of us have experienced a moment in our pasts when we realized our parents weren't as superhuman as we believed. A few years ago, Mom refused to go to church with Dad on Christmas Eve. They had been separated for several months, but Dad was still staying over sometimes, and both agreed to spend the holiday together. Mom didn't want our neighbors to see her with Dad at church. "People will talk," she'd said. Afterward, I remember watching Mom in the kitchen doing dishes and sensing that she wasn't the mighty force who could fix any mess. *She cared what people thought,* and she was proud, which made her just as human and vulnerable as I was. Divorce pushes us to see our parents with the same honesty. Parents are at their weakest. They're not immune from heartache and jealousy. They lose weight. They collapse to their knees in the kitchen and scream.

They fall hard. So hard that they pull away from their adult children to survive. In an attempt to figure out their own feelings, they abandon the nurturing or provider role and look out only for themselves. Adult children are forced to fly solo. Nearly every adult child holds this role reversal against their parents. It seems nothing less than selfish.

When Paige arrived home for Christmas that first year after her parents split, there was not one holiday light hanging on her family's house. In previous years, neighbors would walk several blocks just to catch a glimpse of the sheer number of light strands Paige's father would nail around the windows. The festive mood Paige had come to expect on Christmas seemed forced. Her mother cooked dinner with little flair. Her parents, who had agreed to spend the holiday together, didn't try to alleviate the situation; their disgusted attitudes seemed to inflame it. Changes such as this were overwhelming, and Paige couldn't help her tears.

Neither parent comforted her, which shocked Paige. Her mother's cool behavior was more troubling. "Mom always gave everything to us," says Paige. "Her whole life was us. It was clear that day that my sister and I were unhappy. For the first time in our lives, Mom didn't try to please us." At one point, her mother took Paige aside. "Look," her mother said, "I need to do this for myself. You need to find a way to understand that." When her mother didn't hug or reassure her, Paige was crushed. It was as though some unsigned contract had been broken. Says Paige, "It killed me."

Unmarried adult children may carry larger fears of abandonment. Before marriage, a parent is often our most powerful anchor. Married children will confide in their husbands or wives. Unmarried children don't have a secondary source of undying love on which to fall back so they feel even more lonely. Friends, or a new significant other, are willing to listen to our problems, to an extent. Still, we *want* to talk to our parents. They're the ones who caused our pain. Why can't they acknowledge that and talk to us about *our* feelings?

"Mom never asked once how my sister or I was doing," says Stephanie, twenty-six. Despite the fact that she was in a five-year relationship, Stephanie only wanted to talk to her mother about the divorce. It would be easier, since she wouldn't have to explain the backstory. But her mother wasn't listening. Stephanie's mother would drive two hours to see her. She'd spend a weekend, and they'd talk for hours about all the changes facing her mother. Stephanie would listen patiently, waiting for the moment her mother would finally turn her attentions on her. She never did. If Stephanie tried to bring up her feelings, her mother would change the subject and bring the conversation back to her own struggles. Stephanie wasn't used to being ignored. She grew angry.

Unacknowledged pain causes resentment in the adult child of divorce. It can make a child feel unloved and underappreciated. Typically, parents are the only ones willing to listen to the mundane details of their children's days. After a divorce, the details of our days grow complex and laced with grief. "I know you more than you know you," Mom liked to tell me. Parents know we're upset—they've seen us sulk since we were toddlers. But they also know they're the ones who created this discontent. Hearing about it will hurt too much. So they tune us out. They're preoccupied with their own feelings, which appears selfish to us. We want them to care about our pain, too. Instead, they shift their eyes away and change the subject. They tell us we need to move on. It's *my* divorce, not yours, they'll sternly remind us, recounting their own emotions in an attempt to "outmartyr" us. Instead of validating our heartache, parents only tell us how much *worse off* they are, and our feelings are tossed aside.

Sometimes so is their interest in us.

When I talked to Brittany, a twenty-six-year-old teacher, she was due to have her first baby soon. She assumed her mother would help her pick out colors for the nursery or shop for a snuggly. Instead, her mother is consumed with dating. It's rare that she'll ask about Brittany's pregnancy. Her mother wants to talk about her new love interest, a man she met in a chat room on the Internet. Brittany assumed her mother would throw her a baby shower during her last trimester. "It didn't even cross her mind," says Brittany. Her husband's family had to give her a party at the last minute. "I'm pregnant for the first time in my life," Brittany says, "and my mother isn't there for me. I feel left behind."

Brittany's younger sister just moved to Vermont and complains that her mother never calls to check in on her. Two weeks before Brittany's brother was set to leave for college, her mother still hadn't taken him shopping for dorm essentials such as a shower caddy or towels. Says Brittany, "She's ready to be done as a mom. It's like she shut down that part of herself."

Parents are so weakened by a divorce, they often don't have the strength to be there for their adult children, even in the simplest of ways. Hearing about your new boyfriend for a couple of hours can feel constraining to them. There is so much they need to do to get their life right again. Stress keeps their minds from focusing on any one thing, leaving them forgetful and seemingly unconcerned. They shed their role like a snake slithering out of a dried skin. They force themselves to feel less responsible for their adult children, who don't even know what hit them. We look up and our parents are gone.

This unshackling frees parents. They are no longer bound to anything, which allows them to begin the process of self-reinvention. As parents become new people, adult children watch in shock. I'm reminded of a quote from V. S. Naipaul's novel *The Mimic Men*: "Everything about me became temporary and unimportant; I was consciously holding myself back for the reality which lay elsewhere." That's how I felt—I was a part of my mother's old life, not her new one.

Brittany's father had worked for the federal government for years. He'd often travel, but otherwise, her father led a fairly typical middle-aged existence: thinning hair, gray slacks, a clean shave before work. After he left Brittany's mother, her father became more aware of his appearance. He lost weight and started working out at a gym. He grew a goatee, which Brittany thought made him look sloppy. When Brittany was growing up, he'd have a drink on special occasions. One morning, Brittany found her father hungover after drinking too much at a company party. "It was like he was back in college," says Brittany. "Now he's dating a married woman. He's regressed so much."

It isn't uncommon for an adult child of divorce to feel as if a parent has taken a few steps back. Parents who come home from work and plop on the couch in front of the TV are a relic of the past. To avoid feeling lonely, parents go out and meet people. They live the singles lifestyle. The responsible parent, who puts family and finances first, is gone. Psychologists have long identified regressive behaviors in young children experiencing a divorce. There is a fear the children will resume the behaviors of a previous stage of development, such as a third grader wanting to suck on a pacifier. Adult children watch their parents regress in similar ways. Psychologists say regression is a side effect of stress. When parents divorce, they cope with multiple stresses all at once. They're losing a lifestyle, their home, their in-laws, their closest friend, and sometimes their children—in essence, their identities. They can suddenly find themselves in the throes of a midlife crisis. The weight of the changes transforms how they function and how they see themselves. Their behavior can sometimes resemble that of an immature teenager.

Brittany felt that even her parents' relationship took on a juvenile quality. The day her father told Brittany he'd cheated on her mother again, he called Brittany crying. The indiscretion sent Brittany into an emotional tailspin. She wanted to yell, "You did this! You're the one who hurt us. What right do you have to be upset?" Her parents got back together a couple of weeks later. They came over to her house for dinner and canoodled at the table. Her father explained that he was committed to going to therapy and working things out. Then, a couple of days later, Brittany's mother called her in tears. "He said he isn't sure if he loves me," her mother said.

They were on-again, off-again for several months. Brittany's father was as noncommittal as a twenty-something single male. "The back and forth was almost comical," Brittany says. But the impact on Brittany was real. Just when she'd feel relief that her parents were back together, they'd break up, and she'd find herself grieving again.

Adult children ride the tide of their parents' relationships. When they're up, we're up. When they're down, we're down.

Some therapists say an adversarial divorce can exacerbate regressive behaviors in parents; the process demands immature behavior. "What's mine is yours" suddenly becomes "That's mine, not yours." Parents get caught up in legal proceedings: every exchange is an opportunity to get back at their former spouse. One therapist says that some attorneys encourage a dependency among their clients. They promise them they'll iron out every uncomfortable detail, which makes a parent feel cared for. Then, during proceedings, a parent can go off on a childish rant without a worry. Their even-keeled attorney will still get the job done. In other words, says the therapist, divorcing parents find quasi "parents" of their own in their divorce lawyers, which allows them, often, to act without consequence.

An adversarial divorce is divorce as war. Fathers hide money. Mothers pack up all their husbands' things and have movers deliver them to their law office. Fathers steal their wives' credit cards and charge them to the limit. Mothers smash a figurine treasured by their husbands as they walk out the door. Parents *act* like children in a bad divorce. They have poor judgment and make poor choices.

Carrie, a twenty-seven-year-old marriage and family therapist, was twenty-three when her parents split up. Always the strict and orderly homemaker, her mother was letting things slide now that her husband of thirty years had moved out. Carrie's little sister, Erin, who was in high school, started dating Rodney, who was several years older. Before the divorce, her mother forbade it. Now she didn't even raise an eyebrow. A few months later, Carrie's mother allowed Rodney, who rode horses in junior rodeo, to move into Erin's bedroom. He brought his infant son. Carrie says her mother's new liberal policies were selfish. "My mother was scared Erin would move out if she didn't let Rodney move in," says Carrie. Feeling unsteady, her mother needed her daughter for emotional support and put her own needs ahead of what was best for Erin.

Before heading off to begin her graduate degree in counseling—she had wanted to be a marriage therapist even before her parents split up—Carrie moved home one summer. By then, her sixteen-year-old sister and Rodney were engaged. Carrie felt uncomfortable; she didn't approve of the relationship. She was even less comfortable when she learned of her family's new habit. Every evening, Carrie's mother, Erin, and Rodney would sneak out the back door and smoke marijuana. "They were discreet about it," says Carrie, "because they knew I didn't approve. But I could smell it. I'd hear lighters. I kept wondering, 'Who are these people!?' "

Carrie didn't say anything to her mother for several weeks. She was disappointed—and livid. But she didn't know how to raise the issue without sounding as if she were telling her mother what to do. One weekend, Carrie's boyfriend came to visit. After he arrived, they went to her bedroom to talk. They lay down on her bed and hugged. They'd missed each other. Her mother caught a glimpse of the cozy position from the hallway. She yelled from outside the door, "We won't have that in this house."

All Carrie could think about was her mother's hypocrisy. She had been acting irresponsibly for months, and Carrie hadn't said a word. As far as Carrie was concerned, her mother had lost all authority as a parent. Her opinion and judgment were less welcome in Carrie's life.

"I'm tired of the double standard in this family," she said to her mother, following her into her bedroom. Her mother was less agitated, more matter-of-fact. "You were in an inappropriate position," her mother said.

"Yeah, well I know you're smoking pot," said Carrie, "and I don't think that's right. But you're an adult, so I don't get in your business." Her mother was speechless.

Divorce can equalize the parent-child dynamic. Just as Brittany stopped taking her father so seriously after he grew a goatee and started partying, Carrie stopped believing in her mother's *right* to parent her. Carrie's mother stopped acting like a mother, so Carrie figured there was no point in acting like a daughter. She could live in her mother's house without rules because she no longer respected her mother's choices.

Parents aren't the only ones who change during a divorce. Adult children are transformed as well. In early adulthood, adult children are just beginning to build more mature versions of their relationships with their mothers and fathers. Therapists call this period "renegotiation." Parent and child attempt to shed their old relationship and build a new one based on friendship—not parenting alone. This is a slow metamorphosis. Like two caterpillars snuggling in a cocoon, waiting to molt, an adult child and his or her parent emerge together only when they're ready to. There is no reason to rush; the changes will come as surely as the moon at dusk—in due time.

Divorce breaks open the cocoon. The caterpillars snuggling inside squirm out. They can sense that something in their metamorphosis is premature. They're not ready; they haven't even grown their wings. But they must emerge anyway.

Parents and adult children are forced to fly blindly together during divorce. As during any time they've been unsure, an adult child takes the mother or father's lead. Parents begin to act differently, so their children begin to act differently. If parents pull away from their family, an adult child simply reaches out for them, soaring through the air with the grace of a trapeze artist to grab hold of their hand and swing them back. Prompted by a sense of premature abandonment, adult children are desperate to reconnect to their parents, even if their parents are abruptly shedding old roles. The desperation—or a fear of losing our parents—pushes adult children into a predicament. We must find new ways to connect with parents so we can keep them close to us.

An adult child's role evolves as a parent's needs change. In the initial stages of a divorce, a parent may require a confidant, or someone with whom to share his or her secrets. Later, the parent may simply need someone to iron his or her clothes or repair a leaky faucet, the way the spouse did for twenty-five years. A parent may unknowingly look to his or her kids to fill voids created by the spouse's absence. We rush to our parent's side out of duty and friendship and offer Band-Aids of hope: "You will make it on your own!" "I'll make dinner the next several nights." "I know you still love Mom!"

Adult children want to help, to make themselves useful. They shoulder their parents' worries. They try to be the good son or the loyal daughter, honoring their parents with endless devotion and care. Says family sociologist Teresa Cooney, "Adult children take on pain like it's them hurting."

In the beginning, adult children assume that these new roles are temporary. After the divorce settles down, the roles will start to fade. Things will return to normal. Only they don't.

Household responsibilities are usually divvied up in marriages: Dad takes out the trash and turns on the grill. Mom walks the dogs and pays the monthly electric bill. Husband and wife come to depend on the other to keep the house running smoothly. When one partner leaves the equation, the daily hum of life is interrupted. Mom is left to walk the dogs *and* take out the trash. Dad must ready the grill *and* pay the monthly electric bill. And while each tries to take on the other's burden—if only to prove they can do it alone— they eventually look to their children for help.

I have a friend I'll call Ivy whose parents split up a few years back. Ivy lived at home with her mother. Her father moved into an apartment nearby. One morning in March, several inches of snow fell. Ivy's mother needed to get to work. But before she could get her car out, she'd have to shovel the driveway. Her mother went out to shovel alone but returned after a few minutes. Her toes were numb. Her neatly styled hair was matted down with clumps of snow. She angrily flung Ivy's bedroom door open, demanding that Ivy wake up and help her shovel snow. Ivy reluctantly climbed out of bed and pulled on her snow boots. Outside, her mother kept mumbling, "I'm not the man in this house. I'm just not."

Adult children fill in for an absent parent because *they're the next best thing*. Ivy's father would usually wake early to shovel the driveway and scrape the ice off the cars. Her mother would only have to dress warmly, get in her car, and blow a kiss good-bye. With her husband gone, the task fell to Ivy's mother and then to Ivy. She expected Ivy to take out the trash on Tuesdays and Fridays, mow the lawn once every two weeks, and walk the dog daily.

"I felt like I was her new husband," says Ivy.

One twenty-nine-year-old man interviewed says that whenever he flies home to visit his mother, he spends his "vacation" doing odd jobs around her house. He'll check on her finances. He even made an arrangement with a neighbor to mow her grass. One young woman visited her father's new apartment and made him dinners nightly, including his favorite dishes that his wife used to make. Another brought her father groceries whenever she visited him in a motel where he was staying; her father had always relied on her mother to grocery shop.

An adult child can feel his mother's or father's absence as much as a parent can, which is why we step in. We think, *Our mothers and fathers shouldn't have to take on these sticky new problems alone. We can help.* An adult child reenters his parent's life as a grown-up—as a new partner. Instead of having his wife to walk hand in hand through life with, a father has his adult child. Sometimes we play this role for both of our parents at once.

Sarah, thirty-four, was already married when her father ran out on her family. He left her mother in a fix: he ran up credit-card bills and spent down their retirement money. He borrowed against their home's mortgage. With her father already living on the opposite coast and creditors stalking like coyotes, Sarah knew it was only a matter of time before her mother lost her house. Sarah and her mother conspired about what "they" should do. Sarah also talked to her husband. Ultimately, Sarah and her husband decided to buy her mother's house from her—and move in with her. A joint solution agreed upon by all three. Once they moved in, Sarah, her husband, and her mother cared for the house equally. They were three partners starting out a new life together.

Researchers say parents expect their children to contribute to a household after divorce. A mother who spent years working part-time or earning less than her husband can find herself struggling just to make ends meet. Pressure mounts on the adult child. Instead of their bedroom remaining a rent-free place to crash, an adult child is often expected to pick up the financial slack left behind by a parent. A newly single parent might ask an adult child to help pay the mortgage or the rent. The child may become responsible for paying a utility bill or buying the groceries. These demands are most often made by mothers, for whom divorce is a risk factor for poverty. Many mothers haven't worked outside the home in decades and find themselves combing the classified ads. Even if they don't demand our assistance, we often feel an obligation to help. It's hard to watch your mother or father, who has lived a comfortable existence, suddenly become poor. A parent's new financial situation can cause an adult child to question their life plan: should I quit school and go to work full-time to help pay Mom's bills?

Like any true spouse, an adult child will sometimes take on the whole household. The child's devotion to keeping the family running smoothly is resolute. Their family does not have to end just because one family member walked away. An adult child assumes that if they step up where the absent parent stepped down, it will restore a family to its original glory.

Wendy, thirty-one, was an undergraduate when her mother moved out, leaving Wendy's fourteen-year-old brother and father alone in their colonial home. Wendy would lie awake in her dorm room bunk worrying about her father and brother. She'd call home to check on them. She didn't want to speak to her mother, who, in Wendy's eyes, had deserted her family. Wendy grew homesick. She figured she should be thankful she lived so far away from her parents. But she didn't want to ignore what was transpiring. She wanted to help. "I felt like I needed to go home," Wendy says.

While many of Wendy's friends moved to major cities and took glamorous jobs after graduation, Wendy decided to return home to the small town in upstate New York where she had grown up and attend graduate school at the local university. Someone, she says, needed to "Krazy Glue" her family back together. "No one was asking me to come home," she said, "but a part of me felt like I needed to take care of them. I needed to go home and clean up the mess."

Wendy made dinner every night. She kept grocery lists and did the shopping. She scrubbed the family home from top to bottom twice a week. "I was the only woman in the house," she says, "and I began playing wife."

Being her father's "spouse" was depressing. She missed her mother and her old singleton lifestyle. When she looked in the mirror, she could see only her mother's face. *I'm not ready to be her*, she thought.

Two years into the new routine, Wendy's father decided she

should start paying rent. He wasn't asking for very much money. Wendy was working; money wasn't an issue. But to her, the suggestion cheapened her years of hard work and devotion. She had changed the course of her life to move home. Paying rent, she thought, made her feel like a burden. She had assumed her father realized how much he needed her. "It was like all of these things I did for him meant nothing," she says. Realizing how wrapped up she had become in making her father happy, Wendy decided she needed to separate herself from her "spousal" role and just be a daughter again.

Now, several years later, Wendy laughs about it. "They were absolutely fine," she says. She believed her Dad and brother needed her—but really, she says, she needed them. She wanted to fix their pain as much as she wanted to fix her own. With no other idea of how to connect with her father, she became his caretaker. "It was unhealthy," she says.

When we assume the role of a missing parent, though it is often our own idea, we grow resentful. Anger comes with the realization that we're putting our own lives aside and making sacrifices for our parents. We're thrust into a role that no one else is willing to take on. Sometimes we find ourselves cleaning up the mess one parent left behind.

Bob, twenty-seven, says his mother has been bipolar his entire life. As a teenager, Bob never really saw the effects of the psychological disorder. His father always made sure his mother took her medication. After his parents split up, Bob, then nineteen, says his mother grew depressed. She went off her meds without telling anyone. She started to behave strangely: She partied and blew through her savings account, taking random road trips. She slept with a teenage boy—one of her daughter's friends. With his father gone, it was up to Bob to get his mother back on track. One afternoon, he sat her down and scolded her as his father would have done. He made sure she once again swallowed her pills. His life centered around keeping his mother's life stable. Forget that this was his final summer home before he went off to college. Bob didn't have time for fun. As the summer progressed, Bob felt like a caged bird. *How could Dad leave me with this mess?* he wondered. "It was hard enough just to take care of myself," he says. "I feared I'd have to manage her life again."

Adult kids know nothing of emotional health when they see their parents struggling. Children's initial instinct is to be there for their parents. They want their parents to know that someone will still love and care for them, even if it isn't the other parent. *Who else will love you like me?* Now it's us asking them.

Adult children think they know the intimate details of their parents' lives because they're old enough to remember how and when their parents' relationship changed. Adult children who become their mother's or father's confidant, the keeper of secrets, often learn more than they ever really needed or wanted to know. To have a parent confide in us is problematic, though we don't quite see it that way— at first. In the beginning, we're only responding to our parents' immediate need: Mom is crying in her bedroom. We can't pretend we don't hear her shudders and sniffles. So we walk inside her room. We place a hand on her back and listen. And listen. And listen. Says one young woman interviewed, "I was Dad's only friend."

Parents believe their adult children will understand them like no one else. "You know how your father is . . ." "Remember how your mother used to . . . ?" Yes, we'll say. Of course we do. Adult children know their mothers and fathers to the core. But listening to their pain often means learning things about a parent we don't feel comfortable knowing. We're too connected to the drama to separate ourselves. Hearing parents talk about what was wrong in years past hurts us. Yet we're forced to listen. Sometimes we think we want to know. Children whose parents admit to an affair sometimes seek out this role. They're looking for answers. Listening to a parent talk things out can help adult children understand why their mother or father wandered.

After he left home, Bob's father often talked to his sons to try to make sense of why he cheated on their mother. Electric shock therapy had left his bipolar wife not only emotionally numb but physically numb as well. His father said he hadn't felt sexual fulfillment in a long time. "Can you imagine going several years without physical pleasure?" he asked his sons. While Bob and his brother sympathized, they also felt uncomfortable. Who wants to know the details of their parents' sex lives? Says one young woman, "Many things I learned after the divorce fall under the category of 'things I wish I didn't know about my parents.'" We don't want to know that Mom had an abortion when we were five or that when Dad said he was on vacation, he was with his mistress. Who needs to hear that one parent openly admitted they never wanted a family?

Details of a failed marriage are embarrassing. Parents don't want to share their secrets with just anyone. Says one woman who recently divorced, "Who wants to call someone and talk about how their husband is an alcoholic and cheats on them?" Parents expect their children to offer a nonjudgmental ear. Listening to our parents' problems can be draining. As in any close friendship, problems blur. A child may start to believe that her mother's problems are her own. Says one young woman interviewed, "I didn't know where my mother stopped and I began."

The first week after her father left her mother, Jessica offered her mother a couch in her home. Jessica, then thirty-two, was married with a two-year-old and a five-year-old. She couldn't stay up nights at her mother's and leave her children. So her mother temporarily moved in with her daughter. She'd stay up all night long crying. "Pull yourself together," Jessica would tell her. Jessica talked her mother through every emotional stage. She went from anger—"We just started thinking about our retirement"—to worry. "What's going to happen to the house? Oh, I don't want to lose the house," her mother said. Jessica sat by her mother's side and comforted her, with the attentiveness of a best friend. But she couldn't detach herself from what her mother was saying. A few weeks later, Jessica had a meltdown in her living room after dropping off her youngest daughter at preschool.

Her mother felt horrible that Jessica was suffering because of the divorce. "You need to take care of yourself," she told Jessica. She said she'd stop leaning on Jessica and talk more to her friends. Jessica was relieved. But within days, her mother was harping on Jessica's father again, talking to her as though nothing she could say would hurt her daughter. "I think he had affairs in the past," she told Jessica. "Oh, and I'm going to have to go get an HIV test." Jessica took it upon herself to shield her mother from additional upset. As her parents' wedding anniversary approached, Jessica made sure her mother had plans. If her mother brought up the past, Jessica would try to get her to focus on her grandchildren. "A therapist said I should stop being there for her. But she is my mother. She needed someone to talk to," says Jessica, "so I listened."

Loyalties die hard between parent and child. As much as they don't want to listen, adult children often have difficulty turning a deaf ear. They know their parents have no one else to talk to. For the first few years or so after his parents split up, William listened to his mother bash men repeatedly. "Men think they can get away with everything," she'd say. "Men are such babies. Men need a young wife to make them happy." William says it was hard not to take her rants on men personally. He would listen and think, "Wait. I'm a man, and I don't do that." At first, William listened patiently. He felt that his mother deserved a grace period to release her anger from the divorce. "I'd let her get it out of her system," he says. It didn't stop. "A year and a half after their separation, I couldn't listen to it anymore. It was becoming too overwhelming." William decided to change the dynamic. Instead of putting up with her man-bashing, he'd be there for her in a different way: he'd give her a reality check.

One day, he listened to his mother go on and on about her marriage as if she and his father had the enduring connection of Fred and Ethel on *I Love Lucy*. She'd made it sound as if she never did anything wrong and that she was the ideal wife. Instead of passively agreeing, William spoke up. "It's not like you had a perfect marriage and Dad just decided to leave," William told her. "You didn't share any interests." *Remember?*

When adult children are asked why they're so upset after a divorce, they often find themselves recounting their parents' pain rather than their own. One young woman decided to write in to an online support group a year after her parents split. As she started to write the e-mail, she realized that all the things she was writing were things *her mother* was upset about. Her father left her mother without saying good-bye. She wrote, "He left without saying good-bye." The young woman caught herself. He didn't say good-bye to her mother. But she and her father had talked that morning.

A parent can get used to having a best friend in a son or daughter. As time goes on, an adult child will try to slide back into the old way—a relationship centered around the child's needs—and begin talking about her own problems. A mother or father listens but then adds to the conversation. Think of an exchange between friends: You tell a story. Your friend acknowledges your story and adds a story of his own.

Carrie finally resisted interacting with her mother as a friend after several months of doing so. Knowing that her mother wasn't seeking emotional support from more traditional sources—a thera-pist, a support group—Carrie decided she needed to get her mother talking to someone else besides her. She researched a support group at the local church. She told her mother the date and time to show up and handed her the address. Her mother never went. She kept trying to talk to her daughter. "I can't talk to you about your rela-tionship with Dad," Carrie told her. "I can't hear certain things be-cause you're my parent."

Her mother sniffed. "I listen to things about you and your boyfriends," she said. *But that's not about you and some guy*, Carrie thought. *That's about you and my dad.*

Anytime Carrie started to talk about a guy she was dating, her mother would relate it to her own relationship. "That's like me and your father," she'd say. It could be on any topic, says Carrie. One day, she was talking to her mother about how difficult men are to under-stand. Carrie had been trying to get her boyfriend to see a fault in his personality. Her mother had a story to tell about Carrie's father.

Carrie wanted to rewind time and freeze-frame their old mother and daughter relationship. They had talked often then, but her mother had held some things back to protect her daughter. Now her mother treated Carrie as she did any friend. She told her whatever came to mind.

"Being there" for our parents has some unexpected side effects. A temporary arrangement becomes a permanent change. As each phase of the divorce begins, parents continue to look to us in the same open-ended ways. In the beginning, they want us to bad-mouth our other parent or cry with them over the loss of the house. Then they'll expect us to listen to them talk about their new boyfriend or an argument they had with one of our siblings. Why shouldn't we gossip with them about our other parent? Once we start, parents expect us to keep on listening.

When parents and children interact as friends, issues more commonly associated with friendships surface. Jealousy plagues newly divorced parents, who often feel as if the split reflects their shortcomings. Everyone seems to be better at life than they are, including their adult children.

Adult children sense their parents studying them. They eye our existence like cultural anthropologists searching for the secret to surviving on their own. They want to be our equals. Looking at their adult children's accomplishments with fresh eyes can remind parents of all they haven't done. Parents would never admit they envy their children; it makes them feel like bad parents. But sometimes they do.

One young woman, who is a twenty-seven-year-old graduate student, showed her mother a paper she had published in a journal—a big feat for any aspiring academic—a year after her parents divorced. Her mother threw it aside. Typically, her mother would insist they celebrate with dinner out. Instead, seeing the publication unearthed memories of the things her marriage had kept her from doing. "My mom didn't get to go away to college," she says. "Instead, she married at twenty-one to get out of the house. She wanted to travel and see the world. She wanted to be recognized for her intelligence." Her daughter had done all those things.

Envy runs both ways. An attorney whose parents split up was floored when her mother was engaged a few months later. "I had been in a relationship seven years and I couldn't get the guy to marry me," she says. "Then my mom meets someone and falls in love, and he asks her right away." It made her own love life feel inadequate. Watching a parent skip down the road to happiness can be intoxicating. *I want to be that happy,* we think. The desire might inspire adult children to hold a magnifying glass up to themselves. You might realize you're in a job that doesn't challenge you and feel a tinge of irritation when your father tells you he quit his corporate job to start a sailing school. Immature? Yes. Fun? Yes! Their new beginnings can make ours feel stale. They're coming of age all over again.

When parents act like children, someone needs to step in and care for them. In the same way we crave to be coddled by parents through the difficulty of divorce, parents are hoping for the same level of attention from their adult child. Unlike playing spouse, "the parent role" calls forth a much more nurturing and supportive piece of us. We're not warming someone else's shoes. We're taking on the parents' well-being. Parents come to rely on us in the same ways we've looked to them. We're a fallback to which they can turn if their plans don't work out. We are their lone support as they take *their* first wobbly steps.

Adult children can become chronic worriers as a result. In one study conducted by Pennsylvania State University, researchers found that 77 percent of adult children surveyed worried for their parents after a divorce, as they would worry for the well-being of their own child. The adults in the study were concerned not only for how their parents would weather the divorce but also for how they'd build a healthy future. How will they manage in the long run?

The night Stephanie, twenty-six, found out her parents were splitting up, she kept herself awake all night, fretting about her mother. "I was planning out Mom's life," she says. She worried less about her father. He made more money and had initiated the split. "We should probably move Mom back to the Bay Area," she said to herself. She was preparing a mental checklist. Her parents had recently moved from San Francisco to Sacramento, where the houses were cheaper. All of Stephanie's mother's friends lived back in the Bay Area. *She'll be too isolated and lonely here,* she thought.

Then she pictured her mother in San Francisco. How would she make it on her own? "She can get her old job back," Stephanie reassured herself. "She should be able to afford a condo." These thoughts consumed Stephanie, until the morning, when she called her mother and told her about the plan. Her mother had a different idea: she wanted to stay in Sacramento; she wasn't sure why. Stephanie still worried. She says she won't stop worrying until all the uncertainty ends and she knows that her mother is going to be OK.

"Would you like a snack, honey?" You remember the scene—you're stretched out on the couch, watching cartoons, your broken arm elevated above your head. In comes Mom with a platter and sets it on your belly. Chamomile tea, cookies, all of your favorite snacks. Mommy is here to nurse you back to health. When Marisa's parents divorced, her mother was left with no one to arrange her a tray of tea and cookies. After she had surgery, her mother was told she should take it easy. She called her daughter and asked her to come home and care for her. Marisa was at college, a plane ride away, and couldn't leave school. When she told her mother she couldn't come, her mother wailed. Her mother felt cast off, as any child would have. She yelled at Marisa, calling her selfish and ungrateful.

There are times when our parents stop resembling parents at all, and we find ourselves keeping close tabs on them because we are their only caregiver. This is what happened to David, whose parents split up thirty years ago when he was just out of high school. When David's father moved out of the family's bungalow in a suburb of Chicago, David worried for his father's health. His father was an alcoholic. David and his brother, who were roommates, would often call to check in on their father. They hated going to his apartment. He lived in a tiny, dilapidated place in a rough neighborhood near Wrigley Field. On a weekend afternoon, he and his brother were talking about the legacy of their parents' unhappy marriage when they realized they'd never heard from their father. They had called him a few times over the past several weeks. He hadn't picked up.

They tried him again. No answer. David imagined the worst. "He's lying dead on the floor," David said to himself.

The brothers hopped in the car and drove across town. They rehearsed what they'd say along the way and how they'd ream him out for being so inconsiderate. When they got to his apartment, they pounded on the door. Their father was inside nursing a vodka. "When I saw him," David says, "I wept." His brother hugged his father. "You bonehead," David said, lovingly. "We've been calling you. Why didn't you pick up the phone?" As if he were dealing with a lost child found in a mall, David was gentle, trying to make his father feel OK about his own mistakes.

"We said everything a parent might say to a child," David recalls. They even came up with a signal. David would ring the phone twice, a clue to his father that it was his son calling and not a random telemarketer. Without his sons to check up on him, his father might one day die in his apartment feeling unloved and lonely. David and his brother took it upon themselves to make sure that would never happen.

Because they sometimes feel deserted by their spouse, parents may say disturbing things to get an adult child's attention. Call it the adult version of the temper tantrum. Divorced parents want to feel as though they are still the center of *someone's* world. They want their adult children to be thinking about them even when we should be thinking of ourselves. So they dangle in front of us a terrifying notion—suicide.

Mandy, twenty-seven, had been fighting with her mother on and off since her parents split. She got in to work one morning and found an e-mail from her mother. "I don't know if life is worth living anymore," she wrote. Mandy is a graphic designer. She sat at her desk at the magazine where she works, in shock. Even though she was on deadline, she couldn't focus. She kept hearing her mother's words in her head. *I don't know if life is worth living. Could Mom mean that?* Mandy shook her head. She doubted her mother was seriously contemplating suicide.

But what if . . . ? "It just scared me to death because if she ever did do something, I'd feel so guilty for not calling," says Mandy. The bid for attention worked. Despite the requests piling up on her desk, Mandy picked up the phone. "Oh, hi!" her mother said brightly. Mandy told her she got her e-mail. Her mother made light of her comment. Once she had gotten Mandy's attention, her mother was satisfied. Her instant phone call proved to Mandy's mother how much her daughter cared. This isn't to say suicidal thoughts shouldn't be taken seriously. Many adult kids report hearing their parents speak of ending their life after divorce. But when parents repeatedly make empty threats, they probably just want your attention.

Or your help. Many of us find we must help our parents prep for their new lives. Lara, twenty-five, returned home to Tennessee for one last Christmas with her parents when she was twenty-three. Her parents planned to depart amicably. Her mother would move to Chicago two days after the holiday; her father would stay in their home. "Oddly, it was the best Christmas of my life," says Lara. "My parents didn't want to focus on what was happening, so I got to be the center of attention." They baked cookies, decorated the tree, and opened presents. Her dad gave her mother a stereo system—the same gift he gave each of his daughters as they went away to college.

The following day, Lara helped her mother pack up her car. She set up an e-mail account in her mother's name. Lara acted excited. "Where are you going to find an apartment? What kind of job do you think you'll get?" she asked her mother. Lara showed her how to pay a credit card online. She taught Dad how to use the washer and dryer. "I was teaching them things I'd recently learned," says Lara. "I felt like we were all growing up together."

Two days after Christmas, her father snapped a photo of Lara and her mother in front of her white Ford Taurus, all packed up. Her mother cried as she waved good-bye. "I'm sorry," she yelled to them. Lara and her father went into the house. Without her mother fluttering about, the rooms seemed unusually still and quiet. Lara and her father didn't talk about her mother's leaving. "I wasn't feeling," says Lara. "I was just taking care of everybody." They talked instead about their New Year's Eve plans and took down the Christmas tree. Lara made a slew of dinners, including a huge batch of lentil soup, and put them in the freezer.

Lara and her father sat together at dinner the night before she was to return to college. They ate the lentil soup. They talked about a date her father was going on. Out of nowhere, Lara was overwhelmed with a desire to connect with her father. She grabbed his hand and pressed her own over it. "Dad," she said, "you're going to be OK."

Her father nodded. He took a deep breath, his eyes welling up with tears. Lara was reassuring him as much as she was reassuring herself.

"Yeah," he said. "Yeah. I guess I am." The poignancy of the moment touched Lara.

"That must be how parents feel when their children go into the world," she says. "I had the realization that I wasn't going to have to worry as much as I thought. Dad will make it."

Anyone poisoned searches for an antidote. So the inevitable question is, How do I avoid the poison? What might I do to keep from stepping into one of these roles?

Therapists talk often to adult children about setting boundaries. Think of a boundary as a way to separate yourself from the drama. Boundaries are a loose set of "rules" that you can outline to help dic-

tate your role in a divorce. The hope is that setting up these boundaries with our parents will help them understand the difference between talking to a friend about their divorce and talking to their
child. Parents won't have a clue how difficult it is for you to step in as
their "parent" or "confidant" unless you tell them. The revelations
may keep them from leaning on their adult children so heavily.

All adult children will be troubled by different aspects of the
roles into which they step. Adult children should think about behaviors or conversations that have upset them. What made you uncomfortable? Figure out what's "out of bounds" and what's welcome
territory. Once you're clear on your message, you should try to sit
down with your parent and explain the lines you're drawing.

The teenage Iris in Gregory Maguire's *Confessions of an Ugly
Stepsister* cuts her mother off when she begins to share too much of
the family's problems: " 'Mama,' says Iris. She yawns. 'These are
adult things and I am a child.' " Adult children need to be equally direct with their parents, says psychologist Robert Emery. *But what do
we say?* Keep it simple. "I love you very much, Dad, and I know
you're hurting. But I just can't be there for you in this way."

Parents watch what they say around young children, and they're
forced to confide in a friend or a therapist. But adult kids are a
built-in support system. No, we are not children anymore, but we are
still *their* children. Explain that you can't listen to one parent outline
another parent's shortcomings without the insights kicking up a
tsunami in your stomach. Explain that what they say bothers you.
It's *whom* the stories are about that makes them unbearable. If you're
like me, you could sit for hours and help a friend dissect the weaknesses in her parents' marriage after they divorce. But when it's your
own parents saying hurtful things about each other, it batters you to
listen. They make comments under their breath that sting.

You should set boundaries early. As soon as your parents begin untangling, take a step back. Be the little piggy who constructs a brick wall so that no one can blow his house down. Build up an emotional immune system. Put yourself first. If you don't have the conversation early, the roles into which you fall will quickly become cemented. It's much easier to put your foot down in the beginning than it is to go back to the way it was after you're in the thick of your parents' divorce.

Melinda, thirty-two, learned that she needed to set boundaries after she found out her father was cheating. He left her mother and moved in with another woman. Melinda's mother often called her daughter with "updates," which consisted of any nugget of gossip she'd mustered up since they last spoke. One day, she told Melinda, "Your father told us he had surprise business in Atlantic City when really he was there with *her*." On another occasion, she said, "He left early on Thanksgiving because he said he had work. . . . Hmph . . ." Melinda found the comments infuriating. "I'd have to stop her each time and say, 'No, Mommy, stop. I don't want to hear it,' " says Melinda. Her mother would deflate each time. But Melinda stayed strong. She knew hearing details about her father's indiscretions was too much for her. "I know I'm not a kid. But does anyone need to know her father was screwing his mistress in Atlantic City?" she asks.

For all of the adult roles into which we step during a divorce, adult children still struggle with expressing their feelings to a parent. The "setting barriers" conversation is one of the hardest parts of our parents' divorce. We are stepping up in an adult way, only our parents don't often benefit from the boundaries. They're not going to like what we have to say. They'll feel shut out and abandoned, which are the same emotions of which we complain. Some adult children say the "boundaries" conversation spiraled into a fight about whose pain is more legitimate or who should be listening to whom. Parents often use guilt to reel their children back in. I have a friend who nervously asked her mother to stop bashing her father in front of her. Her mother's gut response: "You better remember who brushed your hair and wiped your nose all of those years."

Her mother saw her daughter's boundary as a breach of contract. I did for you, she's saying, now you do for me. Parental emotions resemble an autumn wind blowing a cyclone of leaves into the air. Picture yourself standing there. Winds laced with loyalty and guilt about being a bad son or daughter spin the leaves around you. The emotions tumble around your feet and try to climb up to your chin. Only you don't let them get that far. You kick the leaves away and step aside. The emotions may continue to stir, but you don't have to watch. This is how you must handle a parent who doesn't respect your request: keep moving in the direction in which you were trying to go. Walk right past the cyclone spun of guilt. Remain firm. You have a right to do this. *You need this to stay sane.* Forget the accusations that you're acting selfish. "Do not take anything either of your parents say personally," says Melinda. "People don't always make sense when they are angry or grieving a loss." But this is always easier said than done.

It's difficult to erect boundaries without talking to our parents about our feelings. And it's impossible to talk about our feelings without hurting our parents. So we often don't say anything at all. While setting up boundaries is useful, parents sometimes don't take our request seriously. Melinda's mother continuously brought up her marriage despite her daughter's requests. Says Melinda, "I just had to keep telling her over and over, 'I'm not listening,' or, 'Is there anything I can do about this? If not, stop telling me. I don't want to hear it.' "

When unsure how to talk to a parent, adult children may stop answering their phone and temporarily erase the parent from their life. Stephanie wrote her father a letter a few months after he left her mother. "I need to separate from you for awhile," she wrote. She felt as if she was too angry with him to see him; she didn't even want to hear his voice. She wasn't ready to talk about boundaries. So she created a boundary, a separation, and vanished. To sit down one-on-one with her father and have a true conversation about boundaries would mean that Stephanie would have to explain that everything he said when they were together now seemed like a lie. She didn't know how to say that without sounding as if she no longer loved her father, and she didn't want to hurt him that badly. Instead, she found relief in temporarily writing him out of her world. The separation did her good. Not hearing her father's sad voice allowed Stephanie to work through her own struggles about her parents splitting up—without taking on her father's emotion.

Your parents' feelings are not your problem. "It took me a long time to realize I couldn't be a therapist to my family," says Carrie. If your parents are upset, it isn't your job to make them feel better. It isn't your job to be the glue that holds a fragile union together. It isn't your job to listen until your heart burns.

So step out of whatever role you find yourself in. Try to set your parents' needs aside. Your emotions are on spin cycle. You'll never acknowledge your pain as long as you put your parents first. Says one twenty-nine-year-old woman interviewed, "My mother expected me to support her. Be her shoulder to cry on as well as help keep the household going. I was miserable, confused, and numb. I wanted to be there for both of my parents. I thought that if I didn't let myself feel, then I could achieve that goal.

"The best advice I have for someone is . . . feel your emotions rather than suppress them. During the divorce, there were times when I could look in the mirror and not see my soul behind the eyes staring back at me. I saw the shattered pieces of my life all around me. It's going to hurt. You will feel despair. You will be angry. But allow yourself to go there and feel it. Only then will you find acceptance and, eventually, peace."

Points to Remember

• Parents expect their adult children to act as their personal support system. They step out of a parenting role, which makes adult children feel alone. In an effort to please parents, adult children will often take on the parents' grief.

• Parents aren't superhuman. They will disappoint you, often acting selfish during a divorce, and it is painful to witness them in a weaker state. They're coping with a very big crisis. So are you. You are entitled to be weak sometimes, too.

• Divorce makes parents reevaluate their lives and often their identities. They may change into someone you feel you don't recognize and often no longer respect. Be patient. Oftentimes this radical change is only temporary. Expect to see your parents regress. In an adversarial divorce, parents can act immature. Sometimes they make poor choices, and an adult child is forced to clean up their mess.

• An adult child's role evolves as a parent's needs change. In the beginning, a parent may require a confidant. Later, parents may need someone to iron their clothes as a spouse used to. You can be there for a parent or, if it's too hard, explain to a parent why you need to walk away.

- Set boundaries early. The earlier you establish rules to manage your role in the divorce, the easier the split will be on you. Don't try to be your mother's or father's therapist or friend. You'll learn more than you should know about their marriage, and you'll only walk away hurt.

3

Caught in the Middle

> I would have died if I did nothing; I would have died if I
> did something.
>
> —JAMAICA KINCAID, *Lucy*

A BAMBOO SHADE NAILED TO THE CEILING SEPARATES Dad's bed from his kitchen table. There are two pictures of sailboats hanging on the walls and two model sailboats in each of the studio apartment's three windows. On the stereo is a four-by-six photograph of me and my sisters in the same battered silver frame it had been in when it was in our living room; it was one of the few things Dad threw into his bag when he left Mom's a year earlier. There is no couch or coffee table or anyplace to sit except the dining table. It's June 2002.

Dad wanted me to come over to his place to show me a few

things: a wall in his kitchen he painted the color of tomatoes; his Fender Strat, a guitar he'd just bought; and a new pair of black, shiny dress boots with pointy toes, which made Dad look like an elf. I smile when I run my hand across the wall. I make him laugh when I hold the guitar and attempt a chord. I tell him the leather boots are stylish. The truth is, I'm bored by instruments, and I think the boots and the wall are hideous. But I want to feel close to Dad and comfort him, so I pretend I like all the same things he does.

I don't have to fake it when Dad hands me a Yoo-hoo, a watery chocolate drink I've loved since I was little. We sit at the table, sipping Yoo-hoos, and talk about the band Dad is forming with a few buddies of his. I ask about each band member and venues at which they'll play and what style of music he likes and then about the band members' children. *Do I ask about their wives?* I draw out the conversation for as long as I can to avoid any awkward silences. Every time I'm alone with Dad, I worry we will not have enough to say. Even a year after they split, I'm not used to talking to him without Mom around. Sometimes I list "fallback" topics in my head before I go to his apartment. Then, if there is ever a lull in conversation, I have ready ideas from which to pull. When things get quiet, I panic and say, "Why don't you get a dog?" Dad mumbles, "Too much work." Then he asks if I want to play SCRABBLE, which shocks me. Mom and I used to beg Dad to play board games with us. He'd always lie on the couch and watch the Sci Fi channel instead. I tell him sure. "I just bought it," Dad says. "I figure it gives me, you, and Chelsea something to do when you come over."

It doesn't take long for the SCRABBLE board to fill up. When Dad spells out the word *S-E-N-T*, we laugh. He earns only four points. As I plan out my next word, Mom's face pops into my head. Mom, with her hair long and blond and pushed back in a headband.

Mom, who now wore plunging necklines even when she cleaned the kitchen. We got in a fight before I left for Dad's that afternoon. All Mom had to hear was that I was seeing Dad for her veins to bulge. Her face turned beet red. "What are you going to do," she said, "go over there and bad-mouth me?" Seeing Dad was like consorting with the enemy to her. She assumed I stole away to say all the things about her that she'd hoped I'd say about him.

"I don't know when you're going to realize that your father couldn't have cared less about you all these years," she said. "He didn't care if you went to college or not. *I* paid for that. *I* made sure we drove you down to Maryland. Do you think your father was the one looking out for you?" Then she laughed, as if what she had just said were funny enough for a stand-up comedy show. "I mean, who do you think did all of that? Who?"

Mom paced up and down the hallways as she yelled. I could hear the click-click-click of her heels approaching the living room. I had a few minutes to think before she click-clicked back up the hallway to my room. *Of course Dad cared about me growing up,* I told myself. *Didn't he?* I reminded myself of a morning Dad took me to breakfast alone when I was five. He was there the day I learned to ride a bike. He stuck his two fingers in his mouth and whistled so loud I could hear him in the cavernous theater where my college graduation was held. *Dad loved me.* But then again, Dad would drink too much on holidays, often slurring his words before dinner. Once, he stung my face with a slap in high school after I called him a drunk. *Did he love me?*

"Do you realize your father is *stalking* me?" she asked. She stood in the bedroom's wooden doorway with her head cocked. Mom's eyes always look like flying saucers painted blue.

"First of all," I said, my voice quavering, "Dad paid for a lot around here. He cared if I went to college. He—"

"*He* hasn't given me a dime to help with this house since he left. He doesn't care if your sister starves. Believe what you want to believe," she said. Her eyes narrowed. "You always do."

"Dad was asked to leave," I yelled back. The more Mom tried to get me to hate Dad, the more it pushed me toward him. Mom hurt me, which made me want to hurt her back.

Mom went into the bathroom and put the blow-dryer away. She folded a towel. "Your father calls me ten times a day at work. I can't even concentrate. It's over. Will you tell him that?" she yelled. Click-click-click. Back in my room. "Do you know what he's trying to do to me? He wants to leave me destitute. Pushing a cart on the side of the road," she said. "He's had the papers for months. He won't agree to anything. Nothing."

"Leave me out of this," I said. "I don't want to hear it."

"You never want to hear it, Brooke. Well, your father, your perfect father, wants to screw me. You want to help him screw your mother? That's what you're doing." Now she was crying.

I grabbed my purse and pushed past Mom. She followed me around the living room as I hunted for my keys. She talked about how her daughters needed to get their priorities straight. After I found my keys, I let the front door's screen slam shut. Mom yelled after me, "That's it. Just run off to your father's. Well, tell him I don't want his money. I just want out of this marriage. Tell him to sign the damn papers."

So there I was a few hours later, playing SCRABBLE in Dad's living room. Invited by Dad, and *S-E-N-T* by mom. Everything Mom said was stirring inside me. I was desperate not to get in the middle. But it felt strange to sit silently with Dad when so much was hanging over us. I spelled *A-S-K* on a triple word score—twenty-one points.

"What's going on with the divorce?" I said. Dad said the lawyers were handling it. I pushed. "But I mean . . . why isn't it over yet?"

Dad explained that he and Mom couldn't agree on the terms. Dad only mentioned one. "Mom wants the sailboat to be considered a joint asset," he said. "That's my boat, not hers." I was beating Dad. The spelling of *O-X* on another triple word score put me up another twenty-seven points.

"You know, Brock," Dad said, scanning the tiles on the board, "your Mom wants everything from me. I worked hard for many years paying for that house. I deserve a fair share of what I worked for."

"Mom doesn't want alimony," I spit out.

"See, that's why I want the lawyers to work out what's fair and what's not," he said.

"But, Dad, you might have to do this yourself," I said. I found myself repeating exactly what Mom had yelled about hours before. I was saying exactly what I swore I wouldn't. "Mom says you call her all the time," I said. "She just wants it to be over."

"I'm not sure why she said that," Dad said. He looked hurt. "I called her at work to try to talk some things over a couple of times last week. You know Mommy. As soon as she hears my voice, she starts yelling."

"The longer you drag this part out—"

"It's not just me," he said.

"Well, the longer you drag this part out, the more you're hurting us. Mom is angry."

The words rolling off my tongue made me nauseous. I was regurgitating Mom's every word. The last thing I wanted was for Dad to move on. The longer he loved my mother, the greater the chance that they might reconcile. So why was I suddenly my mother's voice? Why was I pushing for a swifter end to what I cherished most deeply?

"I still love her," Dad said.

"Find a way to let go," I told Dad. *Mom has certainly let him go,* I thought. Then I spelled out *L-O-V-E* on the board, earning eleven points—nothing much at all.

Adult children are used to standing between their parents. We walked in between Mommy and Daddy, holding both of their hands, for as long as we can remember. Warring parents split an adult child's heart in half. Often the first thing we say to our parents when they announce they're divorcing is, "I don't want to be in the middle." Instincts tell us this is a good idea. But divorce makes the middle an inevitable destination. Children are at the dead center of divorce. Parents can cheat on each other and steal assets and walk away from a divorce feeling victorious. They can wipe their hands clean of their former spouse. But they still have to answer to us. We will always connect them.

Like a glue of sorts, adult children try to hold their parents' hands together after they announce they're divorcing. Parents react differently. They grip one of our wrists and pull us hard toward them. Our body is jerked left, then right. They play tug-of-war with their children as the rope. Parents fear we'll take our love elsewhere. Losing a spouse can make a parent feel as if they are losing us.

The middle isn't such a foreign place for some of us. In high-conflict unions, adult children report being involved in their parents' marriage long before their parents split up. When Jodie, twenty-four, was in high school, her parents often fought about money. Instead of saving and trying to get ahead, her father would plan far-flung solo vacations or shop for designer ties to wear to work. His wife would find out about his extravagant purchases in advance only if she saw his monthly credit-card bill. Jodie's father asked his daughter to hide the mail when she got home from school. Then he'd sort through it and pull out any incriminating statements before setting the mail back out on the kitchen table. "Don't tell Mom," her father made her promise. Says Jodie, "I didn't want my parents to fight, so I went along with it."

When Mandy's parents fought when she was in high school, she'd come into the room and try to defuse the argument. "Everybody calm down," she'd tell her parents. "Mom, you need to stop saying these things. You're hurting Dad." Mandy, a twenty-seven-year-old graphic designer, says her parents constantly pushed each other's buttons. They both looked to their daughter for help. "I always took on the role of keeping them together," she says. And her efforts helped.

Adult children continue their efforts after their parents split up. Parents may not know how to fix their marriage, so an adult child steps in to try to save it for them. Like therapists, we demand that our parents sit one-on-one with us. We coax "what went wrong" out of them and use the information to our advantage. If we know why our parents are so upset, we might talk them back into each other's arms. As much as adult children hate being the go-between, they relish the role. They want to be the superhero who saves the day. If they don't step in between their parents, no one else will. Adult children believe they are the only ones who have the power to help their parents reconcile. We know our parents' shared history. Says one twenty-seven-year-old woman, "I had the outside perspective. I could see things that were wrong and things that could be fixed."

Paige, a twenty-seven-year-old graduate student, had just graduated from the University of Pennsylvania when her mother called to say she was leaving her father. A few months earlier, her mother had gone into the hospital for kidney stones. Her husband didn't accompany or visit her. Paige's mother told her daughter it was a moment of truth. She believed she deserved better. "I'm fifty years old," she told Paige. "I still have a lot of life in front of me."

When Paige learned how upset her father was—he didn't want

the divorce—she sided with him. Her father said he'd offered to go to therapy. He said he kept trying to talk things out with his wife and understand why she was so upset that he didn't visit her in the hospital. Nothing he said helped. His wife was determined to end their marriage. "I don't know what your mother is doing," he told his daughter over the telephone. "Please say something to her." Paige could hear the sadness in her father's voice. "Help me get her back," he said.

Paige called her mother soon after they hung up. "Why are you giving up?" she asked. Dad has the potential to be a better husband, she told her mother. "You don't know everything about our relationship," her mother said. "I was unhappy." Paige had taken medication to treat her depression since she was in high school. Lately, she'd been feeling strong, so she stopped. Hoping to combat any sadness she might feel from the split, Paige started taking her pills again. Paige didn't understand why her mother wouldn't consult a professional, too. Maybe her mother was just depressed. "You're not willing to go to therapy?" Paige asked her. But her mother's mind was made up.

Magical reconciliation is a fantasy many adult children harbor. Most children, even as adults, believe they have a certain influence over their parents. With the tap of a magic wand, they might get their parents to forget twenty-five years' worth of anger and resentment. They prance into their childhood homes filled with as much self-importance as Mary Poppins. *I am their child. They'll listen to me.* Children have no reason to think their parents will not take them seriously. Parents typically give their children what they wish. Why wouldn't they give them this?

When our parents stop talking to each other, we talk for them. We become their voice. Sometimes, we're asked to do it. More often, we mediate on our own. Parents have big hopes. "Get your mother to forgive me," said one young woman's father. Another father told his twenty-seven-year-old daughter, "I think I might move back home. Wouldn't you like me to move back home?" His daughter asked whether he'd asked her mother. "Well, no . . . ," he said, "but I figured I'd ask you first."

Once in the thick of divorce, a parent may look to us to speak for the opposing parent as much as they expect we'll speak for them. And they may mistake our voice for that of the ex-spouse. In an adversarial divorce, a parent cannot call his ex and inquire about the other person's life. Both yearn to know what their husband or wife is thinking, whether he or she is missed, how the ex is coping. So they ask their kids.

As mediators, many adult children admit they aren't entirely fair. They often mediate for one parent—whichever they agree with— rather than negotiating a constant flow of information between both. Adult children continually return to the same parent with the same messages. In a divorce, children are like soldiers trying to win a public relations war. "Dad isn't what you thought." "Mom is willing to go to counseling." We give our parents an image makeover. Sometimes parents listen. Sometimes they don't. Either way, our role doesn't feel so powerful when we walk away with our tail between our legs.

The first Thanksgiving after her parents split up, Jenna, twenty-seven, says, "I came home thinking I'd single-handedly save my parents' marriage." She went to her grandparents' house with her mother on the holiday. Her father wasn't close with his family. He stayed home alone. So Jenna made sure to wrap up a plate of leftovers for him. When she arrived at her parents' house, she found her father sitting in the living room in the dark with candles lit. He was staring at a blank TV screen, and tears were running down his cheeks. When he saw Jenna and her sister, he quickly wiped his cheeks and pretended nothing was wrong.

Jenna decided she needed to get moving on reconnecting her parents. The following day, she asked her mother to meet her at a local restaurant. "I tied the cape on and strolled in like I was some superhero," she says. Jenna scolded her mother. "You're breaking up our family," Jenna told her. She pummeled her mother with questions. Finally, her mother talked about how she resented her husband because he'd been unemployed for several months. Her mother was tired of running the household alone. Jenna felt as if she'd made a breakthrough. "You need to tell Dad all of this," Jenna said. "It could really help." They talked for five and a half hours. Her mother promised she would call her husband the following day. "I went back to my childhood home feeling somewhat victorious," Jenna says. "I told Dad that Mom was going to call him." She never did.

The fantasy that you can mediate your parents' love persists long into the divorce negotiations. It is a very big smack to adult children's ego when they see that their parents' minds are made up. Adult children realize they hold no power over their parents at all. Many times, it is a lost cause.

When the planes hit the World Trade Center in New York, Jenna hadn't given up hope that her parents might reconcile, despite her mother's continued unresponsive behavior. *If we're ever going to make this family work*, she thought, *it's going to be now*. She wrote an e-mail and sent it to her parents and her sister. "We could still save this," she wrote. "We don't know what's going to happen. Bad things are going on in the world. It's time to be a family, just in case. It's time to mend things." Neither of her parents responded. She didn't know at the time, but her mother already had a serious boyfriend.

Trying to pull our parents together is exhausting. "At some point, I had to let go," says one young woman interviewed. "I had to stop obsessing over the details of whose fault it was. I had to try and re-member their separation had nothing to do with me and then realize that their getting back together had nothing to do with me either." There's only so long you can bear the burden of convincing your par-ents they should stay together. You'll drain yourself trying to salvage a relationship that you cannot save.

Siding with a parent who wants what we want is human. You're fighting for what's best for you, too. The parent who wants a mar-riage to heal is generally the parent who is seeing eye-to-eye with their children. Tensions rise in the relationship we have with the par-ent who wants the marriage to end. As divorce proceedings drag on, and more information comes out, our view of our parents can change. Allegiances often shift.

In the beginning of her parents' divorce, Paige immediately sided with her father. He thought his wife was being ridiculous, ending their marriage after thirty years, and Paige agreed. Paige barely spoke to her mother, and when she brought her new boyfriend, Larry, around, Paige ignored him. She reluctantly went to her mother and Larry's wedding a year later. As far as Paige was con-cerned, her father was an angel. He bought out his ex-wife's share of the house. "I want to save the house for you and your sister," he told Paige. When Paige's father announced he was moving back to Nicaragua, the country from which he'd immigrated years before, Paige supported her father. Paige flew from New York to visit him there on vacations. She was polite when she met his new girlfriend.

A couple of years later, her father announced he was selling the house. Paige asked what he was going to do with the money. Her fa-ther said he planned to invest it. Because her father had called the house hers and her sister's, Paige assumed she'd be given part of the money. "Why don't we just split the $300,000 between the three of us?" Paige said. "Then I can pay for graduate school. Carla can pay her medical school loans off, and you can invest yours in what you like." Her father agreed. When Paige's mother got wind of the sale, she told Paige, "You have to get that money for yourself or you'll never see it." Then her mother told Paige about how badly her father had mismanaged money over the years. He had twelve credit cards, and her mother had to pay them off. Her mother hadn't told Paige earlier because she didn't want Paige to think poorly of her father.

Paige called her father a month after the house sold. He didn't return her calls. Finally, she caught him on the telephone. He said he'd been traveling in Costa Rica. "How about we split up the money now?" she asked. He said he planned to invest it in farms in Nicaragua, "which is a horrible investment," says Paige. "Dad!" she said. "We had an agreement." He got angry and started to yell at Paige. They hung up and didn't speak for two and a half months. Paige never got a check. Suddenly, Paige became closer to her mom. Her mom admitted that her father had been a financial drain on her. She talked to Paige about her disappointment in her ex-husband, and Paige shared her own feelings. During her parents' divorce, Paige had favored her father and didn't speak to her mother. Two years later, the situation was reversed. "My relationship with my mother was reinvigorated after I saw a side of my father I never had," says Paige. "Now I understand why my mom divorced him."

Because Paige regarded her father as a victim, she believed everything he said. She ate up all of his sadness and hurt. Now she says, "He was a good actor in many ways. All along, he was taking advantage of the fact that I sided with him." She found out later he had lied to her many times—he told her his new wife's pregnancy was a mistake when it had been planned—to keep her from getting angry with him. He told her what she wanted to hear. It kept Paige on his side, and away from her mother.

The middle is a horrible place for anyone to be. Middle children have cried the blues for years. They're not quite as stunningly perfect as the eldest sibling and not quite as silly and comical as the youngest. They're caught between the two, which makes them unsure of what to be. The same identity crisis faces adult children of divorce, who start thinking of their parents as individuals. Says one thirty-four-year-old woman interviewed, "My first thought was, 'Oh no. Now I'm going to have to deal directly with Dad!'" Who are our parents if they're not together? Adult children who are in the middle think they need to choose between their parents. Am I my mother's loyal daughter? Or am I my father's princess? Early on, you're unsure whether you can be both, especially as parents lobby for your favor.

Some parents use their children as they would a pawn in a chess game. They arm us with feelings and information. If they use us strategically enough, parents can get a child on their side and, even better, use the child to get what they want. Parents often tell their children things they shouldn't know about the other parent. Sometimes, they do it innocently—they need someone to whom to vent. Other times, they leak information on purpose in a hurtful bid for their child's loyalty.

Marisa, twenty-four, was already angry with her father for cheating on her mother numerous times over the years. Then her mother shared what he'd said in couples therapy. "My father said he never loved my mother, and two years into their marriage, he was already having affairs," Marisa says. "He said he stayed because Mom got cancer and he didn't want to be the jerk who left his sick wife. He stayed after she recovered because he knew how much she wanted children and he thought she was too old to meet someone else." After her mother told Marisa these things, Marisa would swear and call him a jerk. Knowing her father was capable of cheating was bad enough. Finding out he had fathered her and her brother out of pity was so much worse.

"The three of us will be a family," Marisa told her mother. "We don't need him. We'll sell the old house, but we'll buy a new house. And it will be ours only."

Marisa's mother appreciated her daughter's support. If Marisa was angry with what her father said, it validated her mother's anger. But Marisa missed her father, and he soon began reaching out to her. After her childhood home sold, he took Marisa on a trip to California to see her grandparents and drove her around the Los Angeles area. Marisa was considering moving there after graduating from Northwestern. Marisa's mother was encouraging Marisa to move home to Denver so her mother wouldn't be alone in her new town house. Marisa's father was encouraging her to take a risk and move to a new city where she knew no one.

Marisa started to see her mother in a new light. Her mother wasn't necessarily looking out for her daughter's best interests. Her mother continued to bring up details of her ex's affairs, which only drove Marisa further away. Marisa hoped one day she'd forgive her father for his indiscretions. "I was starting to get closer to my dad," says Marisa. "But Mom was still attacking him. I didn't feel comfortable talking about him in a positive way around her. I could only call him a jerk."

Parents don't just vent to their kids. Their kids vent to them. Talking badly about one parent to the other is the easiest way to convince a parent you're on their side. Numerous adult kids complain that their parents say dehumanizing things about each other. In the same breath, they'll admit they sometimes talk badly with one parent about the other. The behaviors feed into each other. Think of it as the golden rule: Don't talk badly about one of your parents with the other, and each of your parents will be less inclined to talk badly about the other to you. It won't solve your problems, but it might help.

Once an adult child establishes himself as taking one parent's side, it's difficult to switch. The "out" parent, or the parent with whom you were angry, will be thrilled you've joined their ranks. But it's difficult to reconfigure a relationship with a parent you once favored. In the past, your deep connection with the favored parent was centered around bad-mouthing or grieving the out parent. If an adult child abdicates that role, a favored parent suddenly finds himself on the "outs." Marisa felt as if she were betraying her mother when she reconnected with her father. Some adult children say they had to make amends with an out parent behind a favored parent's back.

Barbara, twenty-eight, says her mother assumed her daughter would take her side once she learned her father had cheated. Early in the separation, her mother dragged Barbara into the middle. She asked Barbara to go to the country house, where her father was living, and take down every picture of the family. She also wanted Barbara to move out some of the furniture on the sly. Barbara refused. She also refused to stop speaking to her father. Barbara says her mother never asked her children to keep their father out of their lives. But if they saw him and their mother found out, she'd get angry. "She didn't want us providing help to him," says Barbara. "She felt like if we talked to Dad, we were cheating on her." Barbara moved a few states away to distance herself from her mother.

One parent sometimes demands we shut the other parent out. They want us to stop loving their ex and build a new life, like they are, without the former spouse. It's an unfair demand, especially when the other parent hasn't done anything to hurt us directly. Accuse one of your parents of trying to wipe the other parent out of your life, and they'll probably deny it. "I never said I didn't want you to love your father," your mother might say. But parents do expect this. They expect us to turn against their ex just as they did. When we feel a parent trying to turn us against the other, we sometimes go out of our way to prove we're impartial. Adult children will refuse to get involved. Even these behaviors can be misconstrued by parents. Parents often equate saying "I don't want to talk about this" with "I'm against you."

Whenever William, twenty-nine, talked to his mother, she'd say nasty things about his father. William says she could be washing the car and she'd think of him. "What an asshole he is for leaving," she'd say. William was angry with his father for leaving, too, but he wanted to keep a neutral position, so he'd stick up for his father. "You weren't happy in the marriage either," he'd remind her. William would say similar things to his father if he brought up his ex-wife.

Whenever William made "neutral" comments, he says, his mother would get upset. "There was so much she'd say about my dad," says William. "Calling him names. So I'd push back. Then she'd swear I was taking his side." William says his mother wanted him to choose between a relationship with her and one with his dad. "I know you're angry," he told his mother one day over the telephone. "But I still need to have a relationship with Dad."

I learned quickly that talking to my mother meant listening to her say things about Dad that I didn't want to know. I'd tell her over and over, "I don't want to hear this." Mom would grind her teeth and accuse me of taking Dad's side. She didn't realize I was telling Dad exactly the same thing. Adult children should not have to explain that continuing a loving relationship with both of our parents is important to us. Wanting to visit Dad or buying Mom a birthday present does not mean we are taking one parent's side. Going on vacation with one parent shouldn't make the other parent feel any less important in our lives.

Parents compete for our attention. They both want us to love them more and spend more time with them. We need to answer to them if we give the other parent even an ounce more attention. They question our motives. Says one young woman interviewed, "If she knew I was with my dad, my mother always said, 'Why are you talking to him?' " It feels disloyal. We're accustomed to giving our parents our all. Now we must divide equally our time, our love, our attention.

One weekend in August, Mandy went to a friend's wedding. During the week, she'd had a job interview. Her father happened to call after the reception. She told him she had a blast and the job interview went great. She said she hoped she'd get the job. A few days later, Mandy's mother called and asked the dreaded question. "Did you hear from your father?" Mandy mentioned she'd talked to him a few days before. Her mother's tone changed. She said she couldn't believe Mandy would call him first after her job interview. "I didn't call him," Mandy told her mother. "He called me!" It didn't matter. Her mother felt betrayed. "Did he tell you about the woman he's seeing?" her mother asked. Mandy was hurt. "Why do you have to say something like that?" Mandy said. "If I had such a good week, why do you have to try and make me feel bad?" Her mother continued telling her about this other woman. When Mandy said she didn't want to hear it, her mother said, "You always take his side."

Two years into their separation, my mom and dad were still arguing. They were legally separated, not yet divorced. As the lawyers continued to renegotiate the terms of the divorce, Mom and Dad kept trying to suck me back into the middle. One day, I got in a screaming match with Mom over the telephone. I'd just told her that no matter what she said, I wouldn't hate my father. "Put yourself in my shoes," I said. "Did your mother ever ask you to turn against your father?" Mom was silent, which is rare. I'd got her thinking. "Your parents never split up. *You* don't know what it's like to have both of your parents pulling at you," I said. Mom told me I was right. She didn't know what it was like.

Parents step outside of themselves during divorce. Remind them of who they are. They know what it's like to be a child. Ask your parents to imagine their own parents saying to them what they're saying to you. They may feel ashamed of their behavior. Every time Mom and I got in an argument, and she tried to pull me over to her side, I reminded her, "Mom, would your father ever have said these things to you about your mother?" Sometimes, she'd roll her eyes and dismiss what I'd said. Other times, she got quiet, which is all I could ask for.

Adult children have something parents want—information. We are messengers from the other side. Not only are we asked to pass things such as bills and speeding tickets back and forth, but our parents hope that we'll share information. They want to know whether their former spouse is dating, where the ex went on vacation. In the same way we always wonder about our exes, parents are curious about how the other one is doing without them. Adult children don't see information swapping as being so innocent.

Mandy says her mother called her every other day during the divorce. She never asked about Mandy's day. There was no "How's work? The boyfriend?" The first thing her mother would say is, "Have you talked to your dad?" The question made Mandy wince. Was she supposed to say he was doing well? Or should she say he was an emotional wreck? "It made me feel used," says Mandy. "I felt like she was calling to talk about my dad, not me. She was calling only to get information." Mandy doesn't think her mother sat in her room conspiring how to pry gossip from her daughter, but it still bugged her. "I don't think she was consciously using me, but I don't think she thought about how it could make me feel, either."

Being the messenger puts adult children in an uncomfortable position. Adult children need to put their foot down early. Tell a parent that you are uncomfortable playing that role. "Ask about me, not Dad," one adult child told her mother. If a parent inquires about your other parent, get off the phone. You don't *have* to answer a parent's questions. If either parent wants you to give the spouse a bill or a note, provide the parent with a mailing address or advise the parent to go through his or her ex's lawyer. There is no reason why an adult child needs to hand-deliver anything. It's only going to incite a parent and lead them to believe you're "working" for the enemy. If the parent promises it will be the last request, still say, "No!" Give dogs one treat, they'll always beg for more. Don't give your parents reason to think you'll give in.

Because both parents are speaking to us, a parent can grow jealous of the attention they're no longer getting from the former spouse. For example, when Mandy would tell her mother that she had spoken to her father, her mother would be angry. Mandy would explain that she had called him to see how he was, and he had called her back. "He didn't bother to call me back, and I called him," her mother would say. "Why did he call *you*?" Her mother felt great pain that her husband was shutting her out. "It was like my dad was leaving her and keeping me," says Mandy. Knowing that Mandy still communicated with him—that he was willing to keep Mandy in his life—hurt her mother. "I don't know if it was jealousy or frustration," says Mandy. "But it was like, why is he talking to you and not talking to me? Maybe she can't accept that I have a much different relationship with my father than she does."

When you're at war, it's natural to like having people on your side. Taking sides is a powerful notion in divorce. Parents often try to get their children to side with them by listing all the terrible things their partner has done. If their children realize their mother is a monster, they'll skip right over to their father's side. Once a parent has you on their side, it's hard for the parent to give that powerful feeling up. An adult child sends a parent a message: You've done nothing wrong, and I know that. Parents are so guilt-ridden once their marriage ends that they fear their children are going to find fault with their actions and shift their allegiance. They cast blame on each other. Sometimes, they say things they don't mean. Other times, they lie.

One day, Mandy was talking to her mother on the phone. "You know, your father never wanted to come visit you in San Francisco last year," she told Mandy. "It was all me. He couldn't care less about seeing you." Mandy acted as though the information didn't bother her one bit. Then she hung up the phone and questioned her father's love for her. *What if what she said was true?* Mandy wondered. Mandy began rationalizing the mean things her mother said. *Well, I know my parents don't like traveling together,* she thought. *So Dad probably didn't want to go to San Francisco—with her. It didn't mean he didn't want to see me.*

A few weeks ago, Mandy got a phone call from her mother. She again began speculating that Mandy's father was cheating on her with another woman. Mandy grew up in a tiny mountain town in North Carolina. Gossip spread like wildflowers in the spring. A week later, her father called her. "I don't know what you've heard," he said. "But there is a rumor going around that I cheated on your mother. I didn't. I want you to know that." Mandy was relieved, but she didn't know whom to believe. "It's hard for me because my mom is good at saying what's on her mind, and so I'll trust what she has to say," says

Mandy. "But Dad was always forthright and honest, too. Now I'm getting mixed messages. What if Mom isn't telling the truth this time? What if my dad is exaggerating his innocence? What's hearsay? What's actual fact?"

Truth is a sticky subject. Send ten reporters out to write a feature article on a six-alarm fire, they'll all return with a different story—or interpretation of the same facts. The same is true in a divorce. I'd witness a fight between my parents. Mom would retell it to me one way; Dad would recount it another. They didn't imagine their versions. They simply experienced the same moment differently. When you're in the heat of any emotional battle, you hardly think clearly or listen well. Resentment bubbles to the surface, clouding how a parent sees a spouse. Simple comments are taken out of context. One young woman interviewed grew so accustomed to her mother and father telling her different versions of the same story, she developed the "Oh yeah, really?" policy. Each time one of them started up, she'd show as little interest as possible. Her dad might say that her mother said she regretted ever having children. "Oh yeah, really?" she'd say. Then she would change the subject. She wouldn't ask a follow-up question or feign interest. She'd shrug her parent off.

Often both parents believe themselves to be the "right" one, or the truth teller. But no one tells the truth in divorce; they just tell their own version of it. We all bring our own personal issues into every conversation we have. Take my situation. From the beginning, I was angry with my mother. She initiated the divorce, and in my eyes, she was splitting up our family. She was divorcing herself from me and my sisters—not just from Dad. She was acting selfish, and I felt as if I were losing her. Because I never talked out these feelings with my mother, I grew more and more frustrated. Everything she said to me was refracted through that prism. Two years after they split up, Mom might be heading to the hairstylist for her weekly comb-out and I'd get irritated. "She'd rather spend time with herself, doting on how she looks, over her own daughters. How selfish!" Then Mom might go out for a friend's birthday, and I'd get perturbed about that, too. Anything Mom did for herself was one more thing she wasn't doing for me. Every fight we had—regardless of how it began—would turn into my bawling about how she didn't care about me.

Parents do similar things as they hash out the end of their marriage. Whatever issues they had before they divorced keep coming up. Adult children will never really know who is telling the truth because there isn't only one "truth." The sooner you understand that, the sooner you'll be able to tune your parents out. You'll stop trying to determine who's right and who's wrong.

Interestingly, that's exactly what parents want us to do. They throw negative information about each other out so they might be exonerated from any wrongdoing. Parents fear our judgments, as though we really will don a black robe, bang a gavel against a towering desk, and hold one of them at fault. Says one twenty-nine-year-old man interviewed, "It was like she was trying a case. Mom was arguing a divorce case in her head and listing all of the reasons why she should win."

Ashley, twenty-four, always assumed her parents would divorce. They fought horribly. But she didn't expect her mother to tell vicious lies about her father. A couple of weeks after announcing the split, Ashley and her siblings learned their mother was pressing child-abuse charges against her husband. Ashley was in shock. She says her father never laid a hand on her. She asked her brother, who was equally upset and also said the charge was groundless. "If Dad was abusing me," her brother told her, "I think I'd know it." Ashley says her mother always talked badly about her father, but she'd never made anything up before.

Ashley saw the divorce papers with which her father was served. She says her mother wanted full custody of her seventeen-year-old son—Ashley and her sister were in their twenties—an outrageous alimony payment, the house, and the cars. Ashley suspected her mother was inventing this bogus abuse charge to gain financially in the divorce. "How could she assume we'd go along with it?" Ashley wondered.

When it came time to testify against her father, Ashley refused. She showed up at the courthouse to give a statement under oath in her father's favor instead. Afterward, her mother called her. "You're brainwashed," she told Ashley. "You're ruining me." Her father was later cleared of all charges and won full custody of his son. Says Ashley, "I wonder: Does my mother mean to lie? Or does she really believe that what she's saying is true?"

Parents sometimes hurt us so they might hurt their ex. An adult child is like a nerve ending leading straight back to a parent's heart. One father told his mediating daughter, "You're just as vile as your mother." Residual anger makes a parent punish their former spouse, sometimes years after they've split up. Parents are too lost in feelings of resentment to realize that when they hurt each other, they hurt their children as well.

Ben, twenty-six, and his sister, Jessica, thirty-two, stepped in numerous times during their parents' divorce negotiations. Their father was an attorney, and he hired the county's pit-bull lawyer. Ben's mother had managed his father's law office for more than twenty-five years. She never collected a paycheck; she didn't need to. Her husband provided for the two of them. She always assumed they would retire together. Then his mother heard the voice of her husband's mistress on the firm's voice mail. Now his father's attorney was trying to cheat their mother out of retirement funds she deserved.

Ben called his father. "You really need to be more generous to

Mom," he said. He argued his mother's case. She was only asking for four years of alimony. She'd never been an "official" employee at his firm, so she hadn't been earning benefits all of those years. She worked long and hard, too, he said. His father listened and said he'd think it over. Later, Ben called again to yell at him after he found out his father was trying to liquidate and hide some of their assets so he wouldn't have to give them up.

Ben's sister, Jessica, now thirty-seven, was involved in similar ways. The divorce proceedings remained deadlocked, and Jessica hadn't spoken to her father in several months. She decided to ask her father to meet her at a local coffee shop. Jessica was seven months pregnant. Her ankles were swollen. She got there forty-five minutes early so she could prepare herself. Her father was already there. Jessica sat down. "What you're doing is not right," she said. Again, she brought up the issue of her mother's alimony. "I need you to back off," she said. Her father was just as direct. He didn't want to give her mother a dime more than he had to. Jessica didn't raise her mother's latest challenges Even though a temporary court order had said he should pay his ex-wife five hundred dollars a week and cover household expenses until terms of the divorce were worked out by attorneys, her father had stopped paying the mortgage and bills. He was trying to prove to his wife she couldn't afford to keep the house so he could buy it from her. "My father had a nonnegotiable attitude," says Jessica. "He also reminded us quite often that 'my attorney is the best, and your mother will be running out of the courthouse with her tail between her legs.' "

Sometimes details that seem so inconsequential to an outsider are important in a family. In the fishing village where Jessica and her family live is a yacht club. Jessica's parents are longtime members; Jessica grew up swimming in the pool there. Now Jessica brought her children. They'd play tennis, swim, or go sailing. The rules of the club clearly state that if members divorce, they need to decide who is getting the membership. The other person can reapply on their own. Jessica really wanted her mother to continue to be a member of the club. Her father would not give it up, which hurt Jessica. Would he bring his mistress to the same pool where she brought her own children? Jessica raised the issue with her father in the coffeehouse. "Let Mom have the club," she told him. "You play tennis at lots of other clubs. All of Mom's friends are at that club." Her father shook his head. "What do you want with it?" she asked. He said, "I just want it." He told Jessica he was moving into a large house in Jessica's hometown with his new girlfriend. He wanted to take his girlfriend to the yacht club. "It was that kind of selfishness that drove me crazy," said Jessica later.

At the end of the meeting, Jessica stood outside the coffee shop with her father. It was cold. Jessica was wearing a purple sweater and no coat. He leaned over to give her a kiss. "I really love you," he said. Jessica hugged her father. "That's why this is so hard," she said, "because I love you, too. But you're not doing the right thing."

Our love for our parents is tested each time they do something to hurt our other parent. We have to watch them hurt the person they vowed to love for a lifetime. They make it difficult for us to love them blindly and easy for us to take a side. No one wants to stand with the devil. "It would not have mattered to my father if she was homeless and had no money for food or clothing," says Jessica. "My siblings and I put ourselves in the middle willingly to protect our mother's future. She was so emotionally disabled at the time, and the attorney could only do so much. When they were at a real face-off and neither side would budge, we got involved."

Money is a contentious issue in divorce. There is no fair answer to questions such as, Who deserves more? Adult children assume assets can easily be split down the middle, but they never are. Even years later, long after the ink on the divorce papers is dry and lawyers walk away with fistfuls of cash once marked for our inheritance, we don't really expect either of our parents to fully abandon the other.

Josephine, whose parents divorced twenty years ago when she was twenty-three, says her father left her mother with little money. "My mother didn't get half," Josephine says. "She got less." Josephine says her mother went from living in a large country house, where her father still lives, to a cheap condo. Her mother still works at sixty-four; her father retired at fifty. When Josephine's mother got a brain tumor several years ago and was unable to work, Josephine hinted to her father that her mother needed financial help. "I felt like he owed her help after twenty-three years of marriage," she says. "I thought this would be an opportunity for him to show that he'd take responsibility and make things right after raking her over the coals." Instead, her father told her she should look into her mother's disability insurance. "I'm sure she has some," he said. Says Josephine, "I would think once you have a child with someone, you will always care."

Our parents will always care about us. That's all we can ask of them. We can't ask them to care for each other. But what's interesting is that Josephine's father took the same hard-line stance against his wife even twenty years later. Sometimes feelings simmer under the surface, even after parents remarry and build new lives.

Melinda's father felt guilty for cheating on her mother ten years ago. Knowing this, Melinda, thirty-two, unconsciously dredges up that guilt to get her mother what she needs. Every time Melinda's parents get on the telephone, they get in a shouting match. Though her mother is a managing editor at a newspaper, she has struggled with money. Melinda quickly tires of listening to her mother's "woe is me" complaints. One day, Melinda decided to call her father. "I need you to send Mommy money," Melinda said. She didn't give him a choice. Melinda told him how much money her mother needed.

Melinda said it was becoming her problem and it shouldn't be, and hung up.

Later, when her mother left her job, she worried about how she'd pay the mortgage. Melinda couldn't pay it. She was an entry-level editor, which pays little. Her mother seemed stressed. Melinda again called her father. "You need to pay Mommy's mortgage this month," Melinda said. "I'm sending you the payment book, and I don't want to hear any more about it." Her father went along with Melinda's requests to please his daughter. Melinda thinks it was partly because he knew that if her mother defaulted on her mortgage, he'd end up paying for it anyway. "Extracting money from Dad was always difficult," Melinda says. "Even as recently as five years ago, my father tended not to pay her regularly. Mom let me ask for it."

Melinda is making her father "pay off" his guilt. *You owe us. Prove you love me by helping Mom.* Parents know we've relied on them in the past to do as we wish and to make us happy. Sometimes they give us lip service to keep us quiet. If they say things we don't want to hear, some parents mistakenly believe we'll stamp our feet and throw a temper tantrum, just as we did in toy stores as children. As much as parents lean on us like adults, they still treat us like children. They fear the repercussions of not going along with what their children say. They aren't sure whether it means we'll walk out of their world forever.

Adult children like to believe that their role as mediator will wither after their parents' divorce is finalized. It doesn't. Congress can pass laws, but they are meaningless without a police force to enforce them. We sometimes find ourselves "policing" the terms of our parents' agreements. Part of our behavior is fueled by our own selfish fears. There are worries about our parents' financial situation. If our mother screws our father on alimony, how will our father make his mortgage payment? Adult children know they'll be the first eyed to help. They worry how they'll handle the financial monkey suddenly on their back. So we find ourselves in the middle once again.

When Kayla was growing up, her father told her that white lies were OK. "Only big lies are bad," he said. Kayla, thirty-one, remembered that when she asked her father why he never sent her mother an alimony payment. Each year on April 15, he was to pay her mother nine thousand dollars. The deadline came and went. Her mother owed her one thousand dollars, which is one reason Kayla immediately dialed her father. "I was angry because he wasn't holding up his end of a contractual agreement," she says. These rules were devised so she wouldn't have to make phone calls such as this.

Her father said that he was waiting for his tax refund. Then he'd send off a check. Kayla asked when he filed. He said April 15. "Why would you wait to file until the day the payment to Mom was due?" she asked him. Kayla wanted to yell at him. "You're the parent. You're the adult. You're *supposed* to live up to your responsibilities." During the conversation, she remembered her father once saying that half-truths are OK, which made her even angrier. He was probably lying. "He did all of it to be spiteful," she says. Kayla believes that her father was defaulting on his payment just to punish her mother. But he was also punishing Kayla.

A parent's financial position changes dramatically after divorce. After my parents first separated, their already slim incomes tightened. Mom, like many divorced women, lived paycheck to paycheck, because she suddenly had to come up with high mortgage payments on her own. If we went out to dinner, we started paying dutch. Family vacations became an event of the past. When I moved into a new apartment, I wanted to ask for help buying an inexpensive couch. How could I ask Mom? She couldn't buy herself a new couch. That's how it is with divorced parents—resources need to be stretched further to cover the expenses of two homes. That means less money is available for adult kids who might need help starting out.

Luke, thirty-seven, is a computer programmer living in North Carolina. Nearly twenty years ago, he was a pimple-faced eighteen-year-old two months shy of starting college at the University of Florida. His parents had agreed to pay his tuition and fees. Luke saw his freshman year at college the same way any teenager does: he couldn't wait to party. Luke threw a party the summer before college while his parents were out of town. They came home early on the night of the party, so Luke had to kick his friends out. Then his parents sat him down and told him they were splitting up. They started to sleep in different parts of the house the following week. They argued violently. One time, his father kicked open his mother's locked door. Then they announced they had more news. It wasn't good. "We can't pay for college anymore," they said. Their money was caught up in legal fees. Luke didn't know what to say. He was in shock. Were his parents trying to ruin his life? "Fine," Luke told them.

He didn't give up hope. Luke talked to a family friend, an attorney, who had put himself through college. The friend encouraged him to go to school and work full-time while attending classes. Luke saved money over the summer for living expenses and books. In Florida, he got a cheap apartment with roommates and a catering job on campus. "It was a big adjustment," he says. "I was focused on doing. I was counting on having time for studies and a social life. It ended up I didn't have time for either."

At thirty-eight, Luke is successful and happy. In retrospect, losing his social life was a good thing; it kept him focused. But he still resents the timing of his parents' split. Losing financial resources forced him to come of age on a faster track than his peers. Researchers in one study found that 60 percent of adult children lost some financial support from their parents after a divorce; 20 percent

had parents who stopped giving them any money. Even adult children who come from less affluent families look to their parents for financial support. A hundred dollars to fix the muffler on a car. Fifty
bucks to buy a college textbook. Six hundred dollars for a security
deposit. Money helps an adult child move toward full independence.
When financial support is lost, whether large or small, our plans
change. Our dreams fall like dominoes. Everything about our future,
which seemed stable moments before, is unclear. In another study
conducted by the University of North Carolina–Chapel Hill, researchers found that two-thirds of the adult children surveyed felt
"their lives were abruptly and unwillingly altered by their parents'
divorce. Insecurity about the future was another common response;
over half of the group worried that because of the divorce their plans
for college and their adult lives would not work out." One nineteen-
year-old in the study said, "I'm not sure of anything anymore."

Divorce creates a ripple effect, says family sociologist Teresa
Cooney. As young people move into adulthood, they depend on a
certain level of stability from their parents. As that foundation disappears, other transitions they're about to make in their lives, such
as finding a career or a new city that fits, seem even less certain than
before. Cooney says the loss of financial support, a common side effect of divorce, can be detrimental to an adult child's future suc-
cesses. In an article in the journal *Human Relations*, Cooney wrote,
"Reduced family income following divorce may force offspring to assume full-time employment, which may interfere with their education. In turn, career entry, marriage, and parenthood could be
delayed or experienced out of sequence." She compares a divorce to a
teen pregnancy. The results change the course of your life. Instead of
finishing college, an adult child might go to work. They might detach from parents prematurely and make poor decisions. One young

woman interviewed says her seventeen-year-old sister got married within a year of her father's leaving. "That would never have been allowed if my father still lived at home," she says.

If not forever changed, our lives are slowed by divorce. Adult children put their own dreams on hold when they tend to their parents' problems. Call it a developmental freeze. Other twenty-somethings, fueled by their parents' unwavering support, are researching tortoises in Costa Rica or toiling in an internship on Wall Street or being encouraged to have more grandkids for their parents to spoil. Thirty-somethings might be forced to evaluate their own marriages in a new light—or decide they don't want to marry at all. Adult children might be less willing to plunge headfirst into a new adventure if that adventure meant abandoning their family in its time of greatest need, or they might make career decisions based more on financial stability than on happiness. You can still succeed and have fun and go on grand adventures after your parents' split. But change feels harder, especially with two parents who pull at you as if you were made of elastic.

Sasha was nineteen when her parents split, and she feels as if she's been stuck in a developmental rut ever since. She had dropped out of college and moved back to her childhood home the summer before her parents broke up. It was bad timing. When her father moved out, she couldn't focus on going back to college or planning her future. Sasha says her parents aren't entirely to blame; she was having difficulty setting goals and focusing on a career before they split. But she felt weaker, even immobilized. There were many nights she'd sit with her mother or father (in their respective living rooms) seeking advice. Should she enroll in the local community college? Should she get a job? Her mother would quickly tell her how little extra money she had. "You'll have to ask your father," she'd say. That didn't answer Sasha's question. She wanted to know what she *should* do. Sasha tried approaching her father. He'd agree to pay for college. Then he'd question the point. "Maybe you should get a good job," he'd tell her. "You don't really like school." Neither parent was willing to sit down with her and discuss all of the possibilities.

Sasha was accustomed to a constant flow of support from both parents when they were together. They'd talk with her for hours about what was best for her. Then they'd head into their bedroom and discuss how they could help. Now Sasha had to jockey for whatever support each was willing to give. She says it always seemed as if her parents were giving advice that suited *them* best. It was, "This is what's best for you under these new circumstances." Everything was suddenly from *the divorce's point of view*.

When a bomb is dropped on your home, your family explodes. Each relationship shatters into tiny pieces that you can't even begin to glue back together. You're blown far apart from one another. Dealing with it takes all of your energy. The rest of you—your dreams, your goals, your plans for the summer—shuts down as you try to process what's happening and how you should react to it. "If divorce occurs, say, during a period when important life choices are being made—like after high school," writes Dalton Conley in *The Pecking Order: Which Siblings Succeed and Why*, "then the turmoil it causes can affect a child's outcomes much more drastically than if it happens when an offspring's path is more or less stable."

Kayla was financially dependent on her parents when they split up. Her father called her out of the blue and said he needed his car back. He said she could no longer use his credit card to buy her books, and he couldn't pay her college tuition. "He was done with helping me," she says. Kayla was in her sophomore year. She applied for financial aid and took out loans so she could continue taking classes. But after two semesters, she was twenty thousand dollars in debt. Her grades dropped—she didn't have time to study because she worked so much. Her mother wasn't doing well financially, so she didn't feel as if she could ask her for help. "I was so angry with my father for putting me in the situation," she says. Kayla dropped out of college and got a second job to try to pay off her debts. Ten years later, Kayla still hasn't finished her degree. Her best friend recently got her Ph.D.—Kayla's longtime dream—and Kayla was so jealous, she says she couldn't see straight. "I don't feel whole," she says. "I feel like I'm not quite as good of a person as I could be. I'm so jealous of that degree."

Money is such an integral part of starting out. Sometimes parents dangle money in front of their adult children to get them on their side. One young woman interviewed was angry with her father after her parents split up because he immediately began dating other women. She knew that he was still "dating" her mother as well. The young woman stifled her feelings for fear of losing financial support from her father. He was paying the rent on her apartment while she was in graduate school. "If I were to tell him how I felt," she says, "he'd say he didn't want to talk to me anymore. I'd rather it not be, 'Hey, I know we're not talking, but can I have my rent check?' There are many times I've sucked up how I felt."

Suzie's father has provided for her and her brother since her parents split up. He pays her tuition and flies her home from college. He buys groceries, and recently, he bought Suzie, nineteen, a new car. Suzie says her mother "doesn't do anything for me and my brother anymore." Suzie isn't just emotionally abandoned by her mother; she receives nothing from her financially. Is it a coincidence that she's always been on her father's side? Suzie says she'd be angry with her mother even if she were the one supporting her. But money can easily control and manipulate adult children, who need it for their lives to move forward. Stories such as Suzie's and Kayla's make me wonder, Can our loyalty be swayed by money?

Teresa Cooney says that at least one college student she interviewed decided to live with his father after the split for financial reasons. "I know where the money is," he told Cooney.

Points to Remember

- Sometimes parents leak information on purpose in an attempt to win an adult child's favor. If you don't take a side, you'll have an easier time staying out of the middle.

- Explain to a parent that you do not feel comfortable passing bills or notes to your other parent. Then stand firm. Do not let either convince you to act on their behalf *one last time*.

- You cannot save your parents' marriage. No one can. They've decided to end it. You'll exhaust yourself trying to save a union they couldn't.

- Don't talk badly to either of your parents about the other parent, and they'll be less inclined to talk badly about the other to you.

- If it seems as if your parents are lying, remember that everyone has their own version of the "truth."

- If a parent disregards your requests to keep you out of the middle, challenge the parent to step into your shoes. It can help to ask parents whether one of their own parents would ever have said to them the things they're saying to you.

4

Without Family

> We would be nothing but for our blood. It's a detestable
> point, but one in which my father and I agree.
>
> —CAMILLE CUSUMANO, "Gods and Fathers"

M om is in the kitchen peeling turnips. Two
large pots of water are boiling. She abandons the
turnips and drops potatoes into the boiling water one
by one. She hums. The stereo is turned up so loud that it sounds as if
an Italian opera singer were performing in the next room. I push my
finger into a half-eaten cherry pie and lick the sweet filling off my
fingertip. Mom pretends not to notice. She hands me a turnip and a
peeler. "Maybe in a little while you could set the table," she says.

On Thanksgiving, Mom is a general and I am her foot soldier.
There are many details to manage. She has to put the turkey in the

oven by 8:00 a.m. so it will be done by 3:00 in the afternoon, which is when we always eat. Sides need to be made. Pies baked. Tables set. Hors d'oeuvres arranged and set out. I'll sit and watch Mom cook, but I've never been thrilled about helping with the turnips. The peeler always slips on the turnips' tough skin, nicking off a piece of your finger. I begin to peel, out of duty, which frees Mom to start on the creamed onions. We prepare a feast for ten, even though we are only three.

The previous two Thanksgivings, we went to my aunt's house in Virginia Beach. Making the trip south isn't Mom's favorite thing to do. Mom always prefers celebrating Thanksgiving at home, where she can direct the cooking. Even when we went to my grandmother's house as children, Mom would prepare a private dinner for our family the night before. After she and Dad split up, Mom admitted it would feel strange to spend Thanksgiving alone with my sister and me. "The house will feel empty with just the three of us," Mom said. This year is different. My older sister, Erin, and her husband, Brian, are visiting from California. Since it has been several months since Erin was home, she decided she'd eat with Mom, Chelsea, and me. Brian would spend the day with his family a town away.

And so there were four.

I stuff white napkins into ceramic holders and place wineglasses at every setting. Mom insists we use the Christmas dishes and digs them out of the cupboard. She puts the parade on the television and turns down the radio. "We have to make this feel a little more like Thanksgiving," she says, brightly. On the screen is a tremendous airborne Snoopy, bouncing its way down Thirty-fourth Street in Manhattan. All I can think of is Dad. He's the one who loved the parade. I'd only watch it so I could sit next to him while Mom cooked. We'd laugh at all the floats and the dancers and the crazy New Yorkers who sometimes lined the curbs even in the snow.

Mom assumed we'd spend every holiday with her after the separation. It made more sense. Dad's entire family lived an hour away while Mom had grown apart from some of her siblings. It was understood she needed us more. I offered to cook Dad dinner anyway. "Spend the day with Mommy," he'd said a few weeks earlier. He was going to Aunt Junie's. "Listen, Brock, make sure she has a nice time. Make it easier on her. OK?"

I'm not sure how I can do that. Facing our first holiday alone at the house is a bold step. There are no cousins around to distract us from Dad's absence. Mom has to gather the wood to start the fire in the fireplace. She has to make the calls to wish friends and family a happy holiday. She has to do *everything*. I cringe when I realize we are going to sit at the same dining room table and eat off the same dishes and sip from the same wineglasses we always use on Thanksgiving. Luckily, we don't have a rectangular dining table where the head seat would remain vacant. Our table is round, so we only have to space the place mats farther apart to make up for Dad's not being there.

The phone used to ring a lot on Thanksgiving. All of Dad's sisters and brothers would call. Then my grandmother, Dad's mother, would have us each take a turn talking to her. Not one of my aunts or uncles called after my parents split up. I have more than fifty cousins. I didn't hear from one. Two years later, still no one had asked how I was doing. Dad's family didn't even call to wish us a happy Thanksgiving anymore. If I wanted to talk to my grandmother or an aunt, I had to call her.

Family members don't want to make situations awkward, so they avoid bringing up an ex-wife or ex-husband. But even my aunt Carol Ann, who visited me in Washington recently without Mom, acted as though the divorce were a taboo subject. She didn't inquire about my father or ask us to say hello. She'd known him for twenty years, and now it was as though he didn't exist to her. To be fair, I avoided my aunts and uncles in the same way they avoided asking me about my parents. Being around them made me feel as if I had something to hide. And without Mom there, to smooth out awkward silences, I often didn't have much to say.

At one o'clock, Mom pushes open Chelsea's bedroom door. She's curled up in bed. "Chelsea, it's Thanksgiving," Mom says. "Get out of bed and get dressed. Erin is going to be here soon." Because she is the only one coming over, Erin is the guest of honor. She gave Mom reason to make the hors d'oeuvres and the cornucopia. Chelsea stirs. "What time is it?" she asks. "One," Mom says firmly. "Now get up." I'm in the living room watching a TV movie when Chelsea emerges. Her eyes are puffy, and we laugh at how raspy her voice is. She slumps onto the couch and pulls a chenille throw from the armrest to wrap around her. "It's cold," she says.

Mom pours olives into a dish and arranges cheese and crackers around them. She lays a nutcracker across a platter of nuts. Both trays are set on the coffee table. A few candles next to the trays are lit. Mom spots Chelsea cuddled under the chenille throw. She winces. "Chelsea, please get dressed," Mom says. "Please!"

I hear a trace of regret in her voice. Maybe staying home with just the three of us wasn't a good idea. Maybe we're not ready. Maybe feelings are still too raw. Mom nearly whispers. "I'm just trying to get through this holiday, too," she says.

And suddenly, I get why Mom couldn't sit still the past few hours. She's trying to make this holiday as normal as possible. Perfect even. She's making the creamed onions and the hors d'oeuvres and putting the parade on because she's trying to prove we can still be a family, even with one person fewer. If she threw her whole self into the day, Mom figured, she'd make up for Dad's absence. But she needed us to try, too. We had to meet her halfway. Chelsea's sitting in her pajamas at one in the afternoon showed little respect for Mom's efforts.

The front door swings open, and Erin walks in carrying a bottle of cabernet. "Happy Thanksgiving!" she yells. I am relieved when I see her.

Later, the four of us sit around the coffee table. Mom pours us each a little wine. We munch on the olives and the cheese and crackers. We talk about our jobs and gossip about friends and family. We reminisce. At one point, we laugh so hard, Erin spits wine onto her shirt. When Mom puts out the turkey, we fall silent. Its skin is crisp and golden brown. Then she covers the table with colorful side dishes—from red cabbage to green beans to orange-colored mashed turnips, our favorite. We raise our glasses in a toast, and Mom says a quick prayer. We suddenly have a lot to be thankful for.

We almost feel like a family.

When parents announce they're splitting up, adult children don't realize how unrecognizable their families are about to become to them. We find ourselves on a high-speed train, and not the fancy kind you board in Europe where seats recline and waiters serve a five-course meal. Ours is more like a commuter train—hectic, uncomfortable, lonely—on a cross-country trek. We embark on a journey with our parents after they split up, and we travel with them through unfamiliar terrain. We don't bother to look out the window. We're so busy making the ride more comfortable for them that we don't notice how much the landscape is changing around us.

So much of an adult child's suffering is immediate. We reverse roles with our parents, we mediate, and we help negotiate alimony. We are so caught up in the details of divorce that we hardly grasp the larger changes sweeping over our families. Only years later, once the arguing settles down and our parents' marriage is officially dissolved, do we find ourselves waking up to the reality of our changed situation.

Everyone knows divorce tears families apart. But you never quite get how broken your family will feel until you find yourself in those shattered circumstances. Parents *are* a family. Once they're officially apart, children aren't sure what to make of what's left. My sisters and I could see there were pieces to pick up. But what were we supposed to do with the shards? We had two of everything: two separate families, with Mom heading one and Dad, the other; two new phone numbers; two houses with one half of our identities attached to each.

Families are disfigured after divorce. Few parents can become friends with each other within a few years after divorcing. An unfortunate side effect: relatives grow distant. Emotions are raw for everyone involved. Parents and extended family members see themselves as being in opposing enemy camps, and sometimes temporary divisions grow more permanent. An adult child is left with dual "subfamilies." Maternal and paternal relatives, who make nice around a young child, don't always hold back around adult children and often try to talk us onto a side. Even grandparents may align themselves with one of our parents. So adult children find themselves managing a divided family, and it's exhausting. Because adult children straddle the divide, it's only a matter of time before our two subfamilies will be forced together.

Lawyers arranged for Jodie's father to come by the house and pick up some things in February 2004, several months after he had moved out. Jodie, twenty-four, was nervous. Ever since she found out her father had cashed $150,000 worth of savings bonds in her name, she stopped speaking to him. It was one reason her mother was divorcing him. He had also squandered her mother's inheritance. "Because you stole that money," Jodie's mother had told her father, "I want the house. The girls are still in school." Jodie saw her father swear on his daughters' lives. "You will have the house," he said.

Three days later, Jodie got home from law school. She noticed that three expensive paintings were missing from the house. Then she found a letter to her mother folded on the kitchen table. "Dear Maria," her father wrote. "Because of your violent and hostile acts, I can't live in this house. If you have any questions, please contact my attorney. I will pay the car insurance and mortgage to the best of my ability." Jodie immediately filled five trash bags full of her father's belongings. She shattered the glass of a frame containing a poem he had written her when she was born: "Butterflies are lullabies . . ." She ripped it up into tiny pieces, put it in an envelope, and inserted a note to her father's lawyer: "Please make sure he never contacts his daughters again."

No one from her father's side of the family called Jodie or her sister. She didn't even hear from her grandparents, who had often checked in with her. Later Jodie learned that her father was telling lies to his family. He said his wife was abusive. In reality, Jodie's mother had quietly put up with her father's extravagant spending habits for years. Her paternal grandparents believed her father and took his side, which, in Jodie's mind, meant they were against her, too. Jodie was upset that they had never called to ask whether the allegations were true.

Jodie's grandmother accompanied her father into the house that February morning. Her grandfather waited outside in the car. They stood face-to-face in the foyer. The silence was deafening. "I guess you've gotten close," Jodie said to her father, pointing to her grandmother. He nodded to Jodie and her mother. "Yeah, I guess you guys have, too," he said. Jodie didn't want to see her grandmother. She'd received an e-mail from her a week before. Attached was an invitation to her grandfather's seventy-fifth birthday party. "I'm sorry, but I do not feel comfortable seeing my father," Jodie wrote back. Her grandmother warned her about taking sides. "There will be consequences," her grandmother said. Then she dismissed her. "Have a nice life," her grandmother wrote.

Divisions destroy adult children's perceptions of their extended family. Aunts and uncles on your father's side show little allegiance to your mother. Maternal grandparents stop speaking to your father. Adult children aren't expecting members of their extended family to stand on opposite sides of their family's rift. When they do, their actions seem disloyal. So does their silence. Neither side brings up the ex-spouse at family events, which causes adult children to feel secretive about their affiliation with the outcast parent. One half of us must be erased when we're around our other set of aunts, uncles, cousins, and grandparents. Oftentimes, we begin to resent our extended family. They seem devoted to only one of our parents—and less true to *us*. Says one young woman interviewed, "Dad's family shunned Mom. My extended family and my parents lived on a few houses scattered along the same dirt road in the middle of nowhere. Mom wouldn't get invited to things. They didn't call her on Christmas. We kids would be invited, but we'd never want to go."

Jenna's father was close with her mother's side of the family. Her grandparents treated him like a son. He was her younger cousins' favorite uncle. "It didn't make sense that they would just shut him out all of a sudden," says Jenna, twenty-seven. But no one asked how he was or where he was living. Finally, Jenna took her uncle Bob aside at a family dinner. Her father and Bob were close friends, but Bob had stopped calling her father after the split. "You can still call him," she said. "He misses you guys." Her grandparents overheard what she was saying. "Why would you call him?" her grandfather said. Jenna understood why her grandparents were siding with her mother: they were protecting their daughter. But she wished everyone would stop acting as if her father had never existed. *You can't just turn your feelings off*. She was relieved when a cousin later confided in her. "I miss Uncle Dave," he said.

Try to think of the divorce from a grandparent's or an uncle's point of view. Extended family members may not call because they don't want to butt in. Maybe they don't know what to say. The situation is awkward for them, too. Chances are, your relatives aren't upset with either of your parents. They're just trying to be supportive of their children or siblings. When your mother's brother stops asking about your father, it's out of loyalty to your mother. Your maternal grandparents aren't going to want to say anything to hurt their emotionally fragile daughter. So they say nothing.

Believe it or not, extended family members may also be looking out for you, too. Sometimes a grandparent or an uncle may not know what to say to an adult child. It's like being around someone whose mother or father recently died. You're not sure whether you're supposed to say "I'm sorry" or "Are you OK?" You're not even sure whether you can raise the issue without making the person uncomfortable. Instead, you act as if nothing had happened and wait for the person to bring up his or her feelings.

I know this because a couple of years after my parents split up, I stopped pretending that one of my parents no longer existed. When I was visiting with Mom's sister, I told my young cousins about Dad's new apartment and his band. When I was with Dad's family, I talked about Mom's promotion at work and how happy she seemed these days. Relatives on both sides would say the same thing: "I'm happy to hear he's [or she's] doing so well." I realized that Dad's family cared about Mom and Mom's family still thought about Dad. They just didn't know how to do so openly without seeming like traitors.

Children in early adulthood are in the most intense period of transition. There are graduations, weddings, babies, and baptisms. A celebration surrounding a special occasion in an adult child's life is often the first time our parents—and their extended families—see one another since they sat across from one another flanked by lawyers. At an event, they face their ex—and the reality of the new dual-family structure. Adult children are equally anxious about seeing the structural changes. The new landscape is hard to accept—and so is a parent's new boyfriend or girlfriend, which adds another layer of complication to our adjustment.

Jenna was hoping only one of her parents would attend her graduate school commencement in San Diego. When both decided to come—her mother said she'd bring her grandparents, who weren't speaking to her father either—Jenna panicked. Her parents couldn't talk on the phone. How would they sit in the same room? Just thinking about it left Jenna "emotionally wrecked." "It was the first time I was going to see my family in this new way," she says. "We were going to be separate. It was like facing my worst nightmare."

Jenna asked her younger sister to fly out to San Diego a week early. She needed help organizing her parents' simultaneous visits. Luckily, they were set to arrive a day apart. Jenna could pick up her mother and grandparents at the airport first. She'd settle them into their hotel—she made sure her father was staying elsewhere—and then take them sightseeing. Then Jenna could pick up her father at the airport the following day without feeling guilty she wasn't spending time with her mother.

When two enemy generals needed to meet during the Revolutionary War, they'd send a trusted subordinate into enemy territory on horseback with a white flag and a message detailing the parameters of the proposed meeting. Jenna didn't want family drama to find its way into her graduation—so like a trusted go-between carrying a white flag, she gave specific instructions to her mother and father to coordinate their individual arrivals at the ceremony.

The detailed planning was exhausting, and it was the last thing Jenna wanted to have to worry about the day of her graduation. Even more stressful was the thought of sitting at a table with both of her parents for a celebration dinner afterward. She knew her parents wouldn't speak at the dinner, and her grandparents probably wouldn't acknowledge her father. Jenna was relieved when her friends decided to forgo the traditional "dinner" celebration and have a joint party. Six friends had recently divorced parents in town as well. No one wanted to deal with the drama of separate lunches and dinners, or scheduling time for each parent on what was supposed to be a joyous occasion.

So the group threw a Dysfunctional Family Graduation Party. Kegs were delivered to a San Diego beach. Grills were fired up. Each family—in Jenna's case, her two subfamilies—was told to bring its own food. Jenna's parents came to the party. They didn't talk to each other. Her father quietly grilled steaks and sausages. Jenna says her father hand-delivered the food to his ex-wife and her parents as a peace offering. They took the food without looking up or saying thank you. "It made me mad," says Jenna. "But I didn't want to ruin the party, so I didn't say a word."

I can't tell you the number of times I lay in bed at night thinking about how my parents would react to seeing each other at my wedding or at the hospital, when my older sister gives birth to her baby. I get butterflies in my stomach just imagining them in the same room. For the past few years, every interaction Mom and Dad had was laced with tension. I didn't know whether they were capable of having a pleasant conversation. Would they say hello? Would my father introduce his girlfriend?

It's inevitable that my parents will run into each other. When it happens, I'm going to have to remind myself that my parents' problems are not my own. Parents may feel awkward around each other; we shouldn't have to feel awkward around them. Too often, adult children, including me and probably you, worry when it's not our job. Parents need to learn how to coexist peacefully themselves. You shouldn't feel responsible for their feelings during a divorce, and you certainly shouldn't feel responsible for them after one.

We allow our events to be poisoned by our parents' forced reunions. Instead of fully enjoying a celebration, adult children go through the motions with a dark cloud over our heads. Previous chapters established the unfair demands parents make on their children after divorce. Seeing each other for the first time—and at subsequent events—will once again raise parents' stress levels. No matter when they see each other, it will be one year too soon. Sometimes a parent will say they're willing to miss a milestone moment in our lives to avoid seeing the ex-husband or ex-wife. Dad will say, "I will only go if your mother isn't there." Mom will flatly announce, "Don't expect me to sit with your father!" These are immature requests, and ones that keep us up at night worrying. *How can I tell Dad he cannot come just because Mom doesn't want him there? Is that really fair?*

Often both parents will attend, despite their demands. And an adult child is forced to function as a stage manager, choreographing parents' movements at an event as though he or she were organizing a ballet. The dance is elaborate: we make sure Mom walks one step in front of Dad or one step behind. We cue their arrivals and departures. We tell them what they can say and what they can't. *Don't bring up how much alimony you're giving Mom.* With careful planning, adult children believe they can defuse an uncomfortable situation, such as a screaming match between their parents on the steps of a wedding chapel.

Barbara's younger brother, Nick, was graduating from a New

York City design college. Their parents, who were married for thirty years, had been separated for six months. Barbara's father refused to go to the graduation because his wife was going. Nick called Barbara. "I really wish Dad would come," Nick said. Barbara knew how hurt she would be if her father were willing to miss such a big event in her life. So she called her dad to persuade him, and after a few conversations, he agreed to go. He said he'd bring their grandparents. Nick recommended a hotel—the same place where his mother was staying. His mother called the hotel and told the receptionist, "I want my ex-husband on a different floor."

The day before Nick's graduation, Barbara and her mother checked into the hotel. They learned that Barbara's father and her grandparents were accidentally given a room on the same floor. "He needs to move," her mother told Barbara. "Call the front desk." Barbara explained the dilemma to the receptionist. Then Barbara called her father. He agreed to move, even though he needed a handicap bathroom for his wheelchair—and his new room didn't have one. Barbara's mother snickered when she heard this, which frustrated Barbara. *Weren't they past this childish back-and-forth?* At the graduation, Barbara made sure her parents were seated on opposite sides of the room. She says it was the first time they were together as two subfamilies. "I kept thinking, *How does this work?*" After the ceremony, Barbara suggested they would have a celebratory lunch with her mother and her family. Then they'd get together with her father and his family for dinner.

Separate celebrations seem like a simple solution, but they're difficult. We never know what might set a parent off. To keep the peace, sometimes adult children find themselves convincing a parent to do exactly what they don't want to do—spend time with a former spouse. "Do it for me," we'll say. One young woman interviewed insisted that her parents walk her down the aisle at her wedding and sit next to each other at the reception, despite the fact that they weren't speaking and had been divorced a year. "As far as I was concerned, this was my day," she said. "They needed to put aside their problems—for me." The strict coordination also allowed her to control her parents' interactions. She didn't have to worry about their running into each other at the bar. They'd be forced to interact and behave at a table surrounded by old friends and family.

Barbara, the same Barbara whose mother forced her ex-husband to switch floors, manufactured a peaceful interaction between her parents when she and her family attended the funeral of a close friend. Her mother made it clear she wanted the entire family to sit together, including her ex-husband. "We knew him as a family," her mother said. "We will sit as a family." Barbara knew her father was going to refuse, and she knew she'd need to convince him. So she waited in the back of the church for her father to arrive; her mother and brother were seated. As soon as Barbara saw her father, she cornered him.

"Mom wants us to sit together," she said. Her father said he felt weird. They *weren't* a family anymore. Barbara wasn't sure how her mother would react to not getting her way. She pressed her father. "There are going to be weddings and all of these other family functions," she told her father. "You need to suck it up to some extent and sit with us." Her father rolled his wheelchair up to the end of the pew, where his ex-wife, son, and daughter were sitting. Her parents didn't acknowledge each other, and her father slipped out quickly at the end.

Barbara has stopped worrying about her mother's and father's interactions since; she grew exhausted organizing peaceful meetings between them. What she was doing was subtle on the surface, even though it twisted her up inside. Her parents might not have realized how much burden she'd taken on. In telling her to "say this" or "do that," her mother and father were thinking only of themselves. It might be uncomfortable and awkward and excruciating to let your parents' time together play out, but you're better off. You send a message early on when you don't get involved. You're saying, "Mom, Dad, you're on your own," which allows you to shrug off the tension between them.

When Mark, thirty-one, got engaged to his girlfriend in Hawaii, he didn't think about the complexities of putting a wedding together with divorced parents. His parents had lived apart for a couple of years by then, and he figured it wouldn't be much of an issue. They'd arrive separately, talk to their own families, and leave. As Mark got more involved in the wedding planning, he began to worry. His parents didn't want to be anywhere near each other. "I'm not comfortable sitting at the same table as your father," his mother said. His father had a similar request: "I don't need to be announced or walk in with your mother." Mark wanted to accommodate his parents, but planning to keep them happy gave him a headache. Who would walk his mother down the aisle? Would his mother be cordial to his father's girlfriend?

Mark decided they couldn't argue with tradition. So he researched appropriate wedding etiquette for divorced parents. His brother could walk his mother down the aisle. At the reception, he told his parents, they'd be announced separately—but they'd sit at the same table.

Juggling our parents gets old. We burn out trying to make their time together comfortable. Every moment is just as uncomfortable for us. This is especially true during the holidays. Unlike young children, whose custody decisions are made by the court, adult kids themselves must decide with whom they'll spend holidays. Choosing is treacherous. Nothing we propose seems fair. Does Mom get me on Thanksgiving and Dad see me on Christmas? If my birthday is

Tuesday, with which parent do I celebrate on the day of rather than the day after?

The first thing to remember is that no matter with whom you decide to spend a holiday, you're going to make someone unhappy—whether it be your mother or your father, or your sister or your grandfather. We often beat ourselves up thinking something like, *If I only said I'd go to Gram's* ... Not true. If you said that, your sister might have wanted you at Dad's. You can't win. Once you realize there is no right or wrong decision, you'll be free of stress. Your time together as a family is not the way it used to be, and it takes a little while for everyone to accept that.

Second, you need to formulate a holiday visitation plan, and you need to be honest about it with both sides of your family. I knew Mom was more sensitive than Dad, so I often consulted her as to what she would *prefer* I do on a holiday—though I didn't always oblige. You might do the same. It helps to get feedback. Perhaps Mom wants you on Christmas Eve and Dad wants you during the day. Well, your planning just got a lot easier. I'd also consult with siblings. Maybe you and your sister can split up and have alone time with each parent, or maybe you decide with whom you're spending what and tell your parents together.

Think about your visitation plan a few months ahead. Early decisions come in handy. If Mom or Dad gets upset when you explain your plan, it won't ruin the holiday. Otherwise, parents will assume you're spending each holiday with them, and it becomes harder to take when you say you're not. You need to be firm and deal with the fallout of your plan. Your parents may get angry with you. They may cry and scream. Unfortunately, you'll have to listen to it. But they'll get over their anger. Weeks will go by, and the reality of the new circumstances will sink in. And you'll have succeeded in taking control of the situation.

For adult kids of divorce, holidays become just one more thing our families don't do together. They're anticipated less. "My siblings and I must have four or more separate gatherings in order to accommodate the different groups of stepfamilies and in-laws who are not willing to interact with each other," says one twenty-seven-year-old man. Another thirty-one-year-old man interviewed said, "Now holidays are just a pain in the ass. They're separate, and you have to schedule everything." Subfamilies tug. Both want equal time. Everything feels different.

Melinda, thirty-two, was glum the first Christmas after her parents' divorce was finalized. Her mother was living in a new house, which made the holiday seem displaced. Typically, Christmas morning had looked like this: Melinda's father would set up a tripod at the foot of the wide, sweeping staircase in their house. As his adult children made their way downstairs in their pajamas, he'd gather them on the steps and snap their picture. "Dad would take our picture the same way every year," Melinda says. Then he'd swing open the French doors to the living room, where a lit tree as high as the twelve-foot ceiling was blinking, surrounded by piles of presents. They'd open their gifts and eat a big breakfast together. "It was our ritual," Melinda says.

Melinda's mother wanted to change the way they celebrated after the divorce. "You'll open your presents on Christmas Eve," her mother said. No picture on the stairs. No twelve-foot tree. Melinda resisted. The holiday was already empty without her father; did they have to erase everything familiar about Christmas? "My mother didn't want to remember the way we used to do it," she says. Melinda wanted everything to stay the same. But that was impossible now that her family had taken a new shape. Melinda's mother knew she needed to redefine her half of the family for her kids. She'd create a new set of rituals, which would become just as special as the old ones. My mother did the opposite. She wanted to keep all traditions the same, which illustrates how differently parents cope.

During the first few years of their parents' split, adult children, such as Melinda, are figuring out how to manage two subfamilies, which can make them dread visiting home. Visits become whirlwind tours with both parents hyperscheduled in equal increments. Parents keep track of how much time we spend with them and how much we don't. Says one young woman interviewed, "Mom gets possessive of my time when I come home. Once she was upset because I was taking a trip with my father over spring break but I wasn't going to come home to see her. I felt so guilty that I shortened my trip so I could go home and spend three days with her."

Liza, twenty-seven, lives in North Carolina, but she grew up in West Virginia. When she and her husband visit home, she says, "Seeing everybody is difficult." Liza's mother lives out in the country. She tells her daughter to come by when she can. Liza usually makes it out for lunch and an overnight on her last day. Liza says her father and his family try to keep her at their house longer. "When I'm leaving," she says, "they'll say, 'Where are you going? Why don't you stay here another night?' " Liza says she'll tell them she's going to her mother's house. "That's when I get the comments," Liza says. Her family gets annoyed. "So you're staying with Mom instead of me?" her father asks.

Leaving one parent to keep an "appointment" with the other feels duplicitous. We rarely share with Mom what we're doing with Dad. Parents don't want to hear about the time we spend with their ex-spouse. So half of our life is one big secret.

Before our parents' divorce, we are often closer with one parent, and that parent sometimes perpetuates our relationship with the other. In other words, if we talk to Mom more, Mom will tell Dad what we're struggling with rather than Dad's asking us himself. A father in this role will rely on his wife for information about his child. He might chat with his son or daughter for a few minutes when he or she calls home, but he's not going to dig. Parents and their children fall into patterns, and once those patterns are defined, they are difficult to break.

These dynamics become even more significant after a divorce. Once a parent loses their "source," they may be unsure of how to interact with the child without the spouse's advice. Adult children notice the absence as well. Suddenly, they need to interact with that parent on their own. One young woman interviewed says she always thought she was close with her father. But after her parents' split, she realized she didn't talk to him much. She'd call home and talk to her mother and *feel* as if she'd talked to *both* her parents. She'd lump them together. "Once Dad couldn't hear about me from my mother," she says, "he took an interest in my life, which he'd never done before."

Researchers have long studied relationships between parents and their young children after divorce. They agree on one point: children of divorce grow closer to their mothers and more distant from their fathers. The distance has long been attributed to custody decisions; relationships falter because kids are generally placed with their mothers. Gloria Steinem was referring to absentee fathers when she said, "It's clear that children suffer too much mother, and too little father."

Many researchers assumed adult children would have stronger relationships with their fathers after divorce because custody decisions aren't involved. Relationships are developed outside of the courts. A study published in the *Journal of Marriage and Family* seems to suggest otherwise. Family sociologist Teresa Cooney examined parent-child relations, with children aged eighteen to twenty-three, after divorce. Whereas the mother-child bond proved resilient, Cooney found adult children were just as likely to spend less time with their fathers as young children of divorce. More than half reported not seeing their fathers weekly; 15 percent were in contact with their fathers monthly. Additional studies can help explain why: ongoing conflict with a parent or geographic distance. "Kin keeping is one task divorced men cannot hire someone else to perform," Cooney writes, citing a study published in *Signs*. In the early 1990s, Harvard researchers found that "for many men . . . marriage and parenthood are a package deal. . . . It is as though men only know how to be fathers indirectly, through the actions of their wives. . . . If the marriage breaks up, the indirect ties between fathers and children also are broken."

A son's bond with his father is often defined differently than a daughter's. In the most stereotypical sense, a father-son relationship centers around simpler topics such as sports or cars, which makes connecting easier. Those subjects are unchanged after divorce. Daughters may have less of an established relationship with their fathers. "I had never really sat down and talked to my Dad," many told me. Because fathers put less emphasis on "human connections and relationship investment," mapping out a relationship with them can be difficult for daughters, who are unsure how to interact with their fathers. *What do we talk about? How do I get close to him?* Fathers struggle, too. Says Cooney, "Even if the father had good relations with his children prior to the divorce, he may find it difficult to manage and foster this relationship on his own."

The studies don't tell the full story. Relationships between parents and their adult children are changed after divorce but not in such rigid ways. Intimacy levels are more fluid. We grow closer to different parents at different points. The quantity of time that adult children spend with each parent, especially fathers, may decrease. But those same children make a conscious effort to reconnect and build a new kind of relationship with parents in subsequent years, and they often succeed. Unlike young children, who have to wait around for Dad to pick them up, adult children can drive over to their father's house. If we want a postdivorce relationship with our parents, we can create one.

After my parents' divorce, I was determined to develop a deeper relationship with Dad. Before they split up, I'd spent most of my visits home with Mom. Dad was usually out on his sailboat. Mom and I would go shopping or visit a winery. Then we'd meet Dad at the boat and go out to dinner. I was never alone with Dad.

After the divorce, Dad and I had to find things to do together. I'd drag him to a movie. We'd go for walks on the beach. Dad would suggest we visit my grandmother together. We'd talk about what went wrong in my parents' marriage, and Dad would ask me about my relationship with my boyfriend. We were getting to know each other, but as with any friendship, it took work.

Dad flew down to visit me in Washington in the winter of 2003—the first time he'd come to see me since Family Weekend during my freshman year of college. Dad and I went to the local aquarium. We shopped and went out to eat. When I dropped Dad off at the airport, I realized how much I was going to miss him. I'd never felt closer to him. Dad was becoming a friend.

Growing closer with a parent is a pleasant side effect of divorce. One young woman interviewed said she tried to find new subjects on which she and her father could connect. She'd inquire how he was doing when they talked on the phone. "How's work?" she'd say. Maybe an adult child asks about a father's childhood or his first love. We build friendships with our parents. And you have your new two-family structure to thank. If I hadn't been forced to create a second subfamily centered around Dad, I might never have really understood who he was.

These changing relationships would be swell if siblings weren't equally involved with our parents. Some level of rivalry always exists among siblings. Rivalries can become heated in divorce. If we grow closer to one parent—or a sibling does—dynamics within each subfamily shift. Parents deny they have favorites, but they often do. Changing relationships can be threatening to those who were previously in favor, dividing an already polarized subfamily.

Relations between Stephanie and her sister, Amanda, grew tense after their parents' divorce. Stephanie was older, and she was always closer to her mother. But after the divorce, Stephanie's mother started spending more time with Amanda because she lived closer. Nearly every time Stephanie called her mother's cell phone, she'd be at Amanda's apartment. "I'd get jealous," Stephanie says. "I was the one who was always closer with Mom. She was *my* friend." Her feelings were heightened when Amanda started to censor Stephanie's conversations with her mother. If Stephanie asked her mother a question about the divorce or the sale of the house or anything really, her sister would shoot her a look. "Don't ask her about that," she'd tell Stephanie.

Stephanie noticed that all their fights centered around the divorce. Amanda and her mother kept secrets. Stephanie found out her father cheated a week after her sister did, which was painful. While her sister was enjoying her newfound affection from their mother, Stephanie felt confused and left out. *How did I fall out of favor?* Stephanie expected her family to divide in half. She never imagined how different the dynamics between her and her sister could be.

Paige didn't approve of her mother's upcoming marriage to her boyfriend. She reluctantly decided she'd attend the wedding anyway. Then she learned her mother had asked her older sister, Carla, to be her maid of honor. Paige was upset. It seemed to solidify her suspicions that her mother and sister had a closer relationship. "Your sister has been more supportive of me," her mother told Paige. Paige had actively pursued a relationship with her father all along, but the news made her even more devoted to him. "After being with Mom, her boyfriend, and my sister, I realized they were getting along so well. I needed to be close to someone, too," Paige says.

Not all subfamilies are created equal. Though Paige and her sister were both a part of their mother's and father's new families, they had different levels of commitment to each. Paige grew closer with her father and more easily accepted her stepmother. Her sister did the same with their mother and her boyfriend. Interactions between Paige and her sister grew strained. She resented her sister's loyalty to her mother, and who knows how Carla felt about Paige's close ties to their father?

In *Brothers and Sisters,* Jane Mersky Leder writes, "The quickness with which all of the 'stuff' from childhood can reduce adult siblings to kids again underscores the strong and complex connections between sisters and brothers. . . . It doesn't seem to matter how much time has elapsed or how far we've traveled. Our brothers and sisters bring us face-to-face with our former selves and remind us how intricately bound up we are in each other's lives." While divorce can polarize siblings, it can also draw them closer. To cope during such stressful times, many of us turn to one another for help. Friends don't "get" our parents the way siblings do. We can vent with them and talk things through without feeling embarrassed or as if we're burdening anyone. So we vent and talk our feelings out. We relate to one another not as children but as adults with a shared problem. Conversations are more mature, and as a result, friendships are deepened.

Siblings sometimes keep subfamilies connected. Within every divided family, one adult child acts as a "kin keeper." Kin keepers take it upon themselves to bring remnants of the old family together. They arrange gatherings or host holidays. They do it because parents often stop doing these things themselves. Mom doesn't have the space to host Christmas at her new apartment. Dad may not think to invite his kids over for dinner. So you or a sibling—in my family, it was my sister Erin—plan events to bring one half of your family together.

"I don't know what I would have done without my siblings" is a line repeated frequently by adult children of divorce. Stephanie remembers a story from her childhood. "When we were little, my sister and I would fight with each other in the backseat of the car," she says. Stephanie remembers her mother's spinning around and saying, "If anything happens to your father or me, it's just going to be the two of you. You will only have each other." Stephanie recalled that memory after her parents split up. She talked to her sister about keeping lines of communication open between them. "We need to support each other," Stephanie told her.

One set of sisters interviewed planned a "sisterfest" after their parents divorced. They rented a hotel room and spent the weekend together, talking out their emotions and making sure they were on the same page. They wanted to ensure that they didn't allow their parents to come between them. Another brother and sister used the "divide and conquer" method when it came to helping their parents. They divided their worries: she talked to her parents about "feely" topics, and he looked out for the financial side of things. They traded off calling home and checking in on each parent. If an issue came up, they took turns being confrontational.

When siblings band together, they can help unite divided subfamilies. Siblings are a constant in one another's lives. If you talk openly about how to handle your parents' divorce, you'll be less likely to take sides—against one another. One of you won't shoulder a parent's pain alone; you and your siblings will share the burden. You'll become surrogate parents to one another.

You'll also have more leveraging power. If you and your brother always take the same position—"We refuse to meet your new wife," or "We're going to Mom's for Thanksgiving, Dad's for Christmas"— there will be less conflict between you. You'll be able to create some semblance of family. One parent will float in and the other out, but you and your siblings will always be together. You are the heart of your new family.

Managing relationships within subfamilies is just as difficult when tensions drive an adult child and a parent apart. The split can inspire secondary divisions among siblings, who, even in our adult years, remain an important emotional safety net. If your sister isn't speaking to your mother, you may feel guilty if you do. Emotions are tabled. You're not going to want to vent about a parent to a sibling who seems to have taken that parent's side. As estrangements drag on, subfamilies become more deeply entrenched. *Will I take my sister's side or my father's?* As usual, we try not to take any, but it's hard to stay neutral.

Adult children who are estranged from a parent often try to reel siblings over to their side. They are insecure about the fallen position in which they find themselves, and they want to feel less alone. Take my family. When my parents divorced, Erin, who is the oldest, sided with my mother, creating one subfamily. I got closer with my father, which established another. Chelsea was angry with both, so she floated in between the two. In the beginning, I never called Erin to vent about my mother because she'd always stick up for her. She never called me to talk about Dad for the same reasons. But if Chelsea had a screaming match with Mom, she'd call me crying and recount in detail every word exchanged. She knew I'd share her anger and feel just as upset. I'd also feel empowered because I wasn't the only one irritated with Mom. A few times, I called Mom to scold her afterward. "You're her mother," I'd say. "You shouldn't talk to your daughter that way." In retrospect, I can see that calling Mom on Chelsea's behalf further divided my mother and me. She could hear how dug into the other side I was. Mom figured if Chelsea talked to me, then Chelsea must be against her as well. Mom felt outnumbered, which strained her affections for all of us.

Rhonda, twenty-eight, called home every Sunday evening, even six months after her parents split up. She was sitting in her computer room, a converted third bedroom, in her apartment near the University of Illinois when her mother picked up. "I'm so stressed," Rhonda whined. "Maybe you should drop your Chinese class," her mother said. Rhonda was a graduate student in computer science. Chinese was an elective in which she had enrolled for fun. Rhonda told her mother it wasn't school that had her stomach in knots. Her mother got the hint. "I don't want to talk about *that*," her mother said. Rhonda hadn't called her mother expecting to get in an argument, but suddenly, she felt so angry, she could scream. "Well maybe I don't want to talk to you," Rhonda blurted out. "I'm going to hang up on you now," her mother said. She never heard Rhonda say, "I wouldn't be this upset if I didn't love you." The line had already clicked off.

Rhonda's sister Lara heard a different story from their mother, who claimed Rhonda yelled "I hate you" during the conversation. Rhonda and her mother still hadn't spoken two months later when Thanksgiving rolled around. Rhonda spent the holiday with her father. Lara and her mother went to a third sister's house for dinner. With all the divisions in her family, Lara says, "it was a respite of happiness." A whole year went by without Rhonda and her mother speaking. They both tried to get Lara on their side. "It got to the point where Mom would say something and I could hear Rhonda's argument back and vice versa," says Lara.

The following Thanksgiving, the three sisters decided they shouldn't be apart. Since Rhonda still wasn't speaking to their mother, they'd spend the holiday with their father. Even though their mother would be in town—she'd recently moved out of state— Lara and her other sister, Rachel, said they wouldn't visit with her. After dinner, the two sisters announced they'd changed their minds. *Why shouldn't I go see my mother?* Lara thought. Rhonda called her sister a moron. She felt betrayed. Picturing her sisters with her mother rubbed the estrangement in her face. "They promised me they wouldn't do that," says Rhonda. "It was like a breach of trust. I was counting on them to support me." Rhonda already felt as if her mother were trying to turn her sisters against her. "After I freaked out," Rhonda says, "my sisters didn't go."

Friedrich Nietzsche said, "All in all, punishment hardens and renders people more insensible; it concentrates; it increases the feeling of estrangement; it strengthens the power of resistance." When Rhonda grew estranged from her mother, she was so hurt, she couldn't think clearly. Both were resentful. It wasn't fair for Rhonda to expect her sisters to stop talking to her mother just because she had. Yet she expected them to do so for the same reasons one parent may expect us to shut out the other—loyalty.

Long- and short-term estrangements are common during divorce. With emotions on overdrive, sometimes the easiest way to stop hurting is to temporarily walk away. Oftentimes, communication is relegated to passive-aggressive and overly emotional e-mails, which only serve to inflame an already tense situation. In e-mails and letters, we can write everything we are too afraid to say in person. This lack of communication is a sort of punishment in itself. It's an adult child's way of demonstrating how easily love can be revoked. Not returning calls sends a clear message: "I don't approve of your behavior. I'm not sure I want you in my life. I'm all grown up, and I may not need you anymore."

The day her mother lost full custody of her teenage brother, Ashley, twenty-six, got a call from the courthouse. It was her brother Toby's court-appointed advocate. "Get your brother out of the house," she told Ashley. "I don't want him there when your mother returns." The court had awarded Ashley's mother and father joint custody, which was bound to enrage her mother. So Ashley drove over to her childhood home and told her brother to throw some clothes in a bag. She took him to an uncle's where her father was staying. Her mother called her cell phone the following day, demanding to know where her son was. "I'm not allowed to say," Ashley replied. She was trying to protect her brother. Ashley's mother yelled profanities. "You manipulate everything," she told Ashley. "You may have just manipulated yourself out of having a mother." The line went dead.

Ashley didn't speak to her mother for weeks afterward. She heard through the grapevine that she had moved to Michigan, which infuriated Ashley. Her mother had claimed she was divorcing her husband to make the family happier. Now Ashley believes she wanted to be free to build a life without her children. Ashley was left with a big mess: a father without a clue as to how to parent his teenage son and a mentally challenged younger sister who needed constant hand-holding. "I worried I'd get stuck parenting everyone once Mom left—and I have," she says. Feeling "ditched" by her mother made Ashley want to cut her out of her life. With so much anger boiling inside her, casual chitchat was impossible. Ashley knew she might say something she'd regret, so she didn't say anything at all.

When her mother called Ashley looking for her brother a month later, they talked for a few minutes. Her mother asked how her brother got to band practice. "Other people drive," Ashley told her. She couldn't pretend she wasn't upset and carry on a superficial conversation. She wanted her mother to apologize and initiate a loving reconciliation. "It shouldn't be me always trying to fix everything," Ashley said later. They hung up after a few minutes. Neither brought up their feelings. And the estrangement endured.

In *The Dance of Intimacy*, Harriet Lerner writes, "Distance or cutoff from family members is always a tradeoff. The plus is that we avoid uncomfortable feelings that contact with certain family members inevitably invokes. The costs are less tangible but no less dear." I've read that estrangements persist as long as the individuals involved have unrealistic expectations of one another. Adult children of divorce have difficulty understanding what is so unrealistic about wanting a mother or father to act like a parent. Parenting is the only context in which we've known them. Was it unrealistic for Ashley to be upset with her mother for moving to Michigan without telling her? Of course not. Was it unfair for Ashley to resent her mother for leaving her to care for her siblings? Not at all.

But there are unrealistic notions in any scenario, and adult children need to look past the details of their anger and study the larger picture. In Ashley's case, Ashley expects her mother to forget all the hurtful things Ashley said to her and mend their relationship, which *is* unrealistic. Both sides are hurt and angry, and until they acknowledge each other's pain, rather than trying to focus on their own, they'll remain deadlocked.

Typically, adult children find themselves estranged from the parent with whom they were less close. "It's easier to disconnect from a relationship that lacks intimacy," writes Barbara LeBey in *Family Estrangements*. This may explain why so many individuals I interviewed stopped speaking to their fathers. Adult kids tend to have less intimate relationships with their dads.

Problems that haunt a parent-child relationship before a divorce don't disappear after one. They might worsen. In the past, if a parent and a child fought often, the other parent might have served as a mediator. Tense situations were defused when the other parent stepped in. After divorce, a child must work out these tensions on his or her own, a role for which the child is hardly prepared. Says one twenty-five-year-old woman interviewed, "I realized there were all of these things that weren't quite right with my relationships with my parents. . . . It was like, 'Oh, we should have been dealing with this all along.'"

After Luke's parents split up when he was nineteen, he called his father several times. Luke, now thirty-seven, never got a call back. He wasn't shocked. Luke says his father never spent much time with his son or daughter—he never attended their sports games or helped them with homework—but he always made sure they were cared for financially. After his parents' divorce, Luke's father cut off his financial support to his son, and they stopped speaking. Five years went by, and Luke didn't hear a word. Luke says he wasn't upset by the separation. "I put off the emotional part for so long," he says. "I never really dealt with any of the emotions as it was happening." He finished college and made a nice living, riding the dot-com boom. Then his mother had a brain aneurysm. She was unconscious in the hospital. Doctors were monitoring her progress in the critical-care unit. Luke was in the room with her when his father walked in. "Hi," he said. Luke was impressed his father had showed up.

Luke's mother died a few days later. His father attended the funeral. "I ignored the past for a little while," Luke says. "It appeared Dad was taking steps to fix things, so I let go of my anger." His father began calling him every couple of weeks. "Let's meet for dinner," he'd say. Luke had never really talked with his father about anything. When he was younger, he struggled with his father. Luke had ADD, which made it difficult for him to concentrate. His father would call him dumb and slow. Now that his mother had passed, Luke felt an emptiness stirring inside of him. So he agreed to meet for dinner. He'd sit next to his father and listen to him rattle on about his business or a recent trip he'd taken with his new wife.

Their meetings grew less regular over time. If Luke called his father to make Thanksgiving Day plans, he wouldn't hear back from him. Luke would later find out his father went out of town without telling him. The relationship proved unsteady. "I really tried," says Luke. "But I realized Dad and I reverted back into a pattern. I was the one putting in all of the effort. It was very one-sided." Today, Luke lives fifteen miles from his father, and they haven't spoken in three years. His sister sees their father, which is hard for Luke. She fills Luke in on his father's visits and what he has to say about Luke. Luke says he gets sad thinking about it from time to time, but he tries to push it out of his mind. "For whatever reason, the momentum could not be sustained," he says.

Healing from an estrangement isn't impossible. If you aren't speaking to one parent as you read this, you have every reason to be hopeful. Nearly every adult child interviewed shut a parent out of their life at some point during a divorce. Sometimes the separation lasted two weeks, and other times, several years. Nearly all of them reconciled with their parents at a later point. They waited until they were ready, after emotions had settled down, and then they picked up the phone.

An important prerequisite to healing an estrangement is knowing when you're ready to sit face-to-face with a parent. You need to be willing to meet a parent halfway and be willing to listen to their side as much as you're ready to spill your own. In *Family Estrangements*,

Barbara LeBey suggests planning a meeting that centers around an activity rather than a discussion. She tells the story of Joe, a father who hadn't seen his son since he divorced his wife sixteen years ago. Joe's son was in college at the time and, over the years, had showed no interest in reconciling with Joe. Then, sixteen years later, Joe's son wanted to see him. Joe asked his son to dinner several times. His son turned him down. Joe's wife suggested planning a meeting around an activity. When Joe asked his son to play golf, he agreed. "They went out to play a couple of times, but avoided any discussion of their long estrangement," LeBey writes. "They just played golf. And they enjoyed each other's company."

When months or years pass by, dredging up the past is only going to bring you and your parent right back to where you left off: arguing. Healing will happen over time. Adult children and their parents first need to remind themselves of what it's like to be around each other. In the end, that's what we want, isn't it? Our mother or father back in our lives so we might see our dad at Christmas or meet our mom for a movie. You need to remind each other that you can be in each other's company without feeling hateful.

Seven months went by and Sarah, thirty-four, still hadn't spoken to her father. It was her choice. She couldn't be on the telephone with him without wanting to scream at him. But her infant son was getting bigger, and Sarah wanted her father to see him. She decided to send her father an e-mail letting everything out. "I just don't understand how you could do this to Mom," she wrote. "It didn't just affect you. It affected all of us." Her father's response was heartening. "I never meant for it to happen, but it did," her father wrote. "If I could turn back time . . . I know what I did was disgusting, and I'll make amends for it." Once Sarah saw her father taking responsibility for his actions, she felt as if she might forgive him.

Sarah brought her baby over to her grandmother's house when

her father was in town a few weeks later. He was on depression medication, so he seemed groggy. But he held his infant grandson and cooed at him. Having the baby around proved a good distraction. At one point, Sarah said, "Do you want to talk about it?" Her father said he wasn't sure what was left to say. "Well, we'll talk at a later date," Sarah said. And she was fine with that. In time, they'd say the things they needed to say. That day, her father could focus on being a proud grandfather. Says Sarah, "You need to tell a parent exactly how you feel. I felt better after I let it out. No holds barred."

But use caution. In real life, there are no take-backs. Once you say something hurtful, those words will sear into your parents' consciousness. It's wise to wait to talk to your parents until you feel your anger has waned.

After not speaking to her father for several months, Kayla, twenty-six, wrote him an e-mail. It was five pages long. She told him he had ruined her life when he stopped paying for her college tuition. She said he destroyed their family. "I know you're physically alive," she wrote, "but you serve no purpose in my life, so you may as well be dead. I've already grieved your death. If I'm being unreasonable, I'd like to hear why." Kayla hoped the e-mail would get her father's attention. She figured he'd see how badly he was upsetting her and call her to apologize. The e-mail had the opposite effect. She received no response. Kayla reread the e-mail and realized how piercing it was. A month later, she sent a second e-mail. "Maybe what I wrote was too much," she said.

Many of us say things to our parents we regret. When I didn't get my way as a child, I'd yell "I hate you" and stomp into my room. Now that we're adults, parents take our words in earnest. They are stung by what we say—and they hold grudges. "You can say some really mean things," Mom told me once, after an argument. "Do you realize how much you hurt me?" The truth was, I didn't. I never really thought anything I said really held that much punch. I assumed Mom shrugged things off the way she did when I yelled "I hate you" as a kid. She took me more seriously than I took myself.

Separations can be a good thing for parents and their children. Says LeBey, "Sometimes it may jolt him or her into examining their role in the conflict. When someone knows exactly what the consequences are of his or her destructive behavior, there is a greater chance it will be corrected."

If you are going to separate from a parent, you might want to make them aware of it. Set a time limit. Briefly explain why you need time apart. "I need a few months away. I'm too angry to talk to you right now." Then the estrangement will have a set end, and it will not take on a life of its own. You don't want an estrangement to become a second permanent divorce. Time apart can be a healthy solution—and a good way to save a relationship with a parent.

Points to Remember

- Parents need to learn how to coexist peacefully themselves. You shouldn't feel responsible for their feelings during a divorce, and you certainly shouldn't feel responsible after one.

- It's normal to feel betrayed when extended family members take one parent's side. Try to think of the divorce from their point of view: if you had a son who divorced his wife, you wouldn't continue to call your former daughter-in-law either. Your mother and father need the support of their relatives.

- If your father is used to hearing about you through your mother, you may find you have less of an established relationship with your dad—and vice versa. Try to get to know your parents as individuals. Building a friendship with each of them will take time and work, but in the end, you and your parents may feel closer than you ever have.

- Keep lines of communication open with siblings. When siblings band together, they can help unite divided subfamilies. You and your siblings are the heart of your new family.

- Adult children shut a parent out as a form of punishment. Remember, though, revoking love is a strategy that can backfire.

- An estrangement isn't always a bad thing. It gives you and a parent time to cool down. But you should explain to a parent why you want to stop speaking to him or her, and for how long. When estrangements drag on too long, you and your parent may grow apart, and it will be more difficult to reestablish a relationship.

5

The Trouble with Stepfamilies

> So just when my love thought he was embarking on a
> new life, his adult kids rose up in one anguished voice.
> They grill him about every weekend we are together. . . .
> They say over and over, "We will never accept THAT
> woman." And of course they call me various and sundry
> things I cannot repeat here. . . . I implore him to be hon-
> est with his children, to defend his love for me, to ask
> them to at least meet me and give me a chance.
>
> —ANONYMOUS POSTING TO A DIVORCE CHAT ROOM,
>   JANUARY 23, 2004

D AD IS GIDDY WHEN I WALK INTO MY AUNT JUNIE'S
house one evening in April 2003. The soft music and
hushed voices inside drown out the rain, which is pelting
the windows outside. It's been pouring since morning. I was reporting a freelance travel story, and I had only one day to do it, which
meant I had to hike trails in a rain slicker and interview surfers hud-
dled under an umbrella at the beach. My hair is damp. The bottom
half of my jeans is soaked.

"You look like a drowned rat," Dad says, laughing, as he walks
toward me. "Hey, honey." He opens his arms and gives me a bear

hug. He kisses my cheek. "How'd your day go?" he asks. It is the wrong question. I complain about the mud puddles, the flooded streets, the fog. My aunt Junie yells hello from the kitchen. "Sounds like a hell of a day," Junie says. She offers enough sympathy to prod me on. "Do you know what it's like to be out in this weather for eight hours?" I say.

Out of the corner of my eye, I can see *her*. She's sitting at my aunt Junie's kitchen table. She's blond and fair. *Like me*, I think, and for some reason, the notion that we might look alike comforts me. As I talk, Dad nods and smiles and pretends he's engrossed in what I'm saying when I can tell he isn't really listening. His hands are folded in front of his stomach as if he were waiting patiently on a checkout line. He seems nervous. His eyes keep darting in *her* direction. He's looking for a natural break in the conversation so he can lead me over to her. Do the introductions. But that's why I keep talking. I'm putting off the inevitable. I want to be ready when we come face-to-face. I can see her raise a glass of white wine to her lips and take a sip. *So she's sophisticated*, I think. *Or maybe not—she could be drinking white zinfandel.*

Who is this woman? I'm so curious that I let myself look at her. The first thing I notice is how skinny she is. She wears a black ribbed turtleneck sweater with dark jeans. Her hair falls in soft curls around her cheeks. She has full lips and a narrow face. She's pretty. Dad sees me glance at her. "Come here, Brock," he says. "Take your shoes off and let me introduce you to my friend."

Friend? I wasn't sure why he was calling her that. Maybe Dad was trying to make it easier on me. If she is just a friend, she is less of a threat. More likely, Dad is so nervous that he's jumbling his words. I imagine the two of them in the car later. "Why did you call me *your friend*?" she'd say. *Of course, Dad had to pick a possessive one*, I think. *Couldn't he just find someone who was nice? Who—*

"Brooke, this is Donna," he says. Then he turns to her. "Donna, this is my middle daughter, Brooke." We say hello. She smiles. I'm relieved to see that she's in her late forties. When Dad told me about her a few weeks earlier, I forgot to ask her age. I worried I'd be meeting a young tart. "I just need to get on with my life and stop keeping secrets," Dad had said when he called. "I'm done with this other life crap. It's not good." He said he'd been seeing a woman for several months. He'd already traveled to Boston to meet her twenty-two-year-old daughter. They were thinking about moving in together. He met her at a support group. He said they laughed a lot, which was important to him. "She thinks like me," he said. They went to Broadway shows together, which stung. *Mom used to practically beg Dad to take her into the city to see a show*. "Why didn't you tell me any of this earlier?" I wailed. It didn't matter, Dad said. "I'm telling you now."

Standing face-to-face with Donna in my aunt Junie's kitchen is overwhelming. *You're my mother's replacement,* I think. *What does she have that Mom doesn't?* I'm struck by how similar to my mother she seems. Neither wears much makeup. Mom often dresses in the identical black turtleneck sweater and jeans. Donna is wearing a silver bracelet and silver hoops; Mom wears nothing but silver jewelry.

Only seconds go by before I'm overcome with panic. *What do I say next?* I don't know what to do, so I open my arms wide, just as Dad did a few minutes earlier. "I feel like I should just give you a hug," I say nervously. "Dad has told me a lot about you." She is startled when I wrap my arms around her. She doesn't hug me as tight. "So you have a daughter, too. Right?" I say, sitting down next to her at the table. Donna tells me her daughter is graduating from Boston University in a few weeks. "Donna has traveled all over the world," Dad says. I love far-flung places, which is why Dad brings this up. I ask where she has been. *Europe. The Caribbean. Canada.*

My five-year-old cousin is coloring at the table. Her twelve-year-old brother is watching us talk. When my father's sister Janice walks in, she greets Donna warmly, and they chat as if they've known each other for months. *I guess they have. Have I really been out of the loop that long?* I think. Then I get the feeling that everyone on Dad's side of the family knows Donna. Dad kept the relationship only from my sisters and me, which is why my cousins are hanging around as I talk to her. We may be gathering to celebrate my grandmother's eighty-third birthday, but everyone is aware that this is the first time I'm meeting Donna. Or at least it feels that way. I swear I can sense my cousins and aunts measuring how much time I spend talking to her.

Early on, I'm not sure whether I like Donna. She seems harmless. During dinner, she is quiet. She politely answers my questions. But then she grows more comfortable, and she begins talking louder, sometimes over me. Donna doesn't ask me much about myself, which I take to mean she doesn't care. Before arriving at Aunt Junie's, I imagined that I'd either immediately hate my father's girlfriend, and refuse ever to see her again, or that I'd love her. As I sit talking to her, I realize Donna lands somewhere in the middle. She is OK. Not extraordinary, but not excruciating.

Any doubts I have about Donna are quelled when I stop sizing her up and look over at Dad. He is laughing at something Donna said. When she turns her head, he crosses his eyes behind her back. She catches him. "Oh, come on. Stop!" Donna says, pushing Dad playfully on the shoulder. Dad puts his arm around Donna, and he smiles. He looks different. Happier. Lighter.

Dad has been acting less depressed for a few months. I just hadn't noticed until now. He'd started sounding brighter on the phone, talking about his plans to buy a bigger boat and to take Chelsea to Puerto Rico. He hadn't trapped me in any impromptu counseling sessions. He'd put on several pounds, which gave him a slight potbelly, and the creases under his eyes had faded. He'd stopped asking about Mom.

Mom had been dating as well. She'd met a man in a coffee shop who sent her roses at work that Valentine's Day. They met for dinner a few times. Mom's dating life was a topic she considered off-limits. She'd offer tidbits if she was in a good mood, but if I asked too many questions, she'd grow irritated. She was always suspicious that I was snooping around in her business so I might relay information back to Dad. She told my sister she'd been on a few other dates, and she wanted to remarry. Mom's "dates" weren't serious like Dad's relationship with Donna. Mom told us she'd only introduce us to someone she really liked. She worried about our reaction. Would we treat her boyfriend with as much disdain as we'd treated her decision to divorce our father?

Donna and Dad trade off sentences as they tell a story about Donna's years as a single parent. Dad wants me to know she paid a mortgage and put her kids through expensive private universities working two, sometimes three, jobs. I stop listening and watch them interact. I see Dad's hand on her thigh. I listen to Donna's easy laugh. Two years ago, I could never have predicted that Mom and Dad wouldn't be together at this party. I wonder, *Who is this woman trying to take my mother's place?*

Watching your mother or father date is surreal. An adult child has known his parents only with each other for more than twenty years. To see Dad kiss another woman's lips or hold another woman's hand, or to sit at a breakfast table with Mom and her new husband, who are both in bathrobes—these are scenes from our very own episode of *The Twilight Zone*. You'll try to awaken from the bad dream: Blink twice. Squeeze your eyes shut tight and pop them open.

But your parents and their new significant others will still be sitting together, introducing you to yet another phase in divorce.

It's only a matter of time before your parents will begin searching for the next Mr. or Mrs. Right. Whether they begin dating as the divorce proceedings drag out or two years after the split is final, you'll never feel ready. When a parent meets someone and becomes serious with them an adult child must abandon any lingering hopes for reconciliation.

We have to watch our parents act like love-struck teenagers. A mother may lie in bed talking on the phone to her boyfriend until 2:00 a.m. A father might send a girlfriend flowers and read aloud to us a short poem he wrote her. Your mother may talk about getting in shape and dress sexier before a date. Dad might slick back his hair and buy a motorcycle to pick up his new lady. Our parents are back on the prowl, but in the midst of a midlife crisis.

Friends will describe love later in life as sweet. And it is adorable—until it's one of your parents locking lips with a stranger on your childhood home's front porch. "My mother got more dates than me," said one twenty-two-year-old woman. Adult children who live at home with a parent may have it worst. They are suddenly taking messages for a parent. "Joan called. Sally called. Justine called." We are protective. We say, "Who is Joan, and who is Sally?!"

If a parent asks his children what they think of his new love interest, adult children are caught in a catch-22—damned if they do, damned if they don't. A negative reaction will elicit anger from a parent. "You never support me," they'll say. If we say we like their boyfriend or girlfriend and we don't, a parent will believe we're supporting their new relationship, which will only cause confusion when the truth comes out. A safe answer is "OK." It's open-ended. It says, "I'm not sure how I feel yet."

Sometimes we witness our parents flirting, which sickens us to the core. One twenty-five-year-old woman had just finished a volunteer shift when she found her father, who had come to pick her up, talking to the volunteer coordinator in the lobby. "See you later," her father said to her. The volunteer coordinator winked back. "If you're lucky," she said. The daughter was in shock. Her father was acting like the guys she dated. *Eew*, she thought, *Dad was just playing mack daddy with some chick.*

No one wants to think of their parents sexually, even together. Once parents split up and begin dating, their sex lives are more obvious to us. We know Mom or Dad is going to have sex with the people he or she dates, which is exactly why we don't always want to hear about our parents' nights out.

Mark, thirty-one, was comfortable talking with his father about sex. After his parents split up, he and his Dad would discuss dates his father went on. Mark couldn't imagine his mother out with someone else as easily. When Mark's mother tried to talk to him about her own forays into dating, Mark would squirm. He couldn't imagine his mother on a date with another man.

When planning the invitations for his wedding, Mark told his father he could bring a guest. His mother couldn't. She called to ask why. "I'm being selfish," Mark said. "I don't want to have to worry about who you'll bring." His mother said she wasn't happy with his decision.

"You hate that I'm dating, don't you?" she said. Mark's mother noticed that if she brought up a boyfriend, Mark changed the subject. Mark explained that it was easier to picture his father dating.

"I don't know why," he told her. "It's not that I don't want you to be happy. I just have a tough time with it."

"Maybe it's just because I'm your mother," she told Mark.

Could it be that simple? I was happy for Mom when she started dating, but I did get queasy thinking about her sleeping at some guy's house. Why was it OK for Dad to move into Donna's house without proposing to her, but it wasn't OK for Mom to stumble in at 3:00 a.m. after a date? My sisters and I would joke about Mom's "getting some." Subconsciously, were we concerned our mother would act promiscuous after the divorce? Did we worry, *Is Mom a slut?*

Previous chapters have outlined the countless ways parents rely on their children after divorce. But what happens if parents start dating—and those needs are met by someone else? When a parent meets someone, that person often inherits whatever roles we were playing. Mom's boyfriend will listen to her. Dad's girlfriend will counsel him on decisions. A new spouse can help a parent financially in ways we couldn't. A lover or spouse will take on our parents' problems for us. We can walk away. Our job is done.

This is often a great relief for the adult child. Some adult children are so grateful to a stepparent or significant other for waltzing in and taking over those roles that they blindly accept them. Says one young man interviewed, "I just felt so much less burdened when Mom ended up with my stepfather. They could help each other out. My brother and I could take care of ourselves." Another young woman said, "As soon as Dad had someone else to talk to, he stopped talking to us."

Before Marisa, twenty-four, met her mother's boyfriend, she'd decided how she felt about him. She was driving to her mother's cabin, which was nestled in the Rocky Mountains, to meet him. "I'm going to like this guy," Marisa said to herself. She needed to accept him. If she didn't, her mother would remain alone. Plus, Marisa wouldn't have to feel guilty if she moved on with her own life; her mother would be moving forward, too. Marisa's mother would have someone else to care for her and travel with.

"I wanted her to have a companion," says Marisa. "I couldn't take care of her forever." That weekend, Marisa's mother and her boyfriend canoodled. Though it was hard to watch, Marisa liked that her mother's boyfriend was loving and affectionate. He and her mother told Marisa about his plans to move from Oregon to her mother's house in Denver, Colorado. Marisa imagined sharing a bathroom with the man when she visited home on vacations. "It will be strange when I go home," says Marisa. But she was willing to accept the changes. The reality of her mother's new predicament—a lack of financial and emotional support—had weighed on her. "I just didn't feel like I would ever be enough for my mother," she says.

Feeling relieved by a parent's new relationship is a phase. When a parent no longer looks to an adult child for help, the child may feel deserted. We're losing a parent's affections all over again. As much as we dislike reversing roles with our parents, the switch often draws us closer to them. During that time, parents and their children always have something to talk about. We feel like an important part of our parents' lives. Once they remarry or move in with someone, we are expected to go back to the old way of interacting.

Lara, twenty-five, and her mother shared *everything* when her mother was deciding whether to leave her father. They'd stay up talking about whether or not her mother was a lesbian. Her mother said she'd never had feelings for a woman before Georgia, but she couldn't mistake her attachment to the woman. Lara helped her mother realize she should follow her heart and move to Chicago, where Georgia lived. After her mother moved in with Georgia, her mother distanced herself from Lara. She had less complex emotions to mull over, and whatever issues her mother did have, she could talk to Georgia about them. Lara stopped feeling important to her mother.

One night on the phone, Lara was asking her mother questions about how it was living with Georgia. Her mother was giving her standard answers. Lara couldn't ignite an emotional conversation—the kind where they talked out her mother's feelings for hours. Lara felt defeated. "You don't need me anymore," Lara told her mother. Her mother didn't disagree with her. She acknowledged that their relationship had changed. "I don't need you," her mother said, "but what we had was inappropriate. It's better this way."

Lara knows that what her mother said is true. But she couldn't help feeling as if Georgia had somehow replaced her. Georgia stole away all of the attention Lara was used to getting from her mother, and she resented Georgia for pushing her into second-class status. "Georgia has done a great service by giving my mother happiness," she says, "but Georgia has been alone most of her life. She doesn't want children. She isn't interested in children." Lara believes Georgia has little interest in her. Lara worries she and her mother will grow even further apart.

Once a parent meets someone they really like, adult children feel threatened. Maybe Dad's girlfriend starts sleeping over at his house. Maybe Mom tells us she's falling in love all over again. Then they announce they're moving in together. When we visit home, we're thrown into the same intimate space as these strangers, which is extremely uncomfortable.

Think of it like this: You and your father are reading the paper on a Sunday morning at the breakfast table. You pour Dad some coffee, and he scrambles you some eggs. You trade sections of the paper and read while you eat. Both of you are comfortable in the quiet. Then the back door opens. In steps a strange woman, carrying bags of groceries. You've never seen her before, but she's unpacking trash bags and cookies and arranging them in your kitchen cabinets. She talks loudly, and she pops a toothbrush in the bathroom. She tells everyone she's making pancakes even though you're already eating eggs.

She's disruptive. You're ready to call the cops to arrest the intruder until your father waves you off. "She belongs here," he says.

She "belongs" in *his* mind—but not yours. Nothing about having a strange woman poke around Mom's kitchen or some guy clean out Dad's garage feels right. Parents welcome these complete strangers into our families and into our homes. They give them free rein. They assume their adult children will learn to accept them. Instead, adult children often respond with resistance. Who wants a strange man lounging on the living room couch, deciding what everyone will watch on TV that night? *That's my couch! My TV!*

Different issues come up when a parent moves into an entirely new house with a girlfriend or boyfriend. Adult children feel even less at home because the house isn't *theirs* at all. It's a space a parent shares with someone he loves. Adult children are the invaders. One forty-two-year-old woman said she always felt nauseous as she drove up the long drive of her father and stepmother's house. She dreaded stepping inside and witnessing her father's new life with this woman: her father took out the trash for her stepmother, and he raised *her* hand to his lips for a kiss. The daughter always left feeling as if she didn't belong. This was her father's new life, and she wasn't sure there was room for her.

When a parent moves into his or her significant other's house, the space is even more foreign. Six months after I met Donna, Dad moved into her tiny three-bedroom rambler in a town forty-five minutes away from where I grew up. My younger sister, Chelsea, was angry Dad had moved so far away. I worried about setting foot in Donna's house. When I met Donna at my aunt Junie's, I was sharing my family with her. Going to her house made me feel less in control. In her house, she could decide whether she wanted to share her life with me.

The first time I went over to Donna's, I was fidgety. Dad wasn't completely comfortable in the house yet—it wasn't his house—so I wasn't comfortable either. On subsequent visits, I noticed I left with a stiff back. I'd sit straight up on the edge of the couch in Donna's living room. I never took off my shoes and curled into the sofa the way I did with Dad growing up. I was too jittery to relax. Dad would tell me to "make myself at home," but I couldn't. Her home wasn't my home just because Dad was suddenly living in it.

From the beginning, Dad said he wouldn't marry Donna. Not because he didn't love her—Dad often told me how much he cared for her. But his experience with the divorce made him fear that the same thing might happen again. What if something went wrong with this relationship, too? Then he'd be forced to split assets once more. "I want to make sure you girls get everything of mine," he told me.

Besides, Dad didn't need to walk down the aisle to feel married. From the moment Dad moved in with Donna, he started to act like Donna's husband, and Donna acted like his wife. Dad put skylights in Donna's kitchen. He mowed the grass. Donna reminded him of his favorite dish at a restaurant and washed the dishes after Dad cooked. They booked cruises and vacations. Dad and Donna didn't have a marriage license, but they might as well have.

In *Step Wars*, psychiatrist Grace Gabe and sociologist/social psychologist Jean Lipman-Blumen say an adult child may feel "five furies" after a parent remarries: a fear of abandonment, a fear that a parent will not remain loyal to a family, a fear that a parent will put their new spouse first, a fear that an inheritance may be lost, or a fear that a parent will focus only on himself. "The new marriage threatens to eradicate that shared history," write Gabe and Blumen. "It's not surprising that the child feels disoriented—the remarriage feels not like a joyous event but more like the loss of everything the child knows."

Many adult children choose to skip a parent's wedding altogether. Going to a wedding hurts too much. You're watching your parent celebrate a new union, which feels like a smack in the face. The parent promises to honor and love *someone else*—someone we barely know—till death do them part, which didn't mean much the first time around. What does it mean now? Remarriages are especially difficult for an adult child whose mother or father exchanges vows with someone from an extramarital affair, which is explored in the following chapter.

In the short term, it may seem like a good idea to skip a parent's wedding. Emotions are on overdrive, and getting through the day seems impossible. But adult children who shunned the nuptials say they regret it. Eventually, most of them came around to accept a parent's new relationship. Not going hurt them more than it hurt their parent—though the reverse was their intention.

Paige, twenty-seven, nearly skipped her mother and Larry's nuptials. At the last minute, her older sister convinced Paige to go. In retrospect, Paige says she would have been sorry if she hadn't. Now that she's closer with her mother, she likes that she was there. It is a memory for them to share. If she hadn't gone, Paige and her mother might feel more distant today.

Remarriage always seems to come too soon. Some parents remarry within a year. Some, several years later. But the sting isn't any less severe. Parents move on once they remarry. They're building a new life with someone else. The authors of *Step Wars* say an adult child can react positively or negatively to a parent's new adopted family. The child might act as the "joiner," who actively seeks out a relationship with the stepparent; the "distancer," who pulls away and develops no relationship at all; or the "destabilizer," who actively tries to disrupt a parent or sibling's bond to a stepparent.

But we don't fit into one neat little category. In my interviews—

and in my own experience—I've found that adult children's reactions are more likely to evolve. Marisa, the young woman who went to her family's mountain cabin to meet her mother's boyfriend, decided up front she was going to like the man with whom her mother was moving in. Marisa is rare. Most individuals start as a "distancer," try on the "destabilizer" role, and ultimately become a "joiner." Or they begin as a "joiner," realize they aren't so fond of a stepparent, attempt to "destabilize" the relationship, and then "distance" themselves from a parent, who won't back off from their new love.

I dreamed of finding a fourth sister in Dad's girlfriend, but after meeting her a few times, I realized Donna didn't want to be my sister. She was Dad's girlfriend, and I could accept her or not accept her. Donna didn't care whether I liked her, in the same way she didn't care whether her twenty-two-year-old daughter liked Dad. We were too old, too independent, to tell either of our parents whom they could or couldn't see. The relationship she had with Dad would exist no matter what, and therefore, I wasn't very important to her. I was merely an adult who lived in another state and floated in and out of Dad's life. She'd be civil and polite. But I wasn't the gatekeeper I liked to think of myself as. And more than that, the importance of the role I played in my father's life was threatened by someone who wasn't interested in having me in *her* life.

When we realize a parent's new relationship will happen with or without our blessing, we grow angry—and territorial. In *Step Wars*, Gabe and Blumen say it's because adult children are drafted into the relationship; they're not voluntarily involved. We have no reason to embrace this new person. We don't yet love them. We know the person only through a parent. Therefore, we feel we can easily walk away.

And compare. We study our new stepparents like microbiologists examining cells. We wonder how they size up to the parent whose place they have taken. Initially, we may distrust their motives, especially financially. An adult child wants to know what kind of job he or she has. We wonder whether the stepparent is trying to move in on our family's inheritance. How will this person's presence change a parent's will? Stepchildren are deemed even more threatening than a stepparent. If a parent has a second family to raise, what will he do to help the first family? Will Dad stop paying my tuition now that he's remarried to a woman with three young children? It's uncomfortable to admit we care about these things, but we do.

We also don't know the rules. Can we tell a stepparent stories of our childhood? Can we talk about our mother in front of our stepmother?

While visiting Dad at Donna's, I'd want to talk about what my mother and I did the day before or this awesome dinner she made me. Around Donna, I kept quiet. Then one afternoon, my sisters and I were sitting on Donna's couch. Erin was reminiscing. She told a story about this time she got caught smoking cigarettes in a field behind our house. "And then Mommy was like . . . ," Erin said. I don't remember what Erin said next because I was watching Donna's expression. *Did it sting her to bring up the past?* She didn't flinch, so maybe not.

I've read since that stepmothers struggle with listening to stories of our mothers. They feel left out. Our mothers don't want to hear about our relationships with our stepmothers, and our stepmothers don't want to listen to stories involving our mothers. So every time I brought up my mother, was I hurting Donna? I didn't want to have to worry about that.

In the previous chapter, I talk about subfamilies—the idea that our family breaks in two, and we often side with the parent who is considered "left behind," versus the one who "left." Often we're more willing to accept one parent's boyfriend or spouse over another, too. The parent who ended the marriage shouldn't be dating. They shouldn't be allowed to have fun. On the other hand, a parent who is left behind is encouraged to date. Adult children see the abandoned parent as a victim.

We've only known our parents in one romantic relationship. We're familiar with all their flaws. Maybe our father talked down to our mother, or our mother could never apologize. When our parent acts differently around a new significant other—Dad is less condescending, or Mom is willing to take the blame—we notice.

We can see how little effort they put into making things work in their marriage. *If Dad can do this for her, why couldn't he do this for Mom?* We realize that our parents were capable of being more mature, just not with each other. I couldn't help but think this way the more time I spent with Dad and Donna. After Dad moved into Donna's house, he started to cook for her and clean. He cut back on his drinking. Dad did all the things for Donna that he had failed to do for Mom. He seemed like his best self. I couldn't help but wonder, if he'd acted this way with Mom, would my parents be divorced?

If you've seen this with your own parent, your observation was astute. Your parent *is* trying to get things right this time. Therapists say parents are so traumatized by divorce that they feel as though they've failed, so they try really hard to be the best spouse they can the second time around. They're also in a honeymoon period. Our mother and father stayed married for twenty years or more. You're seeing the parent in a brand-new relationship.

Jenna, twenty-seven, had heard her mother say "my friend Ray" a lot in the months after her parents divorced. But Jenna assumed that's all Ray was to her mother—a friend. Ray's arrival at Jenna's grandparents' house seemed to suggest otherwise. Ray gave her cousins and grandparents kisses. Ray and her mother acted like a couple. Jenna was in shock. "Apparently, they'd known him for awhile," Jenna says. Jenna's parents had been divorced less than a year when her mother began dating Ray. Jenna was annoyed at her mother. "It seemed too quick," she says.

That Thanksgiving 2002, Jenna wouldn't make eye contact with Ray. She didn't speak to him. Ray didn't push himself on Jenna either, keeping a distance from his girlfriend's daughters. After dinner, Jenna and her sister left as soon as they could without seeming rude. A year later, Jenna still refused to acknowledge Ray. The following Christmas, Jenna managed to wave to him. She felt sorry for treating him like an outcast. So she pulled her mother aside. "You have to understand that I don't have anything against Ray," Jenna said. "I see that you like him, but this is how I need to be right now." Jenna says it was the idea that her mother could love anyone other than her father that was hard to get used to. Jenna knew that her father was still in love with her mother, so she couldn't just open up and accept Ray. If she did, she'd feel she was betraying her father.

Jenna's mother had left her father. So, from the start, Jenna was against her mother's new relationship. In February 2003, Ray and her mother stopped by Jenna's apartment after flying in from Tahiti. Her mother was wearing an engagement ring. Her mother didn't announce the wedding like a blushing bride; she was nervous. Jenna congratulated her mother and Ray. She could tell that her mother was happy. All Jenna could do was think of her father. She wasn't sure how he'd take the news.

Surprisingly, Jenna says, it gave her father closure. "It was final in Dad's eyes once Mom remarried," Jenna says. Soon after, her father met a woman, a widow, with whom he fell in love. Jenna found her dad's love for the other woman a relief. She didn't have to be against her mother's relationship if her father had one, too. "I thought, *OK, now that Dad has someone, I can accept Ray,*" Jenna says.

After the previously mentioned twenty-five-year-old woman watched her father flirt with a volunteer coordinator where she worked, she found out her father was secretly carrying on a relationship with the woman. Her sister snooped around their father's room and found sexy pictures of the volunteer coordinator in his desk drawer along with love letters ripe with sexual innuendo. "You're the stuffing in my turkey," one said. The daughters were livid. The idea that their father was out dating felt as if he were cheating. Meanwhile, the two daughters encouraged their mother to date a man she had met at the doctor's office. "I was all for it," says the young woman. "Mom had my blessing to date. Dad didn't." Her father had hurt her mother.

Here comes the tough part, what I like to call the steamroller effect. Having a stepparent in your life is going to initiate an onslaught of changes. You can lie down, let the steamroller pass over you, and get the flattening over with. Or you can stand up and fight the crushing machine, feeling every inch of its crawl dragging you down. Few of us let the steamroller pass quickly.

It's hard to accept someone's invading your turf. You're going to see the newcomer as a rival who must earn your respect. We share an intimacy with our parents—but we know little about Dad's girlfriend when she becomes our stepmother. Their age keeps many adult children from feeling as if they should call a parent's spouse a stepparent at all. Says one thirty-three-year-old attorney about her stepfather, "I have a hard time with the term *stepparent*. I think of him as my mother's husband."

Adult children are too old to believe in a stepparent's authority—the stepparent has no say in our life—so we see them as an equal. Stepparents are people we can boss around as much as they think they can boss us around. Without an established framework to help a stepparent map out a relationship with an adult child, the stepparent may revert to parenting, even though that is the last thing an adult child needs. We're hardly looking for another parent. We already have two. But a stepparent sometimes crosses the invisible line anyway, making us more resentful.

Liza stayed with her father and stepmother over a long holiday break. It was the first time Liza, then twenty-one, would be in the same house as her stepmother for an extended period of time. Liza assumed her father would make sure she was welcome. That holiday break, Liza played video games with her cousins every night. Sometimes she didn't get home until 2:00 a.m. In the past, her parents were always asleep when she got home. She'd lock up the house and go to bed.

But Liza's stepmother, Ginger, was troubled by Liza's late nights. Ginger kept track of what time Liza got home each night. One day, Ginger tried to enforce a curfew. She told Liza she needed to be home by midnight. Liza ignored her. She wasn't going to listen to some woman she barely knew. Besides, her parents had never imposed a curfew on her. She was a straight-A student. She never partied. Liza was always "the good child." Her stepmother didn't have to worry.

Later, Ginger told on Liza. She explained to her new husband that his daughter got home too late and needed a curfew. Liza's father talked to his daughter. Liza explained that she was at her cousin's house nearby. *Why is this such a big deal? It never was before,* Liza thought. Her father agreed and said he'd talk to Ginger. But the damage was done. Liza couldn't believe Ginger was trying to get her in trouble. She barely knew Ginger, and she was trying to tell her what to do—not to mention that Liza was an adult. "She tried to mother me—and I already had a mother," says Liza, now twenty-six.

Avoiding a relationship with a stepparent is easy for an adult child. We have our own apartment, or if we're in college, we can stay with whichever parent remains single. If we never go home, we never have to deal with the circumstances we find there. Young children are often forced to spend time with a stepparent. They're dropped off at a parent's house for a weekend. They're taught to respect the stranger as another parent—and over time, they often do.

An adult child doesn't have to spend nights or weekends with a stepparent. We don't have a visitation schedule. A stepparent is easily dodged, which is a blessing. Unlike a young child, we can shut ourselves off completely. We can control and determine what kind of relationship we want with a parent's new significant other.

Paige's mother bought a new house after she moved out of Paige's childhood home. She told Paige that "a friend," Larry, was moving into the basement apartment. Larry was dealing with his own divorce, her mother said. He needed a temporary place to live. Within a few months, her mother revealed they were seeing each other and told Paige that Larry was moving upstairs. Paige dreaded coming home. "Not only did I have to go home to a new house, a new bedroom . . . ," Paige says.

There was also Larry. He roamed her mother's house as if he'd always lived there. "I felt like a stranger in *my* house," says Paige. Paige picked fights with her mother so she had an excuse not to go home. She didn't want to be near him. When Larry proposed to Paige's mother a few months later, Paige didn't know him any better than before. She didn't want to. But the more she stayed away, the more Paige grew apart from her mother. Her mother had an entirely new life that Paige was ignoring.

Say you fall in love with a starving-artist type—a shallow mother's worst nightmare. He takes you to art openings and hole-in-the-wall French bistros, and he teaches you how to paint. If your mother disapproves of this relationship, she won't hear about any of the details. She'll shut you out, and as a result, she won't get to know an important new piece of you. That's how it was with Paige and her mother. Paige's mother was changing, and without Paige around to be a part of the transformation, Paige started to feel more and more distant from her mother.

At some point, an adult child is going to need to accept the reality of their new predicament. *Your father doesn't love your mother anymore. He loves someone else.* I had to say those words to myself a lot in the first few months after Dad moved in with Donna. Having Dad living with another woman brought my emotions back to where they were when my parents first split up. I had to remind myself of the reasons my parents broke up and convince myself that they weren't going to get back together. *Mom doesn't love Dad. Remember?*

In *Alcestis,* Euripides writes, "For a stepmother comes as an enemy to the children of a former union and is no more gentle than a viper." Stepmothers can hurt us without even meaning to; it is their presence that makes our hearts rot. Other times, they are so jealous of the relationship we have with our father that they compete for his affection. Take Cinderella. She had a happy life. She lived in a castle fit for royalty with everything she ever wanted under her nose. Then her father remarried, and her stepmother moved in. Cinderella was relegated to ash sweeper, so no one, not even her father, noticed her. "Then began an unfortunate era in the poor stepchild's life," write the brothers Grimm.

A stepparent is an outsider, and you hope a parent will put him in his place. In the past, a parent always reprimanded anyone who hurt you. But this time is different. You're grown up. A parent doesn't want to cause problems in his or her relationship. So you're expected to fight your own battles.

One holiday break, Lara went to visit her mother at Georgia's house in Chicago. She stayed three weeks. On the false assumption that her mother was still picking up after her, Lara left the computer on and made a mess in her bedroom, even though it was a guest room. Georgia grew impatient with Lara. One evening, she came home tired and found Lara and her friend in the living room watching a movie. In Georgia's mind, Lara was making herself *too* comfortable in her house. She pulled Lara aside and yelled at her. Georgia listed all the things Lara had done wrong. Her mother didn't say a word; Lara and Georgia were adults and could figure it out themselves. Lara said she started to cry, and she couldn't stop. "Not only didn't Mom need me anymore," Lara says, "but she had abandoned me for someone who didn't even like me. How could she choose someone who didn't like me?"

When we end up with a real-life wicked stepmother—or "stepmonster," as many of us call them—we blame our parents for making such bad choices. You would think a parent would pick someone who fit in with his or her family. Often we find that parents fall in love with little regard for their children's preferences. They pick whom they like, and adult children have to deal—maturely. Says one thirty-four-year-old woman, "When you are twenty-five, you really don't have the freedom to have a temper tantrum. You have to be extremely civil to a person that you hate on principle."

Mothers are much less likely to remarry than fathers are. So adult children end up dealing with many more stepmothers and fewer stepfathers. Gabe and Blumen write, "The role of stepfather has less emotional charge. This may stem in large part from the fact that the stepfather traditionally enjoys higher economic status than the stepmom. Consequently, he is likely to improve the finances of his stepfamily instead of draining them off, as mythic stepmothers always do."

Denise, forty-two, was twenty-two when her parents split up. For years, Denise didn't accept her stepmother. She resented her presence. Then Denise got divorced and remarried, inheriting two resentful adult stepchildren of her own. Denise is unique—she's a stepmother who was once in her stepchildren's shoes. "I am the one who took things away," Denise says.

Denise's stepdaughter, Bridget, was twenty when her father left her mother. A year later, her father married Denise, and Bridget was livid. She already felt discarded by her father. Now he had a new wife to deplete his already diminishing financial support. Bridget began tracking their money. If she saw anything new at her father's house, Bridget would ask Denise where they got the money to buy it. Bridget demanded that her father take over her car payments. She made him feel as if he *owed* her. He did assume the payments, only he couldn't afford them. Denise uses equity money from her previous home to secretly make the payments for him.

Recently, Denise had a talk with her husband's adult children. "Your father and I are struggling," she told Bridget and her younger brother. "We're giving you what we can." Bridget listened. Then she asked about the porch they talked about building on the front of the house. "Where are you getting money for that?" Bridget asked. Denise recognized the nasty look Bridget gave her; she'd given her stepmother the same sneer. Denise says Bridget was thinking, "You're nothing. You're Dad's second wife. Who are you to tell me how my father spends his money?"

Adult children feel as though they have a right to a parent's financial support, even after they remarry, and they do. Nothing is worse than a stepparent who is draining a parent's financial resources. But consider Denise. A stepparent may be helping your mother or father help you.

If your father marries someone much younger than he is, which is common, a stepmother is sometimes marrying *for your parent's money* and isn't taken very seriously by the adult children. For one thing, if you're twenty-eight and your stepmother is twenty-nine, the term *stepmother* hardly applies. Second, younger women are starting their very first family. They may want to keep an adult child away so their babies will feel special. A young stepmother doesn't want to be reminded of her husband's former life. Sometimes a stepmother intentionally sabotages an adult child's attempt to connect.

Kayla didn't want to invite her father's new wife, Esmerelda, to her wedding. Esmerelda was only five years older than Kayla, which made relations between the two uncomfortable. Ultimately, Kayla decided she'd support her father and invite Esmerelda to the wedding—but she didn't want to invite her stepmother's three children. The guest list was already tight, no other children were invited, and Kayla had never even met her stepsiblings. Esmerelda was furious. She didn't appreciate Kayla's invitation. Instead, Esmerelda saw the failure to invite her kids as a deliberate insult and refused to attend. Kayla attributes this to her immaturity. "She's so young," Kayla says. "It's like Dad married one of my friends."

Relationships with stepparents are tenuous—and tense. Adult children want a stepparent to stand in the shadows and observe. The last thing the stepparent should do is try to dominate. When an adult child or a stepparent is threatened by the other, they may misinterpret each other's behaviors. Insignificant comments are sometimes taken the wrong way. Other times, an adult child downright dislikes a parent's spouse.

Liza used to see her family as a respite. Today, going home is a hassle. Her father married a woman named Ginger, who is a troublemaker. Liza tells the story of her sister, Aimee, who lives down the street from her father and stepmother. When she couldn't get pregnant, Aimee adopted a baby from Korea. When only a few months old, the baby was diagnosed with autism. Thanks to Ginger, the entire block knew in a day. "She's so gossipy," Liza complains.

Ginger and Liza's father fight a lot, which Liza says makes Ginger insecure around his daughters. Liza says her stepmother's insecurity must be the reason she constantly puts them down. Ginger keeps telling Aimee about women who just had babies—"healthy and perfect" babies, she emphasizes. When Liza bought her house, she gave her father and stepmother a tour. "You should see my friend's house," Ginger said. "It's twice the size." Comments such as this are typical from Ginger. "Anything we do," says Liza, "my stepmother wants us to know about someone else who has done it better."

When Aimee decided to hold a yard sale, she announced that any money collected would be donated to help find a cure for autism. The yard sale was advertised as a fund-raiser. Ginger offered to help. She put out some things of her own on Aimee's lawn. As her items began to sell, Ginger said she'd changed her mind. "I think I'm going to use this money to pay for my son's car insurance," Ginger told Liza and Aimee, whose jaws dropped. "You need to stop telling people this money is for the baby," Aimee yelled. Liza didn't talk with her stepmother for a month.

Getting in an argument with a stepparent can be stressful. You don't want to create a headache for a parent. And you're not sure how your newly married parent will react to the disagreement. The idea that your father might take *his girlfriend's* side and reprimand you is illogical.

A stepparent will try to protect his or her spouse, too. Say your stepmother hears you yelling at your father for not giving your mother enough alimony. Your stepmother might step in and tell you to pipe down. Stepparents love our parents, and they cannot bear to see their new spouses' adult children hurt them. So they'll rush to their side at any cost, even if it means alienating us. You'll get angry.

My stepmother needs to stay out of this. It's between me and my father.
You'll feel as if they're ganging up on you. But a stepparent's position
should be expected.

I never talked openly with Dad about my feelings for Donna. I
tiptoed around their relationship. When I went to Donna's house, I
tried to be as polite as I could be. I'd bring my glass to the sink when
I finished a drink. We ordered Italian takeout one night, and I
cleared the table. I always acted excited to see Donna, and I tried to
include her in conversations. I made sure she always knew whom my
sisters or I was talking about.

I feared Donna. Not because she was mean to me—she wasn't.
Donna was one of the nicest people I'd met. But I worried that I'd
make her mad and she'd complain to Dad. I didn't want anyone to
come between Dad and me. So I kept all problems at bay by being
the "superjoiner." If my sisters complained about her, I talked them
out of their annoyance. I didn't want Donna to tell Dad she didn't
want to spend time with us. Then Dad would have to choose between his children and his girlfriend.

When adult children find themselves at odds with a stepparent,
they argue with their parents. *Why does she have to be so rude to me?*
You tell me to make an effort, but why can't she make an effort? Adult
children want to feel more important to a parent. Sometimes, they'll
try to turn a parent against a spouse, by giving a parent an ultima-
tum: Who is it going to be—me or *her*? Adult children will make it
clear that they want their father or mother in their lives, but they
don't want the new girlfriend or spouse. In a desperate attempt to
erase a stepparent, an adult child pushes a parent to take a side. This
is a waste of time, and it's only going to cause heartache.

Asking parents to choose between you and a stepparent isn't fair.
For one thing, parents are going to get angry. They're going to say

they love you equally, and they're going to wonder why you don't want them to be happy. To prove a point, they may choose their new spouse over you. One twenty-eight-year-old woman's father e-mailed her: "If you want me, you must accept my new wife and kids." Asking parents to decide loyalties is like playing with fire. You're only setting yourself up for hurt. Stepparents are an inconvenience in our lives. But they don't have to cause such large rifts—and adult children don't have to widen the divide.

Sometimes, a stepparent's presence changes the way you and a parent interact. Say your father spends all his time with his new wife. Different people bring out different aspects of a person's personality. Maybe your father is silly around his new wife, or maybe he is more serious. Either way, your dad is going to feel different to you. You may feel that a stepparent has changed your parent and that those changes are coming between the two of you. Often, they are. You're going to want your parent to act the way they used to.

As soon as Paige's mother married Larry, her mother seemed less independent. Her mother had always been a high-powered career woman, but she stopped talking for herself once Larry was around. Her mother would say "Larry says we should . . ." so often that Paige wanted to scream, "Mom, what do *you* think?"

They'd been married a year when they came to visit Paige. They were at Babbo, a chic eatery in Manhattan. Paige doesn't remember what she asked her mother; she only remembers her mother saying "Well, Larry says . . ." It was all Paige needed to hear. Paige scolded her mother for always going along with whatever Larry said. Her mother started to cry at the table. "Why don't you leave her alone?" Larry snapped at Paige. Paige couldn't believe he'd talked to her that way. He had no right to get between Paige and her mother. She could talk to her mother any way she wanted. These were their problems—not his. Paige ran outside the restaurant and called her sister, who calmed her down enough so she could return to the table for dinner.

The following morning, Paige and her mother met in front of St. Peter's Church on Fifth Avenue to go shopping. The tension at dinner was weighing on her mother. "I know this has been hard for you," she told Paige, "but I want you to have a relationship with Larry. I don't know what we can do to get beyond this."

"I never thought it was going to be this way," Paige said. "You get divorced, remarry so quickly."

Paige paused, then said, "He shouldn't have spoken to me that way." Her mother agreed, which made Paige feel less isolated from her mother. The talk helped. When her mother returned home to Washington, D.C., that weekend, Paige had a lot to think about. "I needed to work on accepting the new reality," she said. "I couldn't be angry forever."

Because we're grown children, we never expect we'll have to share our parents. But then parents remarry. They inherit young stepchildren or have a child with a new spouse. It's hard to imagine our father reading someone else a bedtime story. Parents *only* do those things with *us*. Our parents are stolen from us.

Young children are more dependent on a parent than an adult child is. There are soccer games and dance recitals. They need advice on how to stand up to bullies and how to say no to a joint passed around at a party. Raising children is exhausting, and our parents find themselves back in the thick of parenthood. Parents table their support for their adult children. They have a new set of kids to put first. Your parents become someone else's parents.

But an adult child's emotional needs are the same as those of a young child. We need to feel loved.

When Paige's father calls, she listens to her father talk about his newborn daughter. *You're so into your little kid*, Paige thinks. Paige's sister Carla reminds her why: Babies don't talk back. They're easy to dote on. They make parents feel young again. "I feel like my father has this new baby, this new life," Paige says. "We don't matter as much anymore. Since the baby, he keeps distancing himself. He is so wrapped up in his own world."

Kayla got pregnant around the same time as her stepmother, Esmerelda. Esmerelda gave birth to a son, whom they named Jacob. Kayla had a baby girl she named Tina. Kayla's father showed little interest in his granddaughter, which hurt Kayla. "This is supposed to be our time," says Kayla. "Dad should be looking forward to seeing his grandchild, hearing about her first words or her first steps. But he doesn't care because he has that at home with Jacob."

Up until this point, Kayla hasn't wanted to see her half brother, Jacob. Even if she wanted to, she's not sure her stepmother would allow it. Having Kayla in Jacob's life would force her stepmother to acknowledge her father's *other* family. Plus, Kayla hasn't thought of Jacob as a brother yet. Jacob is her father's kid.

Sometimes, our parents' new biological children don't feel like a legitimate piece of us. Until the shock of having a new brother or sister wears off, adult children may shun their siblings. One twenty-seven-year-old woman told her father, "You're old. When this child is twenty, you'll be eighty. Don't expect me to take care of this baby when you're gone. This is your mistake."

Early on, Dad talked about taking me on vacation with Donna and her kids. I wanted to go away with Dad, but it would be strange sharing a room with her twenty-two-year-old daughter, Amelia, whom I didn't know. For all I knew, Amelia might hate my father. Would I stick up for Dad if she were nasty to him? Or would Amelia and I sit and complain about this odd predicament we were in? In all honesty, I had little interest in getting to know Amelia. I had two sisters. You can't meet someone this late in life and expect to feel like anything but acquaintances. But I felt evil thinking these thoughts. Shouldn't I embrace this young woman?

I've learned that my reaction is typical. Adult children often don't want to get to know their stepsiblings, even when they are much younger. We don't want to be a big sister; we already are a big sister. And it's hard to see these children as anything but interlopers, sneaking into our lives and stealing our mother or father away. If anything, we envy these children. They take away our resources, our time, our love. And we don't feel so special anymore.

Like a stepmother, step- and half siblings are another drain on parents' resources. In a previous chapter, I explained how we sometimes equate money with love. If our parents don't financially support us, we begin to believe they no longer care how our life turns out. What if your father stops paying your college tuition so he can enroll his kindergartner in an expensive preschool? Resources are reallocated to stepchildren, and adult children lose out.

One twenty-eight-year-old woman wasn't speaking to her father because he'd told his daughter his new wife's pregnancy was an accident; she found out later it was planned. Mapping out a nice life for his new wife and baby, her father stopped paying his daughter's graduate school tuition. Kayla's father stopped paying her college tuition and making her car payment so he could pay a thousand dollars a month to send his stepson to a private military academy.

Holidays are sticky. Your home is invaded by strange bodies under the guise of "family," or you find yourself invading someone else's home. Bonding with intimate family is sidelined. Instead, we trespass on somebody else's celebration. Dad isn't carving the honey-baked ham. Mom isn't making eggnog punch. We're surrounded by people we've never met before—Mom's or Dad's new stepchildren and in-laws. Mom—or Dad, depending on whose house we're at—is rushing about, trying to keep this new blended family content.

Paige decided to go home the first Christmas after her mother married Larry. Her father was already living in Nicaragua. *Where else would she go?* Larry invited his two kids. His son is twenty-one years old, and his daughter is twenty-three. "Everyone was feeling awkward," says Paige. "We're all thrown in together. My grandfather didn't want to speak to Larry's kids." Larry's kids were equally unhappy with the situation. His daughter sat by herself with a look of disgust on her face. She didn't make small talk. Says Paige, "I almost sat down next to her and said, 'I hear you.' "

Holidays are the one time of the year when an adult child *cannot* avoid home. Adult children go home out of a sense of duty. They'll visit with their stepfamilies, even though they're unsure how to act in these adopted homes. A part of us is literally sickened by the idea that Mom or Dad will spend Christmas morning with a second set of kids. *He is my father.* The image is enough to make us want to turn around and fly back to wherever we came from.

Seeing a parent happy on a holiday with his or her new family is a good thing. But it's awkward. A parent seems different, sometimes unrecognizable, when immersed in their new surroundings. We're stepping into the parent's life, and we feel like observers—not participants.

Then there are the details. Do you buy your stepmother a Christmas present? What about her children? Do you show up with a bottle of wine, like a divorced uncle, get buzzed, and watch someone else's family enjoy a special day?

Here's the thing. An adult child should think about what kind of relationship he or she wants to have with a stepparent. Your answer might evolve. Even if you're completely against the idea of a relationship at first, remember that if you want to remain close to a parent, you're going to have to accept his or her new life. You don't have to be best friends with a parent's spouse, but you might make an effort.

The holidays are a good time to open yourself up to a relationship. Bring over a pie or a gingerbread house—a nice gesture that will not go unnoticed by your parent. You may feel smug and believe your stepparent should reach out to you. But he or she is just as anxious. If you want a relationship with a stepparent, you need to initiate one. We're often too lost in our own pain to imagine what life is like for the stepparent. But we should try.

Whenever I'm angry with someone, I remind myself that that person is somebody's sister or someone's daughter, and I soften. We are all human, and we all hurt. A stepmother isn't always as evil as we make her out to be. I did this with Donna. I tried to look at the lay of the land from her point of view. She felt like the odd one out as much as I did. Some stepmothers overcompensate for these feelings by trying to dominate early on. Others remain quiet and don't try to get to know us because they fear we'll push them away.

An adult child needs to be the bigger person and initiate a relationship. Once you and a stepparent are on good terms, holidays won't feel as strained. You can toast with eggnog and open presents—and maybe even laugh a little—with these new faces. Over time, you'll begin to feel more comfortable. You'll come to know the idiosyncrasies of a stepfamily as much as you've known your own. And you might even grow to love them. But none of this is realistic or even possible unless you open yourself up to it.

Blended families don't mix without tension. Even when an adult child is trying hard to connect with a parent's new significant other, the relationship requires reciprocity. Since we are too old to need a second mother or father, we can only hope to build a friendship with a stepparent. If we decide we're ready to pursue a relationship, it doesn't mean a stepparent will embrace the idea. What if they reject us? Then we're left to jockey for a parent's attentions alongside the new significant other. It's an uncomfortable situation, and one in which you don't want to find yourself. If you do, you're going to need to pull a parent aside and confide in him or her. *I'm trying. I want to have a relationship with Pete. How might I win Pete over?* If a parent knows you are trying, he or she may help facilitate the connection. And remember, you need to be patient. You don't just walk up to a stranger in the grocery store and decide to become best buddies. Relationships take time to develop.

When we don't connect with a stepparent immediately, we sometimes want to knock the newcomer out of the picture entirely. It's hard to get used to spending so much time with someone you don't know well. You want your mother or father to yourself. One twenty-five-year-old woman called her stepmother and said, "No one has ever got all of my father's attention—except me."

Between jobs, boyfriends or girlfriends, and kids, time is at a premium for adult children. When we see a parent, we want to spend quality time. But when the parent brings a new significant other around, we're not free to be ourselves. As soon as my father introduced me to Donna, he started to bring her everywhere—even when we met for dinner at a steak house after Dad got off work. Her presence irritated me, mostly because I was used to having Dad to myself. Now I had to share him. I wanted to be able to talk about the divorce proceedings or my mother or anything I wanted to without having to think twice about it. With Donna around, I had to watch what I said. And Donna talked about her job and kids, which was interesting but time-consuming. I wanted to talk about *my life*.

Liza, whose stepmother put distance between Liza and her fa-

ther, says she was really close to her father during her parents' separation and subsequent divorce. When her father remarried, he
dragged his new wife, Ginger, everywhere. One weekend, her father
and Ginger visited Liza in North Carolina. They went to dinner.
Ginger had a problem with talking over people, and she always dom-
inated the conversation. Liza and her father hadn't seen each other
in a few months. They wanted to catch up. Instead, they found themselves listening to Ginger talk about her own family for an hour.

At one point, Liza started to say something about herself and
Ginger cut her off, trying to change the subject back to herself. Her
father got angry. "Ginger! Shut up," Liza's father yelled. He knew his
daughter. She was quiet. She wasn't the type to interrupt people
when she talked. Liza appreciated her father's making sure they
could have a conversation at dinner. But she longed for the days
when he'd visit her alone. "I don't ever have any time with just him,"
she says. "*She* is always there."

Books advising parents how to transition a young child into a
stepfamily say a bedroom should be set aside for the child, even if he
visits only on weekends. They say parents should spend time alone
with the child; don't always include a new spouse. These suggestions
might seem silly for an adult child. Yet an adult child needs to be
eased into a parent's new relationship in similar ways. We are
human. We need to be told we're welcome, and we need to be reassured that we will not lose our parents' love, one of our biggest fears.
The difference between a young child and an adult child is that we
need to ask for the reassurance. No one offers it to us.

One evening, a year after Dad had moved in with Donna, I was
on the phone with him. We were planning to meet for dinner, and I
asked whether Donna was coming. He said no. "Oh good," I said. "I
mean . . . well, Dad, do you think sometimes we could hang out by
ourselves?" Dad said sure. I told him it would mean a lot to me to get

him to myself sometimes. Dad said he understood. We hung up, and I felt incredible relief. One simple question had solved my problem.

I didn't complain that Donna sometimes talked too much, which would've put Dad on the defensive. I turned my issue into a positive. *I want to spend more time with you. You're important to me, too.* Dad didn't have to choose. Any parent, including Donna, could understand why a child would want alone time with a parent. Period.

You're allowed to be happy for a parent when they remarry. Don't feel as though you need to be angry—just because a parent or sibling is. Earlier, I shared Marisa's story. She decided to like her mother's boyfriend before she met him. All of us have the power to choose. Your heart might hurt, but you can avoid drifting further from a parent if you respect the decisions they make. The faster you're able to move on, the faster your relationship will heal. Just because a parent remarries doesn't mean you will lose them. You only have to share them with someone else, which is a big adjustment but not an insurmountable one.

Jenna didn't acknowledge her mother's boyfriend, Ray, for more than a year. After he married her mother, Jenna slowly began accepting him. She couldn't deny how happy her mother was around Ray. She was confident and self-assured. Jenna realized her mother had tried her best to keep the family together over the years. She had tried to be superwoman, working forty hours a week and running a household. But her mother became so focused on her family, she forgot to focus on herself. Early in the divorce, Jenna saw that as selfish. Now she understood. Her mother needed to divorce her father to find happiness.

Once Jenna stopped blaming her mother, she was filled with love for her again. She agreed to go to Florida with Ray and her mother this past year. They stayed in a condo. One morning, Ray ran to the store, and Jenna and her mother went and sat at the pool together.

Her mother painted Jenna's toenails and they giggled about Jenna's love life, the way they used to. *This is the way it's supposed to be*, Jenna thought. Ray might be in her family, but he didn't erase the bond Jenna had with her mother. Says Jenna, "She was the mother I knew my whole life."

Points to Remember

- You decide what kind of relationship you want with a stepparent. You're old enough to walk away or pursue a mature friendship.

- Don't expect your mother or father to fight your battles. Your relationship with a stepparent is an independent one, and it will cause less strain on a parent if you leave them out of it.

- If a stepparent comes between you and your parent, remember that your parent is only protecting the person they love. They're not *against* you. Don't ask a parent to choose between the two of you. They won't, and you'll feel hurt.

- Holidays are a good time to reach out to a stepparent. Build new rituals and attempt to get to know him or her. Open yourself up to the possibility that you actually might like a parent's spouse.

- Try not to resent a parent's happiness. If they seem at peace in the new relationship, it's because the last one was adversarial.

- Let the steamroller drive over you. Try to accept the new people in your family, as difficult as that may be. If you support a parent's decisions, you won't feel so distant from him or her.

- If a stepparent doesn't seem to want a relationship with you, talk to your mother or father. Ask how you might win over a new significant other. Be patient. Relationships take time.

6

Truth, Lies, and Parents Who Cheat

I saw that night, as I'd never seen before, that my father
was living a life that wasn't about us and that threatened
us as a family. . . .

—CHRISTOPHER DICKEY, *Summer of Deliverance*

THE NIGHT WAS BITTERLY COLD. WIND WHIPPED
branches against the side of the house. Mom and I pulled
extra blankets out of the closet for each of our beds. We
tried to ignore Chelsea, then twelve, when she asked where Daddy
was. It was 10:00 p.m. "He's at work," I told her.

None of us could sleep. Chelsea was snuggled next to Mom on
the couch, and I sat with them watching TV for awhile. My stomach
clenched every time Mom turned her head to check the time. *Where
was Dad?* In bed, I pushed my nose against the glass every time

headlights stretched across my ceiling. It was midnight in December 1994. I was a senior in high school.

Dad had seemed depressed lately. The economy was in a recession, and Dad's painting business wasn't doing too well. Dad would drive off if Mom started yelling about money, which is why we'd eaten dinner without him that night. Lying in my bed, the clock nearing 1:00 a.m., I imagined Dad driving home drunk from a bar. *Would he wrap his car around a tree?* More likely, I told myself, Dad went back to work, painting someone's house to earn extra cash. If a house was empty, he would sometimes work late.

At 2:00 a.m., I heard the unmistakable rattle of Dad's pickup barreling up the street and screeching into the driveway. He slammed his car door and jiggled his key in the lock. Mom was already on her feet, walking down the hall toward the living room. She let him struggle with the door. When he stepped in, he said hello. Mom was silent. I sat on the floor next to my bedroom door with a blanket wrapped around me. I imagined Chelsea in the next room doing the same. I almost knocked on our shared wall to say hello. But then I heard Dad fill a glass with water in the kitchen, and I wasn't sure whether Mom was going to take it out of his hand and throw it at him.

"Where the hell were you?" Mom said. Dad told her he went to the house of his customer, Mrs. Laney, to finish painting her sunporch. Mrs. Laney lived on a hill on the main road in my hometown. She worked in the middle school Chelsea attended. When Dad had mentioned he was painting her house, Chelsea had told Dad how nice she was.

"You were painting till 2:00 a.m.?" Mom said. Her tone was sharp. Dad said he was sorry he was late. He said that he painted until about 10:00, and then he and Mrs. Laney grabbed a bite at the local sports bar. Dad stayed for a few drinks after she left. He lost track of time.

"So now you're running around with some divorced tramp?" Mom said. "I've had it with this shit, Dennis."

"Stop," Dad said. "You'll wake the kids."

"I don't care if I wake the whole friggin' neighborhood," Mom said. The argument went on, but I didn't listen. I climbed into bed, grabbed my Walkman, and blasted Nirvana into my ears. *Dad might drink a little too much sometimes*, I thought, *but he wouldn't cheat*. Only slimy husbands who don't love their families cheat. I cried, even though I swore what Mom said wasn't true.

The next morning, Mom and Dad acted as if everything were a bad dream, so I did, too. We ate breakfast together. Dad left first, and he gave Chelsea and me a kiss on our cheeks before he went. On my way to school, I passed Mrs. Laney's house, and I looked for Dad's truck. *What if Mom was right?* Mrs. Laney's driveway was empty.

I looked at that woman's driveway every time I passed it for the next several months. One afternoon, I saw Dad's truck parked there, and I panicked. Would I tell Mom? But Dad came home that night and said he got his last check from Mrs. Laney earlier that day. So it didn't seem like such a secret. No one in my house talked about Mrs. Laney ever again.

But how can I forget her? I drive by Mrs. Laney's house even today when I'm visiting home. Mrs. Laney moved a few years back. I remember seeing the For Sale sign stuck in her lawn. But the memory of Mom's accusation is vivid, especially because Mrs. Laney's house is still the cream color Dad had painted it ten years before. I wonder, *Could Dad have cheated that cold December night?*

I don't want to know the answer, but then again, I do. Is Mrs. Laney one of the reasons my parents divorced? Maybe Mom never believed Dad's story that night. Maybe she carried the anger with her for years, and maybe Dad's possible indiscretion fell into the category of what Mom called "things you kids shouldn't know." Or maybe Dad didn't do anything at all.

Either way, that cream-colored house on the hill haunts me. If Dad did more than paint there, I'd blame him for the divorce, not Mom. I wouldn't believe him every time he said he missed Mom. When he lost twenty pounds after Mom kicked him out, and I walked on the beach consoling him, I wouldn't have shed a tear. You made your bed, I'd tell him angrily, feeling as betrayed as Mom. *This is your fault.*

Dad's larger-than-life presence would seem shrunken and cheapened. He'd be the kind of guy who gives up everything for one roll in the hay. I'd pound my fists against his chest and yell at him. *How could you do this to us? Don't we mean anything to you? What kind of parent cheats?*

Husbands and wives have affairs—not mothers and fathers. Or so we think. Then Mom sits us down and admits that she's been dating another man for three years. She didn't mean to hurt us or Dad. She's sorry. Please forgive her. As she speaks, you picture your mother in ways you never wanted to: in a negligee tumbling around in the crisp sheets at a local motel with some naked, faceless man or scrubbing her lover off her body in a shower before she returns home. As an adult, you understand the gritty nature of infidelity. Maybe you've even cheated yourself. You know your parents kept secrets and lied about their whereabouts. You realize that one of your parents has been leading a double life.

If divorce changes an adult child's perception of his parents, infidelity taints who a parent is to us. It's similar to the point in a movie when you learn something about the lead character that changes how you see him no matter what happens next. A parent's infidelity leaves us with far more questions than we want answers to. Affairs change the backdrop to our lives. Our parents aren't who we thought they were.

It's difficult to know exactly how many marriages end in affairs. Individuals are so ashamed, they sometimes lie on anonymous surveys. A landmark 1995 study by the University of Chicago found that among all married couples, about 25 percent of men cheat on their wives and 15 percent of women cheat on their husbands. Peggy Vaughan's *The Monogamy Myth* claims those numbers are a lot higher, with 60 percent of men and women cheating at least once. According to the American Association of Retired Persons (AARP), 27 percent of divorces at midlife result from infidelity. Says one July 2003 study in the *Journal of Family Issues*, "Although the underlying pattern is not entirely clear, it appears that long-term marriages are especially likely to be disrupted when people seek out new sexual partners (perhaps out of boredom) or become aware of change in themselves or their partners due to the passage of time."

Boomer women are cheating on their husbands more than women in previous generations. The topic prompted a July 2004 *Newsweek* cover story. John Gottman, director of the Relationship Research Institute in Seattle, says working women are most likely to stray. "Baby boomer women are in the work world—and that's where you meet the sympathetic person when you're having a bad marriage. It's opportunity, not biology, and while men had much greater opportunity for cheating in the past, it's far more equal now," says Gottman in the July–August 2004 issue of *AARP: The Magazine*.

"Dad is the last person who would cheat," said Jessica, and many others. No one thinks his or her Mom or Dad fits the profile of a cheater because parents, by nature, aren't supposed to cheat. Only characters in movies stray from their spouses. We put our parents in a different category. Jessica, a thirty-seven-year-old mother of three, says her father was a pillar of her seaside community. He was the most respected attorney in town. On weekends, he'd walk through the village with his ten-year-old granddaughter on his shoulders. He'd play in tennis tournaments. He took his family on skiing vacations and seemed happy. Yet her father had been carrying on an affair with one of his clients for at least a year—maybe more.

Jessica's mother came straight to Jessica's house after hearing a voice mail from a woman on the answering machine in her husband's office. She made Jessica listen to the message over the phone. "Hi, Bill," the woman said in a friendly voice. She said that she was unpacking groceries and was sorry she'd missed his call. Jessica's mother immediately suspected her husband was having an affair. When Jessica's father stopped by Jessica's house a few minutes later, he stood facing Jessica and her mother in Jessica's kitchen. "Where were you?" asked her mother. Her father said he was at the library. "You weren't at the library," her mother said. Then her parents went home. An hour later, Jessica's mother called. "I threw him out," her mother said. "He confessed." Jessica says she knew her parents were in therapy, but she thought they were happy. She never imagined her father would cheat. Says Jessica, "To think of him as a sexual person when I thought my parents were so happy . . . I'm shocked by the deceit . . . the secrecy . . . the dishonesty."

When a parent admits to an affair, our first question is often, How long? The length of the deceit makes a difference to us. If Mom was sneaking off with someone the day after Christmas six years earlier, she has been keeping secrets for a very long time. Our perception of those holidays and every day after is spoiled, which makes an adult child look back on the past with cynicism. A parent's sneaky behaviors, actions that were only suspect before, now seem like confirmations of a double life. How far did Mom go to keep her affair secret?

In a divorce, adult children usually find out about infidelity because the indiscretion ended the marriage. Therapists sometimes refer to this as a "bridge." A bridge affair allows a parent to get out of a marriage by escaping into the comfortable security of another. The parent uses infidelity to avoid facing bigger problems in an existing marriage. It's an easy way out. The admission brings clarity to parts of our parents' relationship.

Then we have questions. How long was our mother plotting her escape? We wonder if the old adage "Once a cheater, always a cheater" is true. Did Mom cheat once before, and Dad forgave her? Was Dad a longtime philanderer or a man swept up by the beauty of *one* other woman? Knowing about a parent's infidelity often means sifting through childhood memories for clues about his or her second life. Sometimes we remember moments we wish we didn't.

Kayla, twenty-nine, found out from her mother that her sixty-four-year-old father had been having an affair with his pretty thirty-five-year-old secretary ten years earlier. Then she found out that her father had cheated before. "Nothing seemed so innocent anymore," Kayla says. Time she'd spent with her father was soured. His actions now had ulterior motives. Kayla remembered going with her father to see a single woman once when she was little. He called her a friend. Her father would sit for hours with the woman and talk. When Kayla hung around him, he'd shoo Kayla away and tell her to go play with the other kids. *Did my father cheat with that woman?* "I can go back and think of things that weren't quite right about it," she says.

In high school, Kayla's mother accused Kayla's father of checking out a curvy foreign exchange student staying with them. At the time, Kayla was angry with her mother for having a meltdown over something so stupid. Now Kayla wonders whether her mother's accusations were true. How often did her father's eye wander? Kayla was especially upset with her dad when she remembered that he'd brought Kayla to his mistress's house a few years earlier. Her father said his secretary was struggling. She had two little boys to feed, and she needed help fixing her plumbing. "We just thought we were being nice," says Kayla, who showed up at the woman's house with her siblings. Kayla isn't sure whether her father was having an affair then or not. Either way, now the visit is a window into her father's other life.

Brittany, twenty-seven, was at college when her mother called. "Your father has been cheating on me," her mother said. Brittany didn't believe her, so her mother kept saying it over and over until Brittany broke down. In time, Brittany learned her father had cheated on her mother often during business trips over the last several years. He was serious with one woman in Arizona, whom he saw regularly. He'd lied and told his wife and daughter he had work there. Brittany's mother found out he was lying when she snooped around in his e-mail account. Brittany was shaken. "It wasn't possible that someone so close to me could do that," she says. Her father seemed like a hypocrite. When Brittany was younger, she remembers watching *Roseanne* on TV. One episode centered around cheating. "Girls," her father said to Brittany and her sister, "don't put up with cheating. You deserve better."

Brittany's mother has since told her that her father's affairs began in 1986, when Brittany was seven. Her mother took him back because he swore he'd never do it again. "I thought my dad was different," says Brittany. Today, Brittany feels as if the happiest moments of her childhood have been painted black. Her father was *always* wandering, *always* bored, *always* looking for another woman and another family.

"My dad seems to be two different people," says one twenty-six-year-old woman. There was the father she thought of as a hero who tucked her into bed as a child and made sure she had what she needed to make it as an adult. Then there was this deviant man who led a separate life with his mistress. It's difficult to reconcile a parent's two faces. Says another thirty-seven-year-old woman, "What I thought Dad was compared to what I think he is now. . . . It's like finding out your father was a bottom-dweller."

One young woman posting to a divorce Web site found out her father had been having an affair with the same woman for more than a decade. She struggles to understand how her father got away with it. "My parents were always together," she writes. "When did he have the time to do this, especially all those years ago when I was living with them?" How many lies had her father told her? Did her father skip her parent-teacher conferences and track meets to have dinner with his *other* family?

Cheating casts a parent in the worst light. We're not even sure we want to love a parent after he or she cheats. Such parents seem like monsters. "I realized my dad is capable of horrible things," Jessica says. "It hit me to the core." Infidelity knocks a parent off a pedestal. We've deferred to our parents and respected their values and authority for a lifetime. When they cheat, we can hardly hold them in the same esteem. One thirty-one-year-old woman whose father cheated on her mother two years ago says, "I see my father more as a man with failings. Somewhat different from just seeing him as my father."

The myth of the perfect parent is squashed. We grow cynical about our childhoods. The daddy who carried us on his shoulder through the park and the mommy who wiped our nose vanishes. We don't want to follow in their footsteps. We're ashamed of who our parents have become. Says one twenty-seven-year-old woman, "I always thought he was the best father. But he's not. He has a lot of qualities I don't like. Everything about him is a model of what you *wouldn't* want to be."

Movies and popular fiction often glamorize affairs. Women are empowered by adultery. Think of Diane Lane's character in the film *Unfaithful*, Gwyneth Paltrow's role in *A Perfect Murder*, or Annette Benning in *American Beauty*. All three women undergo vibrant transformations when they cheat. They're no longer stale or boring. When men cheat on-screen, the affair carries a more negative connotation. They dangle their new trophy wives in front of a former spouse. In the film *The First Wives Club*, Diane Keaton, Goldie Hawn, and Bette Midler take revenge on their cheating husbands, all of whom left them for someone younger.

Parents don't think they're being unfaithful to their children when they cheat on a spouse. As they tear off a lover's clothes, they're certainly not considering the impact the affair will have on their kids. Affairs center around what one parent does to the other—not how one parent's actions influence the rest of his or her family.

But when parents cheat, adult children feel that they're cheating on everyone in the family. Therapists say a parent who is unhappy in his or her marriage may be secretly relieved when a spouse cheats; it gives the dissatisfied spouse a way out of a loveless union without initiating a divorce. Cheating isn't about our father's not choosing our mother; it's about a parent's choosing himself or herself over us. Sometimes it seems we feel more betrayed by a parent's infidelity than our parents do—maybe because there's less to lose in ending an unhappy marriage and more to lose in ending a loving family.

Joanna Trollope's fictional *Marrying the Mistress* follows Alan and Simon, two adult brothers, through their parents' divorce after their father cheats on their mother with a younger woman. Alan sticks up for his father, saying he only wants him to be happy. Simon tells Alan it makes him angry "to hear you saying things like that, as if you didn't disapprove of Dad, as if it was perfectly OK just to duck out on four decades of a relationship because you're bored." Alan says their father wasn't bored. "He's worn out with never knowing what she wants, what makes her happy, what he's doing wrong," Alan says.

Alan supports his father's actions. Simon cannot stomach what his father did. This is one reason why a parent's affair is so difficult. A bombshell like this sends shock waves through a family. Relations with siblings can become tense or codependent, which is the last thing you need when you're dealing with a parent's affair. An affair is one more thing to turn you against one parent and make you grow closer to the other. One more way parents disappoint us.

Sometimes the purity of love seems lost after an affair. A parent's love for us feels less real. *If Mom loved me, how could she hurt me?* We cannot understand how a parent can betray us by choosing a stranger over us. We wonder whether we overestimated how treasured we were to an adulterous parent in the first place. Some adult children say they began to feel like deadweight, like one more thing their adulterous parent is trying to get rid of.

Jessica was driving home from a tennis match on her birthday a few years ago when she thought of her father. She hadn't talked to him in more than a year. He lived with his mistress across town. Jessica and her father always used to play tennis together. For her sixteenth birthday, her father bought her a wooden Chris Everett tennis racket. He was so excited when Jessica had squealed with delight. She loved that racket. "He probably doesn't even remember it now," Jessica thought to herself.

When her father first left, he told Jessica that she'd be over her disappointment in him in six months. "The experts say you'll come around then," he'd told her. Jessica got upset that he was trying to put a time limit on her pain. Six months came and went. Jessica's father grew impatient with his daughter. As far as he was concerned, she was dragging out her feelings. Jessica says her disapproval of his new relationship inconvenienced her father. When Jessica stopped calling, he stopped calling, too.

Several years later, Jessica's father still doesn't call her. Jessica says she doesn't understand how he lives in a house without one photograph of her or her siblings. "He never asked for one picture," Jessica says. She feels as though her father wants to erase his family from his life. Memories of her happy childhood haunt her. The man she once adored doesn't even call her on her birthday. Jessica wonders how someone is able to just "turn off" the past. "What does he do with all of the memories of us as babies, of the trips we took?" she says. "I don't think I will ever get over the pain of being abandoned."

We assume our parents will come running after us after they cheat. We imagine they'll beg us to forgive them. Sometimes the opposite happens. Parents who move in with a lover may cut children out of their lives just as quickly as we cut them out. Cheating parents feel guilt and shame for what they've done, so facing their children is difficult. They don't know what to do with such big emotions. Parents know their adult children are angry, but they're unsure of how to work through it—a common predicament in families after infidelity. "A parent might have the sense that there is nothing they can do to make it better," says Laurel Fay, a therapist in the Washington, D.C., suburbs. So they give up.

Therapists say some parents see divorce as a clean break. They don't necessarily want to have anything to do with the past, including their children. Ian Birky, director of counseling at Lehigh University in Pennsylvania, says that some parents aren't only escaping an unhappy marriage when they cheat. They're trying to escape an unhappy family situation.

A parent doesn't always admit to an affair, which many adult children say is worse than the affair itself. Say your father tells you your mother has been seeing the same man for three years. You confront your mother, and she swears she's never cheated. A year later, she admits she was having an affair all along. Why lie? Parents fear that their children will look at them differently if they tell the truth—which may be true. So they try to save face. But the longer the lies continue, the less respect we have for an adulterous parent.

Stephanie, twenty-six, knew her mother had something important to tell her. A few months earlier, her mother had announced she was divorcing Stephanie's father. Her mother seemed just as serious this time. She turned off the TV, sat down next to Stephanie, and put her hand on her daughter's thigh. "Your dad's having an affair," she said. Stephanie had considered this when her parents split up, but she'd decided her father would never do something like that. Stephanie and her sister, Amanda, had even discussed the possibility. They decided Amanda should confront her father, just to be sure. "I want a one-word answer," Amanda said. "Dad, did you cheat on Mom?" Her father looked her in the eye. "No," he said. That was a month ago. Stephanie and Amanda had believed him until now.

When Stephanie talked to family friends about her father's indiscretion, she found out he'd been seeing this woman for a long time—and they'd been seen together around town. Friends of friends saw them at a conference in New York City. Her father had brought back gifts from his trip: a fluffy stuffed animal for Stephanie and a trendy purse for Amanda. Stephanie and her sister laughed about their father's good taste. "We now realize it was this woman who picked out these things," Stephanie says. There was more proof of her father's adultery. Stephanie says her father got calls from the woman at an aunt and uncle's house—her name was on their caller ID—and one family friend showed Stephanie a picture of her. Her father met the woman through a mentoring program where he volunteered. Family friends knew about her father's affair but had said nothing, which made her feel worse than anything. Stephanie was embarrassed that everyone seemed to know but her. If she were a child, she would have been none the wiser.

Stephanie's father still denies the affair. Stephanie hasn't spoken to her father for two months. The lying hurts more than the affair does, she says. Today, Stephanie wants to make amends with her dad, but she doesn't feel as if she can talk things out unless he admits he cheated. "It would be easier for me to forgive if he'd been honest," Stephanie says. "Why would he choose to continue to lie about it all when it would have been more honorable for him to fess up and come clean? I'm disappointed that my dad carries on a whole other life that doesn't involve what I thought was his family. I want him to know that I know. I want him to know that I know who she is . . . I don't know if that would make it more of a reality for him."

Parents abuse our trust. When tidbits of their double life emerge, we have trouble believing anything they say. It's like listening to a minister preach about values after he's caught reading porn. One twenty-seven-year-old woman's father was cheating for several years before she found out. Her father still denies it. "It's hard to trust someone—especially a parent—when they've broken your trust so blatantly (not to mention your heart)," she says. "Everything feels like a lie. Now I dread talking to my father on the phone because our conversations feel so forced and phony. We skirt around the issues that matter because it's too unpleasant to talk about it all the time. When we get together in person now, it's almost always over drinks, just to loosen the tension."

It's hard to imagine someone so close to you betraying you. In *The Years Between*, Rudyard Kipling writes, "If any question why we died, / Tell them, because our fathers lied." Lies poison, and cheating reveals all the untruths. There is no question about what went wrong in the marriage. Mom fell out of love with Dad and cheated on him. End of story. But parents twist around in their lies and suffocate themselves in untruths. It seems they don't know how to be honest anymore. So they lie and lie, and sometimes claim later that they did it to protect us.

Therapists say parents lie to save face. They're embarrassed. No parent wants to feel looked down on by their child. "They want to protect who they are in a child's eye," says therapist Laurel Fay. Imagine a little girl throwing her ice cream cone at her feet. Fearing Mommy will be angry if she tells the truth, the child swears she didn't do it, even as the ice cream melts on the sidewalk. Denial is a powerful mental state. Parents may actually convince themselves that they didn't cheat. Therapist Ian Birky says that when cheating parents "pretend the situation isn't real, they make their lives easier."

We feel frustrated when a parent won't admit to an affair. Fay suggests an adult child try to be the bigger person. An adult child should say, "I'm sure you denied you had an affair because you feared hurting me. But the most important thing you can do is tell me the truth." The truth is important to us. Many adult children obsessively seek it out. Our relationship with a cheating parent seems to hinge on it. "The truth is a grounding force. It's a way back to intimacy, trust, and faith in a parent," says Fay. "The lying is a big brick wall."

When you realize how easy it was for a parent to lie to you, you wonder how often they lied in the past. The deception makes our childhood seem like a sham. An adult child doesn't know what to believe. *Did Dad ever mean anything he said?* We question the smallest gestures. When Jessica's father cheated on her mother, Jessica stopped talking to her father, who was a revered attorney in her small town. "I expected him to fight to keep a relationship with me," Jessica says. "I think he just gave up. He has a new life."

Her father remarried and moved into a large house near her childhood home. On her birthday, Jessica sifted through old cards she'd saved over the years. There were several from her father on which he'd underlined words that expressed his feelings. "You're a great daughter." Jessica rolled her eyes. Even her father's old cards seemed phony. "I'm so jaded," she says. "A part of me feels like what he felt then wasn't true." If he tried to win her back, Jessica wouldn't believe anything he said. "I would always wonder if he was just saying what I wanted to hear without the emotion on his end to back it up," she says.

The disappointment Stephanie feels in her father is so great that Stephanie wishes her mother had never told her about the affair. A young child can be kept in the dark about a parent's affair. Stephanie believes she could have been, too. Stephanie felt as if knowing only made her hate her father. It forced her to deal with a pain that cut deeper than the initial news of the divorce. Still, Stephanie understands why her mother told her: she didn't want her daughter to find out from someone else first.

Affairs are a favorite topic for gossips. Hearing about a parent's affair through the grapevine is painful. Divorce no longer carries a scarlet letter, but adultery still does. One twenty-seven-year-old woman got an e-mail from an old friend in her hometown who asked her to confirm or deny the rumor that her father was having an affair. The e-mail was the first the young woman heard about her father's indiscretion. (Her father denied the rumor.) Another thirty-seven-year-old woman ran into friends in the grocery store after her father left. They made comments about how unattractive and rude her father's mistress was.

An affair can be "breaking news" in social circles. It's uncomfortable when your family is whispered about. Instead of suffering in private, we are the public faces of our parents' mistakes. Explaining to old friends what happened is equally hard. While shopping in the frozen foods section, nobody wants to get into the details of Mom's infidelity. Sometimes we keep a parent's infidelity secret. "I tell people that they grew apart after twenty-five years, which is, in fact, the reason for their divorce. Infidelity was only a symptom," says one thirty-one-year-old woman.

Adult children are embarrassed to share why their parents are splitting up. "No one wants to air their family's dirty laundry, particularly if it suggests that your parent, your hero, has done something so ugly," says the thirty-one-year-old woman. One thirty-two-year-old attorney's mother was having an e-mail relationship with a high school boyfriend before her parents split up. The attorney felt guilty. She was the one who had shown her mother how to hook up to the Internet and sign on to classmates.com, a Web site that enables people to connect with members of their graduating class, which is where her mother met her old boyfriend again. She tells people that her parents got divorced after thirty-six years and her mom married her high school sweetheart six months later. "Let people infer what they want," she says.

Jessica, whose father is the revered attorney now living with his mistress, says she also couldn't find the words to tell people her dad had cheated. At first, she wouldn't volunteer information to anyone. Over time, Jessica started to tell close friends that her father had cheated. Talking about the affair helped Jessica feel less ashamed. *I didn't commit adultery,* she'd remind herself. "It was not easy at first," Jessica says, "but the more I said it, the easier it got."

Sometimes a parent confesses an affair to us and begs us not to tell another soul—not our mother, our brother, or even an aunt. An affair is a secret for us to keep, which is a great burden. Parents aren't thinking about how hard it is for their son or daughter to keep a secret of this magnitude from the other parent. When they confess, they're thinking only of purging their own guilt, not about the recipient of the information. No longer an innocent bystander, the adult child finds himself tangled in a parent's lies.

One friend of my family, whom I'll call Lucy, was away at college when her father called to tell her he was cheating. He made Lucy swear she wouldn't tell her mother. I'll tell your mother soon, her father said. Over the next year, Lucy would go home and spend time with her mother and father, knowing her father had a girlfriend on the side. Lucy wanted to tell her mother about her father's affair, but how could she? Then she'd betray her father's trust, and her mother would hate her for delivering the news, angry with Lucy for not telling her sooner. Lucy waited a year for her father to break it off with her mother, all the while feeling immense guilt at having known all along.

When I told the therapists I interviewed that some cheating parents confided in their children first, they weren't surprised; they'd seen it before in their practices. Says Tina Tessina, a therapist in Long Beach, California, "When a parent does this . . . it's selfish and downright narcissistic." Parents tell their adult children about an affair before they tell a spouse because they want a chance to explain it before the other parent gets to you. They're hoping to get you on their side. If Mom spins a sob story about how badly your father treated her— "You know he was never affectionate," she'll say—we might be more understanding. Better for you to hear an honest account of an affair rather than hearing about it when you pick up the phone and catch your mother talking dirty, which happened to a good friend of mine. When a parent sits us down and tells us about an indiscretion, he tries to seem like a victim. Cheating parents want us to understand how it happened. "You would have done it if you were me" is their message. "A parent is lost . . . so their moral system collapses a bit," says therapist Ian Birky. They do inconsiderate things.

The secrets we keep aren't always short-lived. A parent's infidelity can drag on for years, and we might know about it for just as long. When we know about an indiscretion before the rest of our family, little in our life feels genuine. Watching Mom act happy with Dad, even though she's leaving in an hour to go to "her mother's," is enough to make you crazy. Your mom seems like a phony, and your dad seems pathetic, like a man too oblivious to notice how unhappy his wife is.

Being an adulterous parent's confidant thrusts an adult child in between her parents. Not telling the secret hurts no one and everyone. What happens once the secret is out? We worry a parent will be angry that we kept the affair from them. It's like learning your best friend knew your boyfriend was cheating and didn't tell you. How do you keep that secret without feeling like the worst friend in the world? And from your betrayed parent's point of view, how can Mom or Dad trust that you won't keep secrets again?

Liza, twenty-seven, knew her mother was having an affair for several years. Liza pieced together the clues. Every night, her mother brought dinner to a man down the street. Her mother invited the man over on holidays. Liza says her father thought his wife saw the man as a father figure—she'd lost her own father as a young woman—and had only a close friendship with him. Liza knew otherwise. When she was sixteen, her mother told her about the affair and made her promise not to tell her father. Her mother said she'd divorce him once Liza and her brother finished college, which Liza didn't take seriously. Liza wasn't angry with her mother for having an affair; she sympathized with her. Even in high school, Liza could recognize how little attention her father paid her mother. But she didn't like knowing what her father didn't. She wasn't sure whether she should tell him. "I felt horrible guilt," she says.

Liza's father was devastated when his wife left him; his wife didn't say she was leaving for another man. When Liza saw how upset her father was, she realized he deserved to know the truth. Should she tell him about the affair? Liza's younger sister ultimately told him. A few days later, her father picked Liza up for an outing. "Did you know?" he asked her. Liza said she did. Her father was stunned. "Why didn't you tell me?" her father asked. Liza said she thought he knew. Her father began to cry. "Please don't keep anything like that from me again," her father said. Then Liza called her mother and told her not to ask her to keep anything from her father again. Looking back, Liza feels as if she played a role in her father's sadness. She wishes she'd told him sooner.

Adult children grasp how serious adultery is. Sometimes we keep the secret to save our family. We realize that if Mom knows Dad cheated, she'll leave him. So keeping Dad's infidelity quiet doesn't seem like such a bad idea. The longer a parent doesn't know, the longer we'll have our family in one piece—even though interactions will hardly feel sincere.

You can do more than refuse to listen to details of a parent's infidelity. Therapists suggest throwing the burden back to cheating parents. Let a cheating parent know you're not willing to carry the secret around. Be bold. "You'd better tell Mom—or else" may seem like emotional blackmail, which isn't wholly unreasonable in a situation such as this. The parent already abandoned the rules by telling us. If this doesn't work, you might try approaching the betrayed parent. If your father cheated and confided in you without telling your mother, tell your mom that your father told you something that you believe she should know. Say, "You need to get him to tell you."

Listening to parents explain away an affair is frustrating. They make excuses. They duck accusations and twist around the truth. They rarely admit they've made a mistake. If our parents seemed to genuinely regret their actions, we might not carry our anger for so long. Therapists say when a parent tells children they should "mind their own business," they're not giving their kids a chance to forgive them. Those behaviors only breed more resentment.

When Jessica asked her father why he cheated, he said, "We were so unhappy. You wouldn't want me to be unhappy the rest of my life, would you?" Every time her father rationalized his actions, Jessica wanted to scream. How can something that hurts so much be explained so simply? *Mom was unhappy, too,* you think, *but she didn't cheat.*

Adult children may get in the habit of sharing their anger with the betrayed parent; we're just as angry as they are. We're in the same boat, and we see a cheating parent similarly: as someone who quit, someone who walked away from the one true thing in his or her life. Rage burns inside an adult child's heart. There is so much we want to say to a cheating parent. Scarred by the parent's indiscretion, we fantasize about vicious confrontations.

Yet so few of us share our emotions. Silence can sometimes say more. One thirty-one-year-old woman told her father he should be ashamed of himself for cheating. Then she stopped speaking to him. "What I didn't say but rather did—ignored him, refused to see him—certainly was the more effective communicator of my feelings," she says.

More often, adult children want to talk to their parents, but they don't know what to say. In the most basic sense, infidelity is about sex. Talking about sex with a parent has never been comfortable. But we also fear telling our parents how we feel. Expressing how angry we are might further widen the rift—so we say nothing at all. Katherine Anne Porter once said, "Human life itself is almost pure chaos. Everyone takes his stance, asserts his own rights and feelings, mistaking the motives of others, and his own." Will our feelings be twisted around? Could talking with a parent make things worse?

An adult child isn't comfortable hanging a parent out to dry. To do so, we have to speak to the parent as an adult about very adult subjects. "We're afraid our parents will get mad at us," says therapist Laurel Fay. "How awkward is it to confront a parent about a moral failure? Parents are supposed to know better." A part of us is so used to being reprimanded by a parent, it feels strange to pummel the parent with all the reasons they disappointed us. At our core, we want a parent to apologize and clean up the mess himself or herself. *Why should I have to tell him what he did wrong? Mom should understand why I feel betrayed. She should come to me.*

So adult children sometimes minimize their hurt. With the admission of an affair, there are so many bigger issues to deal with— your mother figuring out how to pick herself up, your sister calling you crying every day—that you put your own problems on the back burner. Says Fay, "The prospect of dealing with your own emotions and those of your parent [is] so intimidating, you don't deal."

Some adult children want to scream "I hate you. You failed me. Don't ever call me again!" But deep down, we have a reservoir of love for our parents, despite their infidelity; we want them to prove to us why we shouldn't be so angry.

For William, twenty-nine, having an open conversation with his father hasn't been possible. Although his father had been carrying on an affair for several years, his father denies it. His father says he met his girlfriend after he left his wife. William's mother says the opposite. When his parents first split up, William knew nothing about his father's affair. So he was quick to reassure his father he wouldn't lose his relationship with him. Details of the affair have since surfaced. "I think because I acted normal for so long, Dad thought his affair was done and forgotten and he got off the hook," says William.

Now he's ready to confront his father. He wants to know exactly when his father started seeing this woman, tell his father of the proof he has that he's been lying, and accuse him of plotting to leave his mother long ago. William wants his father to admit he left the marriage dishonorably. He wants to hear him say "I ran off with another woman." He wouldn't mind an apology. William has never met his father's girlfriend. He refuses to.

Instead, William and his father talk about football. "How do you bring something up when all of the underlying accusations are against him?" he says. It's like throwing daggers at a dead soldier. So William says nothing.

Beginning the conversation with a parent about an affair is nerve-racking, especially if that parent has avoided the subject. Fay suggests going in with a cool head. Take time to regroup. Think about what has hurt you. "Don't pull a parent out of a store and scream at them on the street," she says. Fay often tells her clients to write a letter to someone with whom they're angry. Write whatever you wish if you're not going to send it. If you are going to send it, be careful: if one day you want to be close with a parent again, writing things like "You're a slut" or "I hate you" is only going to further polarize your relationship. In the heat of the moment, it might seem important to say these things to a parent. In retrospect, you may regret it.

When we realize we may lose a parent to our anger, we often decide to come clean about our feelings. Adult children worry about how the confrontation will change our relationship with our parents. Isn't it easier to talk about superficial subjects peacefully than argue about difficult subjects? Stephanie recently decided to break her silence and talk with her father about his affair after two months.

She's anxious. "The stress is too much for my body to handle. I can't sleep. My depression is worse than ever. My medication has increased. I figured I needed to do something before I fell apart completely," Stephanie says.

Sharing our feelings is an integral part of the healing process. Until we let out all the emotions we're bottling up, carrying on a meaningful relationship with a cheating parent will feel forced. Pretending will only make you feel like an actor in a play. You're keeping your true self from a parent, just as he or she did during an affair.

Brittany kept all her emotions in, even when her father came over to her house at eleven one night to admit his infidelity to his daughter. He wanted her to know it wasn't a full-blown affair. "I didn't sleep with her," her father said. Brittany was angry but not shocked. Her father had cheated a few years earlier. "How's Mom taking it?" she asked. Brittany didn't cry until after her father left.

After the admission, her parents remained in counseling. Her father agreed to stop cheating. As they repaired their relationship, her father decided to move into his RV at a local campground. For a year, Brittany didn't know how to express her feelings. She didn't know how to have a normal conversation with her father. "Every time we spoke, it was very surface," she says. "I'd say that I was upset and that what he did was hard for me. But I never said how I really felt."

Behind Brittany's regretful facade, she felt all-out rage. Her mother constantly encouraged her to share her fury with her father. "He needs to know," said her mother. Her mother said it was for Brittany's sake, but Brittany's mother also gains by her daughter's anger. Brittany is able to scream all the things her mother couldn't. No doubt most parents enjoy the idea of their children verbally skewering their former spouse.

One night, when Brittany's parents came over for dinner, Brittany went upstairs into her bedroom to fold laundry, and her mother and sister followed. Her mother lay down on Brittany's bed and said that a couple of days ago, her husband said he wasn't sure whether he loved her anymore, which infuriated Brittany. Her mother had been physically abused as a child. No one should talk to her mother like that. Brittany's father popped his head in her bedroom and asked what they were talking about. "I'm giving them an update," her mother said. Her father sat down on the bed, quietly, as if he were waiting for a bomb to drop. Twelve months of bottled-up anger came pouring out. Previous chapters explored how tough it is when parents put children in the middle. Brittany put herself there when she exploded.

"How the fuck are you able to live with yourself?" Brittany screamed at her father. "How could you put my mother through this?" Her father sat and stared. Brittany asked whether he regretted his actions. Her mother began crying. "Hasn't she been through enough in her life?" Brittany said. "*She* doesn't deserve this." After a few minutes, Brittany's father rose and went downstairs. "It felt so good," says Brittany.

She saw her dad in the kitchen an hour later. "Thanks for letting me yell at you," she said.

"Thanks for letting me know how you feel," her father replied.

If Brittany had felt uncomfortable around her father when she pretended nothing was wrong, he had probably felt equally awkward around his daughter. "It was very freeing," says Brittany. "It helped me because Dad knew where I stood."

After an affair, we need to treat our feelings as we would in any confrontational situation. If you feel angry, then be angry. You don't have to put on a happy face. When you talk to a parent, don't go into the meeting hoping to convince your father to get back together with your mother or hoping your mother will apologize before the end of the hour. Your only goal is to share your feelings.

A parent isn't going to like what you have to say, but until you share your feelings, your relationship will remain stagnant. You can't heal until both of you know what you're suffering from. Try to listen to your mother or father as much as they're listening to you. Heed the following quote: "Fools think they need no advice, but the wise listen to others."

We're in a state of shock when our parents announce they're remarrying. We didn't expect they'd cheat, and we certainly didn't expect they'd marry the person with whom they cheated. The prospect is scandalous. Says one twenty-five-year-old woman, "I felt like I was in a TV movie."

Adult children often withhold support for a parent's relationship as punishment. They'll refuse to meet a parent's lover. To sit at a dinner table with our father and his mistress feels duplicitous. Not only are we betraying our mother by sitting next to the woman who caused her grief, but we're condoning Dad's behavior. Adult children struggle with wanting to maintain a relationship with a cheating parent while wanting to pretend his romantic life doesn't exist. Parents sometimes push a relationship with their new significant others on us. Parents are tired of their secret life. They want us to approve of their new lovers. Acceptance isn't so easy.

William's mother calls his father's mistress "the whore." William doesn't necessarily disagree. As far as he's concerned, "the whore" played a big part in breaking up his family five years ago. She works in the same school district as his mother. "I blame her," William says, of his father's girlfriend. "She knows who my mom is. She could have waited." Waited to move in on his father, that is. "This woman left her husband at a very similar time to when my Dad left," he says.

The first time William saw his father's mistress was in a bar a couple of years ago. His father and his cousins got together a few days after Christmas. His father had just returned from vacation in Key West. He pulled out a stack of pictures of him and his girlfriend on the beach. *Are you serious?* William thought to himself. His father passed the photos around the table. William refused to look at them. He didn't want to see this woman mugging for the camera in her bikini. He'd made it clear to his father he never wanted to see her, period.

Several months later, William went home again. He met his father at the same bar. After a beer and some sports talk, his father said, "When will you be ready to meet this woman?" William stared at his Miller Lite, thinking he'd need a few more before he'd feel ready to have this conversation. William was put off by his father's tone. *When will you be ready?* His father had cheated, and William was being made to feel childish. "Like I'm an eight-year-old scared to swim for the first time . . . like I am afraid to jump in the pool," William thought to himself. Now he was angry.

"It doesn't feel right for me," William told his father. "What do you want me to tell you?"

"Can you do it for me?" his father pleaded.

He couldn't. William felt that meeting her would lead his father to believe that what he did was OK. He wouldn't shake hands with a woman who had hurt him and spread rumors about his mother. His father's girlfriend wasn't welcome in his life. *She* was why he had to meet his father at bars when he visited home and why his father lived in a dingy apartment. It was her son whom his father took to Little League now.

Several weeks later, William's father called him and left a message. "I got engaged," his father said. William had known it was coming, but he didn't feel any less upset. "I assume Dad will invite my sister and me to the wedding," William says. "What will our presence mean? Does that mean we approve of the marriage?"

Initially, you may feel that a parent's lover single-handedly broke up your family. You'll forget that your mother or father played an active role in the seduction. You see what you're ready to see: you imagine your father's mistress as a cunning vixen who slept her way into your father's heart, tricked him into believing she was more exciting than his family, and manipulated him into lying. *She made my father this way*, you'll think. You picture your mother's beau as moving in on a lonely woman and promising her all the things your father never would. You blame *him* for all your parents' problems, even the conflicts that existed long before he was around.

When we first find out about an affair, adult children are convinced that the intimacy shared in infidelity is only temporary—an easy way out of a marriage—rather than an enduring love. Many of us are knocked unsteady when an adulterous parent chooses to continue an affair rather than repair an existing marriage. *You're going to choose a good screw over our family*, an adult child will think. Nothing is more disappointing. Coming to terms with a parent's infidelity and remarriage is like trying to understand the difference between a person who can pull the trigger and shoot someone and one who cannot.

Watching a parent remarry is tough enough. To see that person marry the person with whom he cheated is unimaginable. "I love this woman," Dad'll say, which stings. Dad fell in love secretly, which is why remarrying seems so bizarre. An adult child will find out about a parent's affair, and weeks or months later—poof!—Dad is remarried to his mistress. Our heads haven't had a chance to catch up to our racing hearts.

Parents sometimes remarry behind our backs, especially if we're not speaking to them. Even when they tell us about an upcoming wedding, they don't always invite us. Melinda, whose father had been cheating on her mother for more than a decade, didn't really want to go to her father's wedding. He was marrying his mistress, Lydia, whom Melinda, thirty-two, resented for breaking up her family. Even so, Melinda was upset when she didn't get an invitation. "I wanted the option to go," Melinda says. Melinda wanted to reject, not be rejected.

A parent may not invite an adult child who is unsupportive of the new relationship. Would you want someone against your marriage at your wedding? Probably not. But being excluded hurts anyway. Jessica's sister was invited to her father's small wedding ceremony in the Caribbean; her sister had kept in touch with her father by e-mail. Jessica only knew about the wedding because her sister told her about it. Jessica was disappointed her father didn't call to tell her he was getting married, let alone invite her. Jessica wasn't sure whether she should tell her mother. The sisters told their mother after the fact. They feared she'd find out from someone else. Ultimately, neither sister attended the ceremony.

If meeting your father's mistress feels strange, attending his wedding to her will feel even more so. You have to watch Dad make the very vows on which he turned his back. A wedding born from an affair seems like a joke, . . . *to have and to hold, from this day forward, for better, for worse, for richer, for poorer, in sickness or in health, to love and to cherish till death do us part. And hereto I pledge you my faithfulness.* You'll think your father is lip-synching. He cannot imagine we're going to believe those words—now.

Going to a parent's wedding takes courage. Nothing forces you to face the changes sweeping over your family more. Says one twenty-nine-year-old woman whose father married his mistress, "I went to the wedding. I sat in the back row, and I cried the entire time. I was trying to be the bigger person. I didn't think it could be real. It was like going to a grave site to finalize things in your head. I thought I would feel closure." A parent's wedding may finalize the end of your parents' marriage in your head, but your feelings will not dissipate afterward. Rather than giving us closure, a parent's wedding only dredges up a new set of circumstances to grieve.

You're witnessing a celebration of the relationship that tore your family apart. One thirty-nine-year-old woman said she forced herself to go to her father's wedding. He was marrying a younger coworker. At the reception, a toast was made to the bride and groom. "You've struggled so much to be together," someone said. The daughter rolled her eyes. She wanted to yell out that they had struggled because her father was married when they met. Their struggle entailed leaving their families behind to build new lives. How was this something to celebrate? They *both* cheated. She felt as if the toast reduced her parents' marriage to an obstacle to true love. The daughter stayed for the whole reception but left with a knot in her throat.

At some point, you're going to have to tell your betrayed parent about the wedding. If you don't, the parent will only hear it through the grapevine later and accuse you of keeping it from them. A betrayed parent may encourage you to attend a cheating parent's wedding. Inside, the betrayed parent may feel deserted. Your attendance is a slap in the face; Dad may understand, but he also feels as if you're supporting the very act that caused him such pain. Even watching you have a relationship with the parent who cheated is difficult for the betrayed parent. Says Jessica, "Mom is sort of happy I don't have a relationship with Dad. It would be tough for her."

When you feel as if you're ready to forgive a parent for his or her infidelity, your betrayed parent may not be ready for you to. Starting a relationship with the person with whom a parent cheated is threatening, too, especially for mothers who are used to being the only woman in their daughters' lives. Your mother might worry that this new woman will take you away from her. If your father's mistress stole your father away, why wouldn't she steal you, too?

If your mother sees you doing things with your stepmother that you used to do with her, she may feel replaced. This is true for any stepparent relationship, but the feelings are exacerbated when a parent marries the person with whom they cheated. The "other woman" stole your mother's life from her. It's a stretch to think your mother will ever accept Dad's lover. If you do, your mother is going to feel deserted. In this case, it's important to handle a parent as you would if your other parent hadn't cheated. Remind the betrayed parent that you're not replacing them. You're simply making the best of an awkward situation. Says one twenty-six-year-old woman, "I would like my dad to share his new life with me," even if that includes his new wife.

Melinda wasn't sure how her mother would react to her father's upcoming marriage to Lydia. She was less sure how her mother would handle her daughter's interest in her stepmother. Melinda decided to be up front and matter-of-fact. "Mommy," Melinda said, "I think developing a relationship with Daddy's wife is a good idea. It's unhealthy for me to keep on like this. She lives with Daddy now." Her mother didn't say anything. Melinda knew what her mother was thinking: *Will this woman take my place?*

Melinda says her mother was hurt that her daughter was choosing to get to know Lydia. "I wonder if Mom thought I was in solidarity with her," Melinda said, later. "Mom didn't want us to know Lydia. To befriend Lydia said we approved."

As Melinda and her stepmother grew close—they shared a love of shopping—Melinda says her mother was jealous. Melinda would walk in the door carrying bags of new clothes, and her mother would ask with whom she'd gone shopping. "Mommy," she'd say. "You know . . ." Melinda didn't want to have to say. Her mother had to accept that she was going to have a relationship with Lydia, and she shouldn't make Melinda feel guilty for it.

Lily, twenty-seven, was twenty-one when she found out her father was having an affair with a woman from work. He moved out of her childhood home and into an apartment with the woman. Lily was so angry he'd found a new family that she didn't talk to her father for a year. He didn't call Lily either. Lily's coworkers noticed her bad mood. Her supervisor talked with her about it during an annual review. Lily realized it was time to make up with her father. "I decided he was the only dad I had and I needed to have a relationship with him," she says. Almost two years after her parents' divorce, her father married the woman with whom he had been cheating. Lily decided to attend the wedding.

Lily didn't block out her anger. Therapists say erasing something from our minds temporarily never works. The issue will come back to haunt us. Lily accepted that she could be angry with her father and love him at the same time. Therapist Ian Birky says that many of us think anger is expressed by screaming and yelling and then slamming the door on our way out. Infidelity stirs up contradictions so complex that our reactions become equally complicated. You can say, "I love you even though I'm angry." Says Birky, "You can have both emotions at the same time."

The same lesson applies to Lily's stepmother. As Lily got to know her stepmother, she realized she kind of liked her. "I just can't let myself think about the role she played in the downfall of my family," Lily says. A stepparent remains a fixture on holidays and get-togethers. Sooner or later, you'll call each other "Judy" or "Jeff"—not the one who broke up my family. As with anything else, it will take time.

Lily learned that her mother needed time to get used to the idea that her daughter liked her stepmother. At first, Lily felt as if she had to hide the relationship from her mother. Then her mother met a man and fell in love. With her mother more stable, Lily talked more openly about her stepmother. Her mother became jealous when Lily got married. Lily's father offered to pay for the wedding. Because he was writing the checks, Lily planned much of the ceremony and reception with her father, which meant her stepmother helped, too.

The planning was good bonding time for Lily, her father, and stepmother. But Lily's mother had little say in her daughter's wedding. She wasn't going to drive around with her daughter and her husband's mistress to help find a reception hall. Says Lily, "Mom felt left out."

Our own romantic relationships seem less certain when our parents' marriage fails. Almost all of our romantic cues come from watching our parents interact over the years. We assume that our parents' marriage is strong. If we act as our parents did, we will have equally fulfilling relationships. We'd like to believe that the love between our parents is bigger than any problem. After an affair, we see our parents reduced to baser urges and impulses.

When a parent cheats, the lessons learned aren't encouraging. We realize that we can never know what's really going on in someone's head and heart. A person may say one thing and do another. No one can be trusted. These are all damaging, cynical thoughts for a young adult searching for a soul mate. Says psychiatrist Frank Pittman, author of *Private Lies,* "Children who experience secrecy and lies cannot trust what they are told; they become insecure and dependent. When the framework of the family finally collapses, there may be no honest relationship to fall back on."

Adult children feel less innocent going into relationships, as if their parent's affair marked them in some way. We worry that telling someone why our parents divorced makes us less desirable. Do people assume that we'll cheat, too? Says one twenty-nine-year-old man, his dad's affair "reflects poorly on me as a potential mate. It's something I can't help, but it's there."

Marisa, twenty-four, was studying abroad in London when she found out her father had an affair. A few weeks later, her boyfriend back in Chicago wrote her an e-mail. He'd cheated, too. "I can't trust my father," Marisa thought. "I can't trust my boyfriend. Screw men. I'm done." Marisa says she started going out more and spending the night at the apartment of strangers. She wouldn't have sex with them. "I'm going to reject them before they can reject me," Marisa told herself.

A few months later, Marisa returned to college in Chicago, where she started dating Ron. Marisa had been friends with Ron for a long time before they got serious. A year later, they moved in together. Marisa thinks Ron's "the one," but she worries about infidelity. "I'm more like my Dad than my Mom," Marisa says. "What if I do the same thing Dad did? I'm so scared that I'll hurt someone the way Dad hurt Mom." Ron's parents divorced a few years before Marisa's. Ron's dad also cheated. Says Marisa, "I feel loved by him and secure. It's the best relationship I've ever been in . . ." But.

The fact that one of them might cheat at any point worries them. Neither of them wants to be with anyone else, but someday they might. Thinking ahead is like a defense mechanism. If they expect adultery, maybe it won't hurt as much as last time.

The two joke often about infidelity. "You've got to get out of here before my other girlfriend comes over," Ron will say. Sometimes their fears turn serious. One night Marisa ran to Target for a quick shopping errand and left her cell phone at home. Ron called her six times. When she got home, her phone rang again. "Where were you?" Ron demanded. "Were you out with some other guy?" Marisa laughed and said she was at Target. Then Ron laughed, too. "But there was something in his voice that made me think he was serious," she says. "He was worried."

Studies that have attempted to determine whether children are more likely to cheat if their parents do are inconclusive. Therapists skirt around the issue. Most say adult children may react in one of two ways: a parent's affair opens up the door or slams it shut. Maybe adult children have fantasies of being with someone else in their own relationship, but they've been controlling their wandering eye. Birky says as long as a child holds on to a belief that a parent is virtuous, the child feels he can remain under control, too. But if a parent breaks away from that image and cheats, an adult child will feel as if all is lost. The child's beliefs don't feel so strong anymore. "Then you think, 'Mom gave in to her urges. How do I not give in to mine?'" says Birky.

Pittman says that adult children can be so disgusted by a parent's infidelity that they often go out of their way to act completely the opposite way. They are extremely faithful to their spouses. Fidelity becomes as much a part of their identity as is their nationality.

Nearly every adult child interviewed feared that a significant other might cheat on them after finding out about a parent's affair. "This is normal," says Fay. "You're thinking about affairs more. It's in your consciousness." If your mother cheated, you might have learned that every time she said she was going to the store, she was really sneaking off to a local motel. When your husband says he's going to the store, how can you not wonder what that means? Your cheating parent showed that you really have to watch someone's behaviors. *Is my husband leading the same double life my father did?*

Brittany was engaged to a man when she found out her father was having an affair with a woman in Arizona. Her father told her, "Not all men do this." But Brittany no longer had any idea who was capable of cheating and who wasn't. She never thought her father could, and he did. "It made me instantly paranoid," says Brittany. If her fiancé came home late from class, she'd wonder whether he ever actually went to class. She'd think, "Was he really late from work, or was he somewhere else? Who is he talking to on the computer?" Brittany didn't confront her fiancé; she knew her fears were unwarranted. But she couldn't control her worries. Ultimately, Brittany broke off her engagement because she didn't feel ready.

Adult children with cheating parents can act extremely possessive in their relationships. They may check in with a significant other constantly. They might track the sites their partners have visited on the Internet. Being vigilant is smart, but hypervigilance can scare a partner away. A significant other may feel watched and suffocated. Some partners walk away.

Many more partners try to help us work through our fears. Jessica, whose father was the attorney who cheated with his secretary, was married for several years before her father left. Still, Jessica says, she suddenly started worrying about her husband—even though they'd been happily married from the start. "If it can happen to your parents," Jessica says, "it can happen to anyone." She says she'd often ask her husband for reassurance, which therapists say is a healthy way to cope. "I could never just walk away from my wife and kids," her husband would tell her. Jessica couldn't hear it enough.

A parent's affair may temporarily prompt feelings of insecurity in our own relationships. It will also teach us about the underbelly of relationships—the dark secrets that no one shares with us before we marry. The illusion of the perfect relationship is broken, says Birky. "They're able to see what real life is." An affair forces us to grow up a bit. We're wiser. And we'll approach our own relationships with more savvy and finesse. *No one is going to trick me!*

What if your husband did cheat on you? Would you take him back? We expect a parent always to walk away after infidelity. Sometimes the parent doesn't, and that can also be disappointing. Many of us find out a parent knew about the other's indiscretions and believed he or she wouldn't do it again. Parents who tell their kids they should leave a cheating partner seem like frauds.

Brittany, whose father was cheating with a woman in Arizona, said her mother always told her daughter she shouldn't accept a man who cheats. Her mother said if Brittany's father ever cheated, she'd leave him. But when her mother learned about her father's affairs, she told Brittany she wanted to work it out. "We've been together twenty-three years," her mother said. "I can't imagine life without him." Not only did her father disappoint Brittany; her mother did, too. What kind of an example was her mother setting? She seemed pathetic—not the strong woman Brittany thought she was. "It was like she was desperately clinging to him, saying, 'Please stay. Please, please stay,'" says Brittany.

Brittany made a point to tell her husband she'd act differently. She didn't want him to think he had license to cheat. "I would never put up with that," she told him. "If you cheat, I'm out." Her husband is frustrated by the situation. He feels as if Brittany's father's affair somehow cast him in a negative light. He told Brittany that he's afraid there will never be a time when he comes home even an hour late without her questioning him, which makes him resentful of his wife's family. "She's always going to think I'm out with another woman," he says.

It's reasonable for a significant other who hasn't experienced infidelity to grow frustrated with our insecurities. They may be entering the relationship idealistic, whereas we come in cynical and broken. If you worry about your partner every time he or she leaves the house, you've probably developed a distrust in all relationships, not just your own—and it's not going to feel good to date you. Imagine if your boyfriend or girlfriend interrogated you every time you arrived home. You'd feel as if you were always suspected of doing something wrong. You might try working with a therapist. Making sense of your parent's indiscretion may bring you and your partner closer together. More important, you'll learn to trust again.

Try to think of the biggest mistake you've made involving family. Mine is easy. When I was twelve, I sat reading in a rocking chair in my living room. My younger sister Chelsea was six at the time. A hyperactive six. She kept jumping on my lap. She wanted to hug me. I wanted to read. "Leave me alone," I yelled at her, pushing her away. Chelsea tumbled to the ground and knocked her head on the rocking chair leg. She was bleeding. We rushed her to the emergency room. She needed several stitches. When Mom narrowed her eyes at me, I knew I'd messed up big-time.

Chelsea still tells this story. We laugh about it, but the emotions are real, even though I didn't intend to hurt her. At the time, she felt as if I didn't love her, so I felt as if I had to spend the rest of our childhood making it up to her. She may carry a lingering bit of resentment, but today, we're best friends.

Healing after a parent has cheated is a bit like this. You coexist knowing the past is laced with hurt, and you grow closer despite it. A parent cannot take back his behavior. You cannot erase what the parent has done. You don't have to accept the affair to move on. You simply intermingle love and anger, merging both emotions into your relationship.

You may *never* forgive a cheating parent. You may always harbor some resentment toward him. Therapists say if you try to heal prematurely, you may act nice and happy toward a parent, but inside, you'll feel as you always did. "Do you need to forgive a parent who cheats?" says Laurel Fay. "You may want to make it better and have it all go away. Maybe there are some things that will never be OK."

When Jessica took her ten-year-old daughter to church for her first confession, Jessica ducked into a confessional herself. Something was bothering her. Jessica had been raised to follow the Ten Commandments, but she felt as if she couldn't follow one: *Honor your father and your mother.* "How do you honor a father making such poor choices?" she'd wondered on her way to church. In the booth, Jessica found a visiting Italian priest who didn't know her, which was a relief. Her eyes welled up with tears. "Father, I'm having a really hard time. I'm breaking a commandment," Jessica said. She told the priest about her father's affair and how angry she was at him. The priest quieted her. "We need to talk about forgiveness," he said.

And so we begin. Forgiving a parent for cheating—and a parent's lover for tearing your family apart—will probably be one of the greatest challenges of your life. And yet you must forgive a little if you want a relationship with one of the people whom you cherish most. At confession that day, the Italian priest told Jessica she needed to forgive her father for herself. Until she let go of her anger, she'd find herself emotionally frozen. If telling her father she forgives him means condoning his behavior, the priest said, then don't tell him. "Forgiveness is for you," the priest said.

To find forgiveness, you might consider the following points:

- *A cheating parent may never apologize.* As much as we dream of a parent's sitting us down and saying that they are sorry, they probably never will. The parent may not beg for our forgiveness. Your mother or father knows cheating is shameful. Parents knew what they were doing when they started an affair, and they were willing to live with themselves. In their eyes, they did what they needed to do in order to make themselves happy. An adulterous parent may be sorry that a son or daughter was caught up in the lies surrounding an affair. But the parent isn't going to apologize for falling in love and marrying a new spouse. Says Fay, "A parent feels like an apology is saying I wish it didn't happen. They don't feel that way. The affair helped them out of the marriage."

Fay adds that it isn't a bad thing when a parent doesn't apologize. The parent is giving you an honest response, which is what you're asking for.

- *A parent didn't intend to hurt you.* Our parents were happy when they ran down the aisle hand in hand on their wedding day. Who could've predicted that in twenty-five years, they'd be lying next to their spouse but craving someone else's affection? When they commit adultery, parents don't consider the feelings of a child, especially an adult child. They feel guilty later only because they love us so much.

- *Your parents' problems were not caused by a cheating parent's lover.* A parent cheats because something in his or her marriage isn't right. Your mother and father should have had an honest conversation about their marriage. Instead, they stayed together and one parent took the easy way out. If your mother and father had a perfect marriage, neither would be looking to shack up with someone else. A parent's lover is the outcome of your parents' discontent; that person didn't initiate the unhappiness.

Your stepparent didn't seduce your mother or father with the intention of breaking up your family. Your mother or father played a role in this relationship, too. You don't know what your parent said to get this person to date them while your parent was married. One adult child found out that her father had lied to her stepmother and told her he was separated for the first several months of their relationship. The young woman saw her stepmother differently after that. It's easy to blame someone we don't care about, but a stepparent isn't always the guilty party.

- *Like it or not, your parent's lover is often here to stay.* Your mother or father fell in love with someone else. It's unfortunate, but it happened, and now you have to deal with it. The longer you hate this man or woman, the more estranged you'll become from your parent. You can meet your father's mistress and start down the long road toward accepting her or refuse to be around her and risk losing a relationship with your father. It's your choice, but you should make that choice knowing you have to live with the outcomes. Says one twenty-seven-year-old woman who hasn't spoken to her father because of his cheating, "I have this little hole in my heart."

- *Happy endings are possible.* The possibility that you might actually like the woman with whom your father cheated may initially seem crazy. But as the reality of your situation sinks in, you may decide you want a relationship with the new spouse after all. Emotions will subside. You'll stop seeing that person as a home wrecker and instead start seeing him as a parent's spouse.

Take Melinda. She blamed her father's new wife, Lydia, for breaking up her family and avoided being around her. Everything about Lydia rubbed Melinda the wrong way. Lydia was uneducated. She wore high heels and painted her face with makeup.

Melinda would go to her father's home and ignore Lydia. Lydia started sending Melinda care packages filled with candy. When Melinda graduated from college and moved home, Melinda was forced to see her stepmother more frequently. One day, Lydia stopped Melinda in the hallway. "I love your father," Lydia said, "and I love your sisters, and I don't know why you don't let me love you."

Melinda was touched. The moment sparked an epiphany on Melinda's part. This woman was a mother, too. She'd been through her own divorce. Melinda was tired of being so angry. "This isn't her fault," thought Melinda. "My father did this. Dad is the one who left. Dad is the one who found someone new." She'd been blaming her stepmother when she should have been blaming her father.

Now that Melinda accepts her stepmother, she has developed a wonderful relationship with her. "She's like a second mom," says Melinda. "Only I can tell her things I can't tell my mom." The two talk often about Melinda's sex life, which is something she'd never feel comfortable discussing with her own mother. They go shopping together. When adult children are ready to heal, we find the smallest pieces of a person to which to attach ourselves. Plus, Melinda couldn't ignore her father's happiness.

Melinda still grieves. Sometimes she gets angry. There will always be a longing for what was. But accepting her stepmother has helped her feel less twisted inside. Says Melinda, "In the end, I've found there are so many more people to love."

Points to Remember

- Infidelity taints who a parent is to us. It's normal to stop trusting your parent and wonder whether *any* of his or her actions are true.

- When you're ready to talk to a parent about his or her infidelity, try to go in with a cool head. Think about what he or she has done to hurt you and be careful of what you say in the heat of the moment.

- Finding out your parent has been cheating may cause you to reevaulate your childhood. Don't let a parent's indiscretion spoil the good times you've spent with them.

- Sometimes parents deny they're cheating for fear that their children will look at them differently. An affair is selfish, so parents may try to save face.

- Initially, you may feel as if a parent's lover single-handedly broke up your family. Remember that your parent played an active role in the seduction.

- It's normal to feel ashamed or humiliated by a parent's behavior. Your parent didn't just cheat on you; he cheated on the family.

- Don't allow a parent to confide in you about his or her infidelity. The burden is too heavy to shoulder, and you will betray your other parent by keeping such a big secret.

- Our own romantic relationships sometimes seem less certain when our parents' marriage fails. You may consider therapy to help you learn to trust again.

7

Love Can Last

> I looked at older couples and saw, at best, mutual tolera-
> tion. I imagined a lifetime of loveless nights and bicker-
> ing days and could not imagine subjecting myself or
> someone else to such a fate.
>
> —KENT NERBURN, *Simple Truths*

M OM AND I ARE STRETCHED OUT ON LOUNGE CHAIRS at the beach. It's August 2003. The sun is high even though it is 5:00 p.m. and most people have packed up and left. Erin and Chelsea rode their bikes back to our hotel on this tiny New England island an hour ago. Mom and I are the only ones who like to stay on the beach all day. I read. Mom closes her eyes and thinks. We have sporadic conversations. A half hour before, Mom told me she had reconnected with a man with whom she was in love as a teenager. She was giddy when she spoke. Then I went back to reading my book.

"You and John have a good relationship, right?" Mom says. I'm surprised by the question. I put down my book and sit up. Mom and I don't usually talk about things such as this. I'll tell her something John and I did, or I'll mention something funny he said. But we don't generally analyze my relationship with him. I don't want Mom to know too much about us. I fear she'll find a hole—a reason why my relationship might fail.

Mom is an expert at picking out unhappy couples. Her views on men are cynical. She once told my older sister that every man has the capability to cheat and that it's the men from whom you least expect it who eventually do. Erin swore to herself that her husband never would, but the conversation gave her doubts. I have my own doubts. I've had regular nightmares about John since Mom and Dad split. It's always the same scenario. John and I are out at a bar or a club, and I look over and he's talking intimately with someone else. When I confront him, he says things he'd never say in real life. "I'm just not in love with you anymore," or "You and I are over."

I wake up from these dreams scared that John is going to change his mind about me the way Mom changed hers about Dad.

John and I have always been a happy couple. We don't have big fights. We like to act silly and have deep conversations. Unlike my parents, we get along really well. We had been together five years when Mom and Dad broke up. Early on, I was needy, so I latched onto him. I never wanted us to be apart, even though I wasn't much fun to be around. We'd go out to dinner on a Friday night, and before we got our drinks, I'd start crying about a fight I'd had with Mom. If he went out with his friends and didn't invite me, I'd take offense. *Is he trying to get away from me?*

Nothing in our relationship changed when my parents split. But deep inside, my perception of love did. I've never been the kind of girl who dreamed about being married. I only wanted to find the kind of eternal love I'd heard about in fairy tales. When John walked into my math class in college, I was instantly attracted to him. He was different from other boys I'd met: his cocoa skin shined like silk, and when he smiled, his teeth glowed like white pearls. I remember calling Mom after our first date my sophomore year of college. "He said he loves the way *I think*," I'd said. Most boys were annoyed by how much I overanalyzed people and situations.

By the time my parents split, John and I were deeply entrenched in each other's lives. We were dating, but we seemed married. We had keys to each other's apartments. We had a dog. We talked about our life plans and dreamed about which cities we wanted to live in and what vacations we'd take after he finished dental school. We came up with scratchy and haggard voices to imitate how we'd sound when we were old. All of our plans included each other. Though Mom's question makes me uneasy.

"Do we have a good relationship?" I say. "Yeah—we do. Why?" *I am always happy with John,* I think. It's only when I let "what-ifs" infiltrate my heart that I grow anxious and begin to question my relationship. I've always believed that he was the man with whom I was meant to be. But since my parents split up, our lives together seemed less certain. I looked for things wrong in our relationship. If we bickered about something, the conflict began to feel a lot bigger than it had before. Every argument seemed like the beginning of *our* end. *Is this a reason why our love won't last?*

I knew that John and I didn't have serious problems. Still, I couldn't help but wonder, if Mom and Dad couldn't make it, why should I believe that John and I could? My parents thought they would stay together forever when they were twenty-seven and idealistic about what life brings, too. Now their lawyers were splitting up their assets.

I glance at Mom, who is staring at a sailboat in the distance.

"Why did you want to know?" I ask.

"No reason," Mom says. "Do you think you'll get married any-time soon?"

"Maybe," I say. Many of my friends are engaged. I'm too scared to get married. To be legally bound means, if things don't work out, we'll have to be legally unbound. Marriage seemed to change relationships. It made people take each other for granted and have unrealistic expectations of each other. John and I had a good thing going. Why ruin it?

"You know, lots of my friends envy our relationship," I say, suddenly feeling as if I need to convince Mom that John and I are nothing like her and Dad. "We have the kind of connection everyone wants. I cannot imagine my life without him."

I want to talk with her about other things—such as how much I fear that divorce will surprise John and me down the road, how I can possibly believe love lasts even though hers didn't. I fear she'll think I'm blaming her for my anxiety, and I don't want to get into an argument. So I say nothing.

My mind is flooded with images: John in a tux at the altar. Smiling faces staring up at me as I walk down the aisle. A priest nodding me on. Then I remember Mom throwing a phone book at Dad. I think about how Dad's face looked when he'd get flushed with anger or the way Dad's eyes fell when Mom put him down. I'd hear Mom crying in her bedroom after a fight.

I couldn't think about choosing the flowers or a reception hall without thinking about the possibility of screaming and fighting.

Walking down the aisle was like walking off a cliff. In a lacy dress with a veil covering my face, I imagined turning my back on the priest and facing the crowd gathered in the church. "How do you get married when you know most marriages fail?" I'd yell.

"How do you believe in love when your parents stopped loving each other?"

Adult children face an overwhelming realization after their parents divorce: love isn't always blissful. It is complicated. After kids and jobs and worries about money, you can fall out of love as quickly as you fell into it. You can say "I love you" your whole life, but it doesn't mean you'll feel it. *Dad told Mom he loved her on Christmas*, we think. *By Valentine's Day, he was gone.*

Few of us would call our mothers and fathers romantics. Before they divorced, you probably saw your mother buy your father the same boring sweater every Christmas. Maybe your dad dutifully brought home roses every other Valentine's Day. Parents are hardly the googly-eyed twenty-somethings they were when they met. As adult children, we sense the spark has faded between our parents, but we assume they feel a deep, enduring love anyway. We tell ourselves that love *looks* different when you're older. Just because Mom doesn't stare longingly into Dad's eyes doesn't mean her heart doesn't swell with love when she sees him.

We assume that parents were magically drawn to each other when they met years ago—that their love lasted because they found the perfect person the first time around. As children, we are unconsciously wrapped up in how fate brought our parents together. Think about how much you loved hearing your parents talk about the first time they met.

Even as an adult, I'd ask Mom questions about that night in 1974 when she saw my father playing guitar onstage in a bar. "He came up to me," Mom would say. "He was trying to act really cool, and he asked me if I wanted to go out sometime. I was actually on my way out of town to see a man I'd met in the Caribbean. . . ." The story made me giggle. I'd picture my father sauntering up to Mom, who was sitting on a bar stool. I'd imagine Mom shyly blowing him off at first. I loved when Mom softened. She'd say my father's persistence won her over and she finally agreed to go out with him.

Nothing was more romantic. This story was the beginning of my parents, which meant it was the beginning of me. Ten minutes in a bar became a moment that created life the way I knew it. It was serendipity.

Divorce diminishes any romantic visions we may have of our parents' love. You learn that feelings change over time. Long-term intimacy doesn't seem like such a guarantee. "Your parents' marriage is your first imprint of love," says Julia Stone, a marriage and family therapist in Falls Church, Virginia. "They are your universe. If they don't love each other forever, then the universe feels like it's on shifting sands."

From the time we're young children, we're told stories of true love. Disney alone may have defined our earliest romantic notions. Take *Cinderella, Snow White, Sleeping Beauty,* and *Beauty and the Beast.* Each cartoon centers around a young maiden finding the man of her dreams, the perfect match who brings her grand happiness. Each cartoon has the same romantic premise: when you meet your perfect match, the two of you will live in bliss for the rest of your lives. True love solves all problems and is bigger than anything we've ever experienced. Even in our twenties, stories all around us fuel our need for romantic inspiration. Movies feature men chasing women down for a passionate kiss; books such as *Bridget Jones's Diary* and *The Girls' Guide to Hunting and Fishing* became chick-lit classics on the notion.

Twenty-somethings need to believe in love. Shuffling from one apartment with roommates to the next, we want to know that one day we'll find someone with whom to buy the fluffy couch and dishware. We want someone with whom to read the paper and sip coffee on Sunday mornings. Many of us share a similar dream for the future: white picket fence, giggling children, dashingly handsome husband or adorable wife.

We are young enough to believe in soul mates. We are old enough to conjure up romantic visions of locking eyes with the cute guy at the drugstore and falling in love at first sight, or asking a girl to dance at the bar and leaving knowing you've met your future wife. Those of us who are married strive to feel as if everything with our partners is as fresh as the day we met. We want our hearts to race and our knees to get wobbly every time we see our significant others, just the way it happens in the movies. It's why I've always loved the popular quote "Once in a while, right in the middle of an ordinary life, loves gives us a fairy tale."

And yet all of it—the wobbly knees, meeting your soul mate, and the white picket fence—feels stale after parents split up. The fairy tale ends. You continue to search for your one true love, but you enter relationships filled with doubt. Being head over heels in love with someone doesn't mean as much anymore. You think, *Mom and Dad thought they had it, too. Didn't they?* Therapist Laurel Fay says adult children's definition of love is hazy after their parents' divorce. "They think, 'Wait, this is the foundation I built my life on,'" Fay says. But the foundation is buckling. Adult children have trouble reconciling what their parents taught them about love and what the realities are behind the emotion.

Lara, twenty-five, didn't date in high school; she was intimidated by boys. But she often talked to her mother about falling in love. "You need to find someone opposite from you so it works," her mother would say. "His strengths will pick up on your weaknesses." Her mother used her own marriage as an example. Lara put her parents' relationship on a pedestal.

Lara fell in love for the first time when she was twenty-three. She'd had other suitors. But with her mother's voice in her head, Lara had a mental checklist she'd go through with every guy she met. Unless they fit the right criteria—opposites, similar values—she didn't give them a chance. "For so long, I was trapped," Lara says. "I thought my parents had it perfect. I was searching for that same perfection." When her parents divorced, much to Lara's surprise, she didn't know what perfection meant anymore. She was angry with her mother. "I felt like I'd been lied to," she says. So she started allowing herself to date different kinds of guys, which is how she met the guy with whom she fell in love. Now Lara realizes she had no idea what love was supposed to look like. She's still figuring it out. All of the relationship advice her mother had given her over the years seemed feeble; her mother and father hadn't truly been in love for years.

Marisa, twenty-four, found herself redefining what love meant to her after her parents divorced. She'd always envisioned herself getting married and having kids. "I'd find my soul mate," she says. Marisa dreamed of finding a man who would make her as happy as her father made her mother; she'd always believed her parents were destined to be together.

After her parents split up, Marisa developed a more simplified view of love. The idea that she was meant to be with one person suddenly seemed naive. "I believe there are right people for different points in your life," Marisa says. "I no longer believe in soul mates."

As a culture, so many of us want to think that there is one person with whom we're meant to be. Monogamy is the heart of our romantic mythology. Films such as *Sleepless in Seattle* and *You've Got Mail* perpetuate the idea. In a March 2004 article in *Jane*, Meg Ryan, who is divorced, says, "The romantic mythology is that there is such a thing as happily ever after . . . and that you'll find a guy who's gonna give that to you. We don't question that mythology." When parents split up, adult children find themselves trying to make sense of a broken myth. Long-term monogamy isn't so romantic when you watch your parents weasel their way out of it.

The idea that we're fated to be with one person brings us a certain level of security. *When I find that person, I'll never be alone again,* we think. Parents shake up our worlds when they divorce. Previous chapters illustrated how abandoned adult children feel by their parents. To believe there is someone out there who will help us feel anchored again would be a relief, which is why adult children worry about their love life after parents split. There is a lot more to lose. If our own relationships don't work out, we no longer have our parents to fall back on as a default. Sometimes we abandon our fantasies about love and approach romance more practically. Says one thirty-eight-year-old woman about her twenty-eight-year-old sister, "She has become more critical of men, to the point where she's not dating at all. It's almost as if she's thinking, 'Why bother?' "

Joel, twenty-three, has come to see romance as silly—a fleeting, childish emotion that is hardly the basis for love. He's felt this way since high school, a time when his parents fought incessantly. He believes his parents' marriage failed because his father wanted to feel the adolescent thrill of falling in love. After his parents divorced, his father moved in with a woman named Kathy. He calls Joel to talk about how in love he is. "She completes my soul," his father will say. "You need to find a woman who loves you more than she loves herself." Joel says he rolls his eyes if his father preaches about intimacy. "My father has unrealistic expectations of love," Joel says. "Love doesn't mean you just sit and stare into each other's eyes."

From watching his father, Joel fears relying on romantic love to define a relationship. "The romantic view is selfish," he says. Romance is nice, Joel says, but it's too sappy and sentimental to sustain long-term love. Love poems won't get you through the tough times. Since his parents split, Joel has changed the way he meets girls. He ignores the ones to whom he's most attracted physically. He looks for women who stand out mentally. A woman who makes his heart go pitter-patter is dangerous. To Joel, romance is an illusion of love— not the real thing.

Adult children's definitions of love come from watching their parents interact when the children were growing up. We are unconscious anthropologists, immersed in our families but also observing the behaviors around us. Our attitudes are intertwined with theirs like a Christmas tree laced with lights; we are separate entities that exist together. Earlier, I discussed how hard it is to understand how one parent stops loving the other—a distressing reality of divorce. What's interesting is that sometimes the loss is so great that we deny it altogether.

In an effort to preserve a piece of the romantic mythology with which we're raised, adult children may continue to believe that their parents still love each other, even if their parents fought their way through a hard and nasty divorce. We counter our doubts about love by writing them off. *A marriage may end*, we think, *but love is unbreakable*. Parents sometimes fuel these ideas.

Dad always told me he'd love my mother—no matter what happened between them. I took solace in his words. As long as Dad always cared for Mom, I knew he'd always feel connected to us as a family. If Mom got sick, Dad might help me care for her. I didn't feel so alone. More important, Dad's saying he *would* always love Mom meant that Dad *had* always loved her. His feelings hadn't changed. It was easier for me to understand that my parents' marriage wasn't working than it was to accept that Mommy and Daddy didn't love each other anymore.

Therapist Julia Stone says the distinction is important. Adult children will always see their parents as a duo. In your psyche, she says, your mother and father are always together. This isn't so odd. They raised you side by side; you'll continue to imagine them that way. If parents divorce, the idea that they are a pair is taken away from you—unless you can somehow salvage their broken love.

That's why we need to believe parents still love each other. They can abandon each other, divorce, and remarry other people, but if you believe they'll always hold a soft spot for the other, you can always hold them together in your heart. In other words, not having to separate Mom and Dad in your mind tricks you into feeling that love isn't so trifling. Their love never changed; their marital problems only got too big. It's unhealthy to hold on to this notion too long. In doing so, you're not facing reality. But it's easy to understand why we do: we are comforted by the idea that our parents will remain a part of each other's lives.

Divorce shows us all the ways marriages go wrong. Sometimes parents fall out of love; sometimes they just grow apart. They develop different dreams. Individuals you expect to hurt each other least have the power to hurt each other most. Knowing what to expect is hard for any newlywed. No one tells us that there will be good years and bad years—that marriage might mean settling for good enough. We often hear about the beginnings and the endings of people's lives, little about the in-between.

Everyone takes a leap of faith when they marry. But the jump feels a lot riskier when you know firsthand how terrible relationships can feel. Every time you visit your childhood home, you see the leftovers of a marriage undone: Mom's refrigerator is nearly empty; she cooks only for herself. Dad's dresser is being used as a de facto filing cabinet; his belongings are at his girlfriend's.

When parents divorce, a door to the past swings open. We find out that times we thought were happy were riled with tension. Times we thought Mom and Dad made up after an argument turned out to be another example of postponed resentment. Looking at your parents' relationship with an enlightened set of eyes makes their marriage feel like a tornado. Discontent was spinning inside them for a long time. You have trouble distinguishing the good parts of their marriage from the bad. Both blend together in one confused mess.

Therapists say parental divorce shatters an adult child's idea that marriage is a utopian state. This sounds almost silly. Television shows and movies love to poke fun at the glum marital households dotting suburbia. But most adult children believe marriage connects their parents in a way even we cannot understand. Dull domesticity in late life is considered comfortable cohabitation. Parents don't need sweet nothings or active sex lives. They have retirement packages, beach houses, and tee times.

Rather than looking forward to a time when we'll hop on the road in an RV with our spouse, we worry that old age will bring us bad fortune as it did our parents. Our views on marriage become cynical. Do we spend twenty years with someone for nothing? We wonder what the point is in beginning something we're not sure we'll finish. Says one twenty-seven-year-old woman, "I realized there was never a point where you could think, 'We've been married long enough that we are safe.' "

The statistics are against us. Half of all marriages end in divorce—a number that never really caught my attention until my parents split up. I always wrote off divorce as something that happened to somebody else. When your parents are happily married, you have no reason to question the institution of marriage—no reason to doubt that your own future marriage won't last. When parents split up, you start taking note when friends complain about their young relationships. Every magazine you flip through seems to have an article related to divorce. Uncles divorce their wives; friends leave their husbands. Divorce begins to feel inevitable. *Is marital discontent as ubiquitous as sliced bread?*

Carly, thirty-eight, was living in Chicago and working as a flight attendant when her parents split up. They put her family home up for sale. The only explanation she got was in what she saw: they had seemed miserable in each other's company for a long time. When Carly went home to pack up her things at her childhood home—she was twenty-eight at the time—her parents weren't speaking.

Watching her parents divorce made Carly hesitant to marry. She'd been with her boyfriend, Keith, for seven years by then. They lived together. Family members kept asking when they'd get engaged. The last thing Carly wanted to do was walk down the aisle. "When you see a bad marriage," she says, "you don't want to rush into *any* marriage."

As the years went on, Carly's fears of marriage deepened. Keith applied to law school, which was a good excuse for her to put off an engagement; he'd be too busy for her, and they wouldn't have much money to pay for a wedding. Carly was scared that getting hitched would change things between them. Keith wasn't in a rush either; his parents had split up when he was young. "For me, marriage was something that wasn't worth going through," says Carly. "What's the point when things could change?" Making their relationship official, Carly adds, "only makes things more complicated if someday we want to split up."

Moving in together is the first logical step for the marriage-weary. It's a way to feel rooted without feeling pinned down. We might have been less inclined to experiment with cohabitation before our parents split. Maybe we would've jumped right into marriage. After their divorce, moving in together seems like the safest bet. Parents often suggest it; moving in together is engaging in a "tester marriage." Some therapists say it isn't always such a good idea. Couples who cohabitate before marriage divorce in disproportionately higher numbers. Many marry because they're afraid to turn back—not because they're right for each other.

In May 2003, I decided I was tired of living apart from John. I missed him during the week; we lived forty-five minutes away from each other. Friends and family wanted to know whether something was wrong in our relationship. We'd been together seven years and still lived in different cities. Everyone feared I was wasting my time, like an old maid waiting for a ring. I was too chicken even to encourage John to propose. I liked us the way we were.

I did, however, need to feel more committed. Moving in together had great symbolic importance. It announced to the world we were serious about our relationship. I called family members with the news. "John and I are moving in together!" I'd said. It was as if I were announcing our engagement. The step felt that big.

It's naive to think that reciting marital vows somehow solidifies two persons' feelings. It's equally silly to think that those vows somehow ruin a relationship, which is exactly what I'd come to believe after my parents divorced. I attended numerous weddings in my midtwenties. I was rarely touched by the fanfare. Instead, I'd feel depressed. Weddings seemed like a joke.

Therapist Julia Stone, fifty, says her parents' divorce made her more realistic about marriage. Stone's parents divorced when she was twenty. "I didn't care about some big fancy wedding," says Stone. She didn't want to pretend she had a perfect marriage if she didn't. It was a way to protect herself, she says. If she expected less, she'd be pleasantly surprised if her marriage delivered more. "I was less interested in faking it," Stone says. "I wanted to know about relationships—warts and all."

Choosing a life partner around the time your parents divorce is overwhelming. Before, you were looking for someone who met your current needs. The adult child with recently divorced parents thinks more about the future. *Will this person please me twenty years from now? Will this person rob me of my lifestyle?*

One of the most dramatic parts of a divorce is watching parents sell their belongings and split their assets. It's difficult to see a parent who used to have a summer home living alone in a crammed one-bedroom apartment. Fears for our financial future play a role in our fears of divorce. Says one twenty-two-year-old woman, "I would've never thought of signing a prenuptial agreement before. It's planning for your divorce, and it's cynical. But now going through all of this stuff with Dad, I wonder if you need one."

As a generation, we've embraced marriage more than our parents did. In the late 1990s, demographer Pamela Paul noticed an interesting trend. Unlike our mothers, who dreamed of careers and independence, Generation Xers dreamed of domesticity. Forget Murphy Brown. We wanted to be Donna Reed. In a 1999 poll by a national market research firm, 57 percent of Gen Xers said they "would like to see a return to more traditional standards of marriage." We don't want to juggle home, family, and career as our parents did. We want to be there for our children in all of the ways in which our busy parents couldn't be there for us.

As a generation, we're also believers in divorce. Paul's book *The Starter Marriage and the Future of Matrimony* cites a 2001 survey by the Centers for Disease Control and Prevention stating that one in five first marriages ends in divorce within the first five years. "Americans are diving in and out of matrimony with a seeming ease that belies the premise of the institution. Is this, one wonders, how the tensions between our optimistic yearning for marriage and our darker, childhood experiences with divorce are meant to play out?" Paul writes.

Therapists debate the extent to which parental divorce makes children themselves more likely to divorce. Many say divorce impacts children only as much as they allow it to. I've found that adult children fall into one of two categories when their parents split: they fear matrimony because they fear divorce, or they vow to avoid the mistakes of their parents by being the perfect spouse. Or both.

The latter swear to themselves that if they take the plunge, it's going to be forever. No easy way out fifteen years down the road. They're going to go to therapy and try to be the übercommunicator with their partner. They vow not to act as selfish as their parents, who thought only of their own happiness when they chose to divorce. They will avoid all their parents' mistakes. Says Stone, "When I got married at twenty-one, I thought to myself, 'This is a long-term thing. The only thing that's going to drive me out is if I'm bored to death.' We had this breach in my family when my parents split up. I thought, I'll heal it." She'd do it the right way.

Research suggests parental divorce has a concrete impact on children's relationships. One 1999 study by the National Marriage Project found that children of divorce are two to three times more likely to split than their peers from two-parent families. But these studies don't really apply to adult children. Young children of divorce grow up in a fractured family; we face marriage with our childhoods intact. Adult children remember how special it felt to have a cohesive, supportive family in our formative years. We know what it looks like to be happy in a relationship, even if it means recalling our parents ten years ago. It seems that more than any other age group, adult children have the maturity and foresight to react proactively to their parents' divorce. They can learn from their parents' mistakes. Says one twenty-eight-year-old woman, "I grew up in a very loving family, and although my parents' marriage didn't last forever, I did see them in an extremely loving relationship for most of my life."

A few studies suggest that our attitudes about marriage were formed *before* our parents divorced. A study in the *Journal of Divorce and Remarriage* compared how 444 unmarried, young, white adults, aged seventeen to twenty-three, viewed marriage. Half the sample came from intact families; the other half had experienced a divorce in the last fifteen months. Participants were asked to describe their parents' marriage as high-conflict or low-conflict. Then they answered five questions about cohabitation, commitment, singlehood, and divorce. The findings surprised even the researchers. Individuals from intact families who identified their parents as having a high-conflict marriage were just as likely to believe in cohabiting as individuals from divorced, high-conflict families. And when individuals from both groups were asked whether marriage is a lifelong commitment, the answers differed only between high-conflict and low-conflict sample sets. There was no correlation between those with married or divorced parents.

In other words, if your parents fought often while you were growing up, you may have developed cynical views of marriage long before your parents split up. Likewise, if your parents rarely fought in front of you, their divorce may have no impact on your outlook on marriage at all. You believe that you can be happy in a long-term commitment because you watched your parents in one. You'd feel this way even if your parents had never split up.

Therapist Julia Stone says that fearing marriage comes down to one thing: a lack of trust in ourselves. We're not scared that the institution of marriage will let us down. Adult children worry that we'll fail our partner in the same way our parents failed us. We never want to hurt someone as much as our parents hurt each other, and we don't want to hurt our kids the way our parents hurt us.

I've always thought all of my fears centered around John's leaving me someday. But the more I think about it, the more I realize how much I'm scared that I'll leave him. I believe in divorce. When a good friend confided her marital problems to me, I encouraged her to separate before she sought counseling; I just didn't understand how a couple could make their marriage better. In my mind, if problems got too big, they were unfixable.

Even before my parents split up, I'd tell myself, If you're ever unhappy with someone, you'll get out. In my mind, there is no reason to struggle on and make a marriage work—just because. Now that I see how much happier my parents are unmarried, I'm even more convinced they made the right decision.

Deep down, I don't trust myself in a long-term marriage. I fear *I'll* grow bored or restless. *I'll* become resentful of compromises we made along the way. I'll let our children come between us. Worst of all, I imagine I'll lie in bed one day and wish I were lying next to someone else.

How much was I willing to commit of myself? For so long, I'd only go so far, thinking my love could be thrown back at me. John had no reason to think we wouldn't last. His parents have been happily married for more than thirty years. I should have been inspired by them. Secretly, I wondered whether his parents were still together because they were too scared to be alone. Maybe they weren't as in love as they seemed. I've said these things to John about other couples we know. He'd say, "Or they could get along great, and they could really be in love." I wish I saw love so simply.

John was willing to take a risk in marrying me. I needed to consider: Why wasn't I willing to do the same?

Mom always had a sign hanging in our kitchen that read, "At 8, children have all the questions. At 18, they have all the answers." Adult children believe they have some understanding of relationships—until their parents divorce. Then everything our parents taught us about marriage and relationships seems insignificant.

Mom's opinions and Dad's advice didn't work even for them. Why would it work for us?

Without our parents' marriage as a standard to which to hold ourselves, marriage is much less defined for us. We no longer have a model. Says one twenty-seven-year-old man, "I just don't know what brings happiness anymore. I don't know what the criterion is for a good relationship."

There is a fear among adult children that we will not fight hard enough for our marriages—that we'll let our unions slip away. Therapists say these concerns sometimes have troubling side effects. We may try to persist in a relationship that isn't right for us or, in the rarest of occasions, stay in an abusive one. "I've been treated poorly in relationships," says one twenty-seven-year-old man, "and I've held on much longer than is necessary in fear of being a quitter like my parents."

If you're unsure of the limits of love, it's hard to enter a relationship feeling confident. You probably have as many questions as an eight-year-old. You may wonder: When am I asking a partner for too much? How much is a couple supposed to fight before they call it quits? Which problems am I supposed to endure, and which are considered the deal breakers? Says one twenty-seven-year-old woman, "Sometimes I wonder, Do I need too much? Do I want too much? I don't have an example to go with. I don't know what's right."

Adult children are trying to create a new vision of what's true and what's real. "They're rewriting history," says Stone. "The past is all up for questioning. They think, 'I've been trying to be happy based on what my parents' marriage looked like.' " And that union failed. One twenty-four-year-old woman finds herself "testing" her boyfriend. After her father left her mother, she wasn't sure how much conflict was healthy and what was abnormal. So she'll get really angry with her boyfriend or act obnoxiously to see how much he's willing to take. "If I'm mean," she wonders, "will he be there the next day?"

Bob, twenty-seven, knows his father left his mother because they were no longer intimate. Bob's father made it clear to Bob that he needs to marry a woman with whom he has great sexual chemistry. Bob always wanted a woman whom he could "dig into the guts of life with and have serious conversations." His father's words haunt him. Unless he finds a woman he lusts over emotionally and physically, Bob has come to see his relationships as doomed. "Often I let great relationships go in the pursuit of a better match, fearing anything less than perfect increases the chance that an eventual marriage will fail," he says.

Bob tries to talk to the women he dates about his ambivalence toward marriage. "There are so many factors out of your control," he'll say. Girlfriends encourage him, but he's frustrated by his own expectations. The last girl he dated he really liked. Then she entered a self-discovery phase and decided to break things off. "I was somewhat going along with it in my head," says Bob. "Then I thought, 'Wait, am I giving up too easily? I should be able to endure changes. What am I going to do when I'm married?' "

Adult children sometimes believe they're destined to divorce if they notice themselves mimicking their parents' behaviors. Whether we're married or dating, finding similarities in our relationships makes us uneasy. When you're able to understand all of the ways Mom ticked Dad off, you're able to recognize that you could drive someone away for the same reason. Many of us find ourselves comparing our parents' relationship to our own. We question our behaviors and try to keep them in check. *Am I being as demanding as Mom used to be? Would Dad say I'm acting needy?* You don't want your significant other to think of you the way you watched one of your parents think of the other.

Then again, repeating the behaviors of your parents is normal. They raised you. When you watch a parent deal with conflict by running from it, it's likely that, almost instinctually, you'll do the same. Even facial expressions are acquired from watching Mom and Dad over the years. At our core, we are our parents. Still, we believe that if we catch their mistakes, we can make our own relationships more peaceful. Says one twenty-nine-year-old woman, "My parents' divorce forced me to take an honest look, [make] a deep examination of my relationship. It scared me silly that the same thing might happen to me, and I was able to see some of their mistakes in my own behavior."

Mandy, twenty-seven, feels strange whenever she argues with her boyfriend, Chris. A voice in the back of her mind reminds her to be careful. Her parents fought often. Her mother would harp on an issue until a disagreement turned into a screaming match. Then her mother would escape into her bedroom and slam the door. Mandy doesn't want to act like her mother, so she tries to catch herself in a disagreement. "Let's stop," she'll tell Chris. Her mother was never able to do that. "I know I am a product of my parents," says Mandy. "Even when Chris and I argue over something totally unrelated to my parents, it sometimes ends up being about my parents."

Mandy says she'll realize she's done something her mother used to or said something her father would say—and she'll feel guilty. "It scares me that I'll turn into them," she says, "not Chris and I becoming *them* but me alone being the two of them wrapped in one package."

Many of us try to "unlearn" the hurtful behaviors we watched our parents engage in. Paige, twenty-seven, has struggled a lot with men since her father left her mother. She felt lonely. She'd latch onto boyfriends. Her therapist told her she fears that men are going to leave her. "I do what I can to keep them, even when things aren't working out," Paige says. She attributes this fear to her father. He left her and her mother and moved to another country.

Over time, Paige has realized that the source of her problems lies deeper. Over the years, her father was never emotionally available to her mother. She watched her mother try to connect with her father, and he'd never reciprocate. Ultimately, her mother gave up and filed for divorce. "I have this pattern where I date guys who are unavailable and I try to get them to love me," Paige says. Paige was fascinated by the revelation. It's exactly how her mother had interacted with her father.

Parental divorce inspires adult children to hold a microscope up to their significant others. Some therapists say we choose partners like our parents. It can be upsetting to see a boyfriend acting like your mother, and vice versa. You want your significant other to be different so you can reassure yourself your relationship will be different. In an attempt to look for hints, or reasons why your partnership won't last with a person, you may nitpick at them, or try to get a rise out of them. Finding red flags is a defense mechanism. Like Julia Stone, you want to know what you're getting into, even if it means discovering a partner's dark side.

In some ways, learning what didn't work from our parents actually helps us be better partners. We don't go into our relationships with false expectations. We have a more realistic view of coupling. "I'm much more aware of what goes wrong in relationships and why people get divorced," says one thirty-one-year-old woman. "I'll see things in people I date and realize they're not going to get better. It's made me think a lot more about what I want."

We can also recognize that problems that fester only become

worse. Barbara, twenty-seven, got mad at her partner for rebuilding a utility closet in their house without consulting her. Typically, Barbara wouldn't share what was bothering her, just like her mother, who also let things fester. When Barbara saw the closet, she decided she should break with tradition and speak her mind. Keeping emotions bottled up hurt her parents' marriage. Barbara didn't want her own relationship to suffer from old resentments, too. "I want to deal with these things now and not let it come out in thirty years," she says.

Many of us wish we could "divorce-proof" our marriages. We dream of a secret formula that holds the key to a successful, long-lasting partnership. Howard Markman, a psychology professor at the University of Denver, has responded to those fears by offering preemptive counseling. Markman analyzes the way couples interact before they marry. Couples may be doomed to divorce, he says, if they engage in any of the four signs of bad communication: They allow an argument to escalate. They attack a partner's weaknesses. They think the worst of their partner or interpret their feelings negatively. They withdraw from an argument rather than engage in a conversation.

Almost any marriage and family therapist with whom you speak will say the overwhelming problem facing couples is learning how to argue. People just don't know how to communicate. John Gottman, a psychologist at the University of Washington, has studied seven hundred couples over three decades in his "love lab." He's produced a mathematical model that can predict whether a husband and wife will divorce within four years based on how they interact. He found that all couples fight, but to be happy, they must share positive communications five times more often than negative ones. According to an October 2004 article on Gottman's research in *Health* magazine, happy couples show interest in each other's thoughts and feelings, share their joy, show affection, listen without being defensive, joke around, prove they care by checking in, demonstrate empathy (use words and facial expressions to show they're trying to understand), and accept and respect each other's feelings.

If you're like me, you just read each suggestion and mentally checked off those that applied to you. You also should've relaxed a bit. Hearing about the latest in relationship research should demonstrate how little power your parents' divorce has to make or break your love life. Every couple creates their own chemistry. It simply isn't realistic to assume that your partner is going to be just like your father and you are going to be your mother and because of that, your marriage is doomed.

You and your partner are your own selves. You each bring a unique set of expectations and experiences to your relationship. Therapists say no one's relationship is perfect, and we need to believe them. There will always be disagreements and challenges. But they will be your own.

One thirty-eight-year-old woman, who had been married for fourteen years when her parents split, says her parents' divorce colored her relationship with her husband. They'd fight over money. She'd constantly associate his views on finances with her father's; she'd get defensive, as her mother used to. Over time, she realized the comparisons were causing larger rifts in her marriage. In projecting her parents' marriage onto her own, she was seeing bigger problems than were actually there. "Gradually, I realized my husband is *not* my father," she says. "He is a completely different person. Our relationship is different."

You need to remind yourself that you are not your mom or dad—and your relationship isn't the same as theirs. Comparing is exhausting. And it's certainly not going to help you put the changes from your parents' divorce in perspective. Robert Emery, a psychologist at the University of Virginia, says adult children are coming of age in a time when many of us harbor a cultural distrust of marriage—regardless of whether our parents are divorced. We have the same worries as our friends who have married parents. "Fifty years ago, you didn't have to figure it all out," says Emery. "There were roles for men and roles for women. Today, each couple needs to decide what commitment they're going to make." In other words, your fears may have less to do with your parents' marriage and more to do with a societal shift in the way we see marriage.

Your parents' divorce will not only affect the way you view relationships; it may also test your relationship with your partner in a more immediate sense. Parental divorce takes a toll on us, which takes a toll on our own marriages. Some adult kids find themselves fighting more with a spouse. If our partners don't react the way we want them to, we get angry.

Kayla, twenty-nine, and her husband got along well until her parents split up. Then things between them got tense. When Kayla would vent about her parents, she felt as if her husband wasn't listening. If she said she was going to stop talking to her father, her husband would tell her she was being unreasonable. If she snapped at him, he'd say, "You're acting like your mother," which Kayla says is an insult. Her mother is passive-aggressive, always depressed, and she often jumps to conclusions. Kayla became concerned that she and her husband were becoming her parents, who fought constantly. She convinced her husband to go to couples therapy. "We're a different couple now," she says. "I'm getting better at getting rid of my negative feelings. He's more understanding."

While Rhonda, twenty-eight, openly contemplated suicide after her parents divorced, her husband kept quiet about his own problems. He didn't think Rhonda could handle hearing about them, which polarized them. Rhonda was fine spending time without him. Being around her husband made Rhonda's skin crawl. Not because she didn't love him but because she felt as if she were dealing with something so big that she didn't have any energy left over for him. "We avoided each other," Rhonda says. "I didn't want to be around him, and he didn't want to be around me."

Our worlds may stop when our parents divorce, but our partners' lives move on. You may be so wrapped up in your own grief, you don't realize how much it's impacting your spouse. You are his life, and you're not the easiest person to be around right now. It's hard work being around someone who's depressed. You know this from spending time with your divorcing parents.

If a spouse encourages you to let go, try to understand that he or she is only trying to help. Kayla says she realizes now that when her husband said she was being unreasonable, he was only encouraging her to see another point of view. It was his way of supporting her. "He was trying to bring me out of my rut," Kayla says. "He reminded me, you still have a life."

Therapists suggest that you try to find positive marital role models after your parents split up. Ask your grandparents, or a good friend of the family, to talk about their relationship. You don't want to hear a sugarcoated version. Hearing a realistic portrayal of love will help you rebuild your trust in romantic relationships. You'll see that just because things don't feel the way they do in the movies doesn't mean they aren't going right. You'll have someone to whom to bring your big questions: How much fighting is too much fighting? Should I stay with someone I love but I'm not in love with?

In February 2004, I pulled up in front of a contemporary house to do an interview for my job. A petite old lady answered the door in a two-piece turquoise suit. "Oh, hello, dear," she said, holding open her screen door. "I'm Sylvia." Sylvia took my coat and led me to her kitchen table. The house was so quiet, the water boiling on the stove sounded like a symphony. Sylvia was eighty-three. Her husband, Ray, whom she had met in an orphanage at the age of fourteen, had died a few weeks before. Sylvia poured me a cup of tea. "As you know," I said, "I'm here because I want to tell your love story—how you and Ray met; how you created such a beautiful life out of nothing, as two orphans; how your marriage lasted; how you said goodbye when he passed." Sylvia nodded.

It wasn't a coincidence that I found myself in Sylvia's kitchen. For the past year, I'd informally studied any couple I'd met, wondering what their secrets to happiness were—looking for loopholes in their love. Old couples were the most intriguing. As much of a cynic as I'd become about love, I couldn't deny that an eighty-year-old couple walking hand in hand maybe had something my parents didn't. I convinced my editor that people would be comforted by a positive story on marriage, which is how I ended up drinking tea with Sylvia on this Tuesday morning. I wanted to know Sylvia's secrets to lasting love.

"I fell in love with Ray the moment I saw him standing on the basketball court. We were at the orphanage. He was so tall and dark and handsome," Sylvia said. "I loved him like that until he died." Sylvia said she missed him terribly. She'd often lie in bed and stare at the indent of his body on their bed. She still baked every day, but she froze her cakes instead of setting them on the table for Ray. During one interview, she retrieved his hat out of a closet, pushed the brim to her nose, and inhaled.

When it was time for lunch, Sylvia prepared a three-course meal. She wanted to know about me—my job, my boyfriend, my hometown. I told her my parents had split up a couple of years before, which made her frown. "That must be very hard," Sylvia said. "Two of my grandchildren are going through the same."

I told her how scared I was of getting married—that I feared I'd one day stop loving John. I don't usually share so much with someone I'm interviewing. But Sylvia was different. She'd lived through a sixty-two-year marriage. I needed her help.

Leave it to an eighty-three-year-old woman to start with sex. "It is so important," she said. She told me I had to be a "tiger" in the bedroom, and I was afraid to ask what that meant. She said that without sex, a couple drifts apart. "I never once turned Ray away," she said. She wasn't ashamed to admit that she'd put the kids aside if Ray needed her. She never wanted him to feel alone. They were partners—not two people living individual lives in the same house.

Then she paused. "There will be times when you'll want to leave him," Sylvia said. "I almost left Ray once. We got in a terrible fight, and I went for a long walk around the neighborhood—for hours." When Sylvia got home, Ray hugged her. It was the only time Sylvia saw him cry. "I always stayed because I knew I'd never love anyone like I loved Ray," she says.

I read once that the secret to a good marriage is learning how to renegotiate who our partners become as they change. It was the way Sylvia described her relationship. Love is an organic matter, like a shell on the beach. Outside forces—wind, tides, rain—might change it over time, but the shell's essence, like love, will always be the same.

I left Sylvia's house that day with this thought running through my mind: if love is always evolving, then I needed to be open to evolving myself. I can't lock my relationship with John into a box and throw away the key, hoping that everything between us will remain the same. Saying you want things to stay the way they are is missing the point. Maybe I needed to accept that I couldn't freeze time: John and I wouldn't always be the same people, and our relationship wouldn't remain the same, either. Instead, it's that very evolution that makes sharing your life with someone so special.

Change is what allows a relationship to breathe and grow. You know someone so deeply that "relaxing" means simply being in each other's company. You face all the different phases of life together. You accept each other transformed.

"Let's get married and have babies," I say to John one Sunday afternoon, a few months after meeting Sylvia. I'd just put down *The Time Traveler's Wife*, which I was reading for a book club. The words had crept inside my heart, and I couldn't get the characters out of my head. I crawl onto John's lap. The book isn't about divorce but rather Henry and Clare, a couple who meet at different points in time due to Henry's "genetic disease"—he time travels with no control over when or where he goes. Henry may be alongside Clare as she is giving birth to their baby when he vanishes from the hospital room. Moments later, he finds himself meeting her for the first time in a café ten years earlier.

The urgency of Henry and Clare's love makes me cringe at how scared of marriage I've become. They had to savor every second together because they never knew when Henry was going to disappear and for how long he'd be gone. I rarely think anymore about how much I love John today. I only worry I won't love him tomorrow.

We've all experienced moments when we realize how unfair or stupid we've been acting. This was one of mine. I curl up on John's lap like a cat, and I cry. "I need to stop thinking my parents' breakup says something about me," I say, "and stop wondering if our love will last or if our marriage will fail."

John laughs. He agrees and seems relieved. Over the past few years, he's listened to me hash out my concerns about marriage. He has always believed in us. He kisses my forehead.

I need to focus on how in love I feel right now, I think. I should revel in our closeness, treasure it, and not always think of ways life might spoil it. Everyone knows the future is unpredictable. You could lose what you had yesterday with a simple twist of fate. Would I rather spend my days worrying that my future marriage won't work or take my days with John as they come, as Sylvia did with Ray? In the end, I might wind up with something greater than I could ever imagine.

Points to Remember

- It's natural to feel cynical about "true love" after watching your parents' marriage end. Allow yourself time to grieve and think things through—and try to keep perspective. Just because their marriage failed doesn't mean love doesn't exist.

- You may feel uncertain about marriage after you've watched all the ways your parents' relationship went wrong. Try not to let their example ruin the idea of marriage for you, especially if it's something you value.

- If you find yourself mimicking a parent's behavior in your own relationship, it is not doomed. You and your partner are *not* your mother and father. Try to recognize the pattern into which you are falling and figure out the reasons behind it.

- Your parents' divorce may impact your romantic relationship in a very immediate way. If you are becoming increasingly depressed, agitated, or despondent, try talking to a friend or therapist. Your significant other can only take on so much of your pain before it affects your relationship.

8

Going Home

> Oh, Ben, how do we get back to all the great times? Used to be so full of light, and comradeship, the sleigh-riding in winter, and the ruddiness on his cheeks. And always some kind of good news coming up, always something nice coming up ahead.
>
> —ARTHUR MILLER, *Death of a Salesman*

I AVOID SPENDING TIME ALONE WITH MOM WHEN I'M VISIT-ing home. This trip is no exception. It's August 2004. I've been home three weeks, and I already feel as if Mom is looking forward to the day I leave. We cannot be in the same room without making everyone around us slightly uncomfortable. On the surface, we act as if nothing were wrong. We gather with my sisters and go to the beach or the pool. When Mom gets home from work, we talk about her day. But anger traded between us these past few years simmers just below the surface. I'm beginning to think the air between us will always feel this saturated.

Before I came home this last time, I thought I was over my parents' divorce. I was on my way to Kenya in an airplane when my parents met around a conference table with their lawyers and finalized things. Being out of the country was a blessing. If Mom and Dad got in an argument at the proceedings, or if Dad got in his truck and cried afterward, I didn't have to hear about it. I knew when I got back, they would officially be apart. Mom would have moved out of my childhood home and into her new condo. Dad, who bought the house, would step inside for the first time since he left three years before.

Kenya provided a good distraction. I didn't have to think about my parents as I zigzagged the African plains, searching for lions and elephants, and interviewing local children who ran barefoot through the savanna. Visiting a place so far away makes it easier to step outside yourself and reflect: I decided I'd been angry about the divorce for too long. I was tired of it. I wanted to be free and feel as pure as I did when I stood in the tall grasses of the Masai Mara and listened to the breeze whistling through the reeds. I left Africa feeling reborn, as if I'd shed an old skin. I told myself that when I got home, I'd move on.

"Want to take a ride with me?" Mom asks the last Saturday I'm visiting home. I'm leaving on Tuesday. Mom says we'll drive along the north fork, a sliver of land that stretches its neck into the Long Island Sound. We'll grab lunch, stop at the farm stands and maybe a winery. Chelsea is already at work, so it's just Mom and me, which makes me nervous. I'm scared I'll say the wrong thing and we'll get into another argument.

In the car, Mom talks about how her shirt isn't fitting right, how she wants to go to Europe this fall, how she feels about Chelsea's plans to go back to college. I want her to ask me deep questions about my writing or John or my trip to Africa, but she doesn't. I fall into journalist mode, as if I were interviewing a stranger, and ask

Mom lots of questions. Around noon, we stop for lunch at a country café, where Mom and I sit across from each other, which feels adversarial. Every time we make eye contact, I tuck my hands under my thighs. We gossip about anyone we can think of so we don't have to talk about ourselves.

Back in the car, I ask Mom about her brother. When I joke that he has bad teeth, Mom doesn't laugh, and I realize I've said something wrong. Mom's mood changes instantly. "If you have something to say to me, then just say it," Mom says, angrily.

"All I said was that your brother has bad teeth," I say.

"You need to stop saying horrible things about my family and me," Mom says. "Just say what you really want instead of making these little comments to dig into me."

I deny I do such things.

"You're always looking at me like I'm doing something wrong, like you hate me," Mom says.

"I don't hate you," I say, laughing. I tell Mom she's crazy, which incites her more. She starts yelling about how she's tired of hearing how terrible she's been, how all she's trying to do is live her life. I laugh again, but I realize I sound like a woman in a horror film who laughs before she really loses it, because inside, my heart is trembling and my hands are beginning to shake. I look out the window.

"I just don't think you're much of a mother to me anymore," I say.

A year earlier, I'd promised myself I'd never say things like this to Mom again. I told myself there was no point in being honest because the truth would hurt her too much—as it has just now. Mom makes a quick U-turn in the middle of the two-lane highway, and I yell at her for nearly killing us. Mom is crying, screaming, turning to me to make her points, not looking at the road in front of us. I don't listen to what she's saying. I just yell over her, which I've never done before. I tell her that she's selfish and self-centered, that she never asks me about myself. "You always say you're the kind of mother who puts her kids first," I say. "You don't even love me. You couldn't care less about me."

When we pull up in front of the condo, I get out of her car and slam the door. I'm planning to take a walk on the beach. I change my clothes, and when Mom still hasn't come inside, I think she's left, which ticks me off more. I'm on my way out the door when Mom walks in. "Where are you going?" she asks. When I say the beach, Mom pleads with me to stay, to sit and talk things out instead of putting off our feelings—again. *I am over my parents' divorce,* I think. But I guess this isn't about accepting that my parents are no longer together. At some point, the way Mom acted during the divorce became the source of my anger—rather than the divorce itself.

We settle into the living room on opposite couches, and I keep my dog at my feet and pet his head. Mom is calm. "This divorce has been the hardest thing I've ever had to do," Mom says. "If I've been wrapped up in myself, I'm sorry, but I needed to be. I've been trying to build a life from scratch. I'm learning how to be alone and how to date. I moved out of my house. If I haven't asked you about you, it's because I'm trying to figure out how to be me right now. I feel like you're always judging me. Like no matter what I do, it's the wrong thing."

I've never heard Mom sound so vulnerable and honest, which makes me listen more closely. I admit to myself that I've been terrible to her. I tell her I just want her to be happy—that I just want all of us to be happy. Mom moves toward me and stretches out her hand, then pulls it back. "Sometimes I just don't know how to be around you anymore," she says. She's crying again. "There have been so many times I've been close to you and I just want to hug you and I don't know how."

I feel the same. I used to climb into Mom's bed and we'd talk for hours before Dad came in. Now we share so little intimacy, I often look forward to leaving home just so I can hug her good-bye.

"We used to be so close," Mom says. I tell her that I'm ready to be friends with her. We'll get to know each other all over again, since both of us are so changed by the divorce, I say.

I move next to Mom on the couch and fall into her arms. She squeezes me. "I just want to feel like you love me again," I say. "That you care about me." We're crying and Mom is rocking me. "I'm sorry that you ever thought I stopped," Mom says.

Then we're laughing about how silly we must look, two women holding each other tight—trying to make up for years of things done wrong.

Neither of us wants to end the conversation, so we stay on the couch and talk about things we've been holding back. I admit how scared I am to get married. Mom says she feels as if her married friends are threatened by her single status; divorce makes everyone question their own relationships, she says.

The afternoon feels like a cliché movie when the sky turns black and lets loose with wind and thunder. It rains as hard as Mom and I have wept. I stand at the glass doors of Mom's hilltop condo and imagine all I've said and all I've felt over these years. I want all of it to be carried away with the rain, flowing over the cliff outside, dissolving into the Long Island Sound below. I want my anger to be gone, and for the first time in three years, I realize that it's finally lifting.

Moving on from your parents' divorce doesn't happen overnight. Healing can take years. Since your parents announced they were splitting up, you've probably journeyed from grief to anger and back again. As much as you try to will your feelings away, they'll stubbornly remain. There is no mysterious formula for you to solve in order to discover eternal happiness. Your life is constantly unfolding, and so are the lives of your parents. For awhile, there will always be something that will make you curl up in a ball and cry. And there will always be moments that bring redemption and joy. Our lives are intricate patterns, woven from ups and downs. Getting to the end of our grief isn't an organized process. It's erratic.

Many of us hold on to our grief longer than we need to because we don't want to move on. Moving on means letting go, and the last thing adult children want to do is say good-bye to everything they consider true. Adult children don't want to accept that their homes and families will never feel as safe and secure as they once did. They don't want to look back on their memories as relics of happiness.

Yet, they're forced to. Reality sets in all around adult children in the years after their parents' divorce, enveloping them like thick morning fog. To see their parents, they must face these changes. They visit with stepfamilies and spend time at a parent's one-bedroom apartment. Adult children long for the way things used to be. They say they'll let go when they're ready.

In the months after September 11, many of us struggled to get on with our lives. Our collective fear was so big and anxiety so heightened that half the people I knew worried about driving across bridges or taking the subway, and the other half pretended nothing much had happened at all. They went about life as they always had, writing off the event as a hiccup. "If I were to think about it all the time," one colleague told me, "I'd go crazy. I'd be scared all the time."

Adult children's feelings break down similarly after parental divorce. One half of us push through life with the stamina of a long-distance runner. We dig into daily routines to remind ourselves things aren't *that* different. We pull inward, tucking away all our emotions, and focus on our own children, our careers, our relationships. To think about our parents' divorce all the time would make us crazy. The other half of us allow our parents' divorce to define us.

We grow resentful and angry. We are so buried in our own grief that sorting through it feels impossible.

None of us in either category are facing our feelings head-on. We're pushing the present away so we don't have to think about the past, or we're holding on to the past as if our life depended on it. None of us are letting go.

Often, we hold on to the past so we don't have to accept the future. As childhood homes are being packed up, many adult children walk through and collect mementos: one young woman saved a music box her father gave her mother, another salvaged furniture from the den she'd grown up with, and another rescued her mother's wedding dress and several family photo albums. Our parents may want to discard their shared history—it hurts them too much—but we hold on to as much of it as we can. We become tenders to the past.

We guard our mementos and memories not because we believe our parents will get back together. It's because we need to believe that who we were—who our families were—mattered. That all of those moments were special then and still are now. Photographs of laughing parents show us the past. Keeping your mother's music box on your dresser makes you feel your history.

The items we take from our childhood homes decorate our own apartments and dorm rooms. Like an urn containing a loved one's ashes, a painting from our parents' living room or a family photo album is a gateway to what we've lost. Every time one twenty-seven-year-old woman opens her mother's music box, she hears "I Left My Heart in San Francisco" and she's reminded of her parents together. The memory comforts her.

We know it might help to take down framed pictures of our parents together, but we leave them up. Our parents are preserved in them. A shot of Mom and Dad laughing and holding hands at a graduation captures happier times. Watching home videos Dad took over the years is like reconnecting with a former self. All of these things make up our identity. *This is who I am,* we think. I am these videos and photographs. I am my mother's living room furniture and my father's toolshed.

We cannot let go of any of these things. They represent us too much. So we try to save as much as we can.

In books about grief, psychologists offer techniques for moving on. Some suggest that widows pack up a husband's closet and get rid of his belongings, such as books or a shaving kit. Keepsakes from a person's life enable us to pretend he or she hasn't passed. Your days should reflect the truth, the book says.

Visual reminders of your family might be reconsidered, then. If you really want to move on, those mementos may be doing more harm than good. Saving your parents' wedding album and flipping through it once in awhile is OK. You're reliving your history as you do when you look through an old high school yearbook. But keeping reminders of your family, especially if you're carrying a lot of anger toward your parents, may be unhealthy. Looking at a picture of Mom and Dad smiling at your graduation is going to feel antagonistic—a reminder of all you've lost rather than a keepsake of the past.

To move on, you don't have to forget your childhood or who your parents were—together. You'll always revisit your childhood in day-dreams. No divorce can take that away. Moving on doesn't mean say-ing good-bye. The past isn't who you are, it's *a part* of who you are. The past can coexist with the present. You don't have to choose one or the other.

Your family's shared history will always live in the background of your life, like a sound track to your days—no matter how far your parents stray. Memories of your family will come to you in the years ahead, and at times, you'll shed a nostalgic tear. But you won't grieve for long. By then, your two selves—"you before the divorce" and "you after the divorce"—will have learned to balance each other out, like the Taoist symbol of yin and yang. Together, each will make you whole.

Although there is no secret to moving on, most of us follow a similar road map to get there. To start with, we must want to. There will be a point in the yelling and tears and silence when you'll tire of all of it. You'll want your life back—your family back, even if it is in pieces.

In *The Wizard of Oz*, Dorothy and her friends spend days searching for the Emerald City. When they arrive, they speak with the wizard, whose voice echoes through the cavernous visiting room. Dorothy's voice shakes when she speaks. The lion nearly runs away. Everyone is scared. Then Toto accidentally uncovers the man behind the curtain.

Perspective opens our eyes to all we *haven't* been seeing. You can look at a divorce from a dozen points of view. A fresh perspective allows us to separate ourselves from the drama. We become outsiders looking in—journalists writing an ever-changing story about our own lives. Guy Finley, author of *The Secret of Letting Go*, says that sometimes individuals need to develop a new perspective on a situation to conquer it, sort of like Dorothy. Once Dorothy saw the man controlling the levers, she was no longer scared. If you could see the divorce through your parents' eyes, maybe you'd see things differently, too. Maybe you'd be one step closer to moving on.

Seeing the drama from your own point of view keeps you from seeing anything at all. You're never challenging yourself to understand a parent's mind-set. You're only listening to something he or she says and processing how it affects you. Says anthropologist Ruth

Benedict in *Patterns of Culture*, "No man ever looks at the world with pristine eyes. He sees it edited by a definite set of customs and institutions and ways of thinking."

Your mother might say, "I need to sell the house." When you process that, you'll think, *I'm losing my home.* You've made the moment about you, even though it's not. I'm guilty of this. When Mom said those very words to me, I never thought about how hard it was for *her* to have to sell the house or to tell me she was going to. I only thought of how *I* felt at that moment.

If someone asked your father how he was doing now that he was divorced, imagine his answer. *Things are a lot better for me. I feel more alive than I have in a long time. I felt lonely in my marriage. My new life is exciting.* If a friend told you this, you'd probably cheer him or her on; say, "Congratulations!" But because we're filtering all of a parent's words and actions through our own perspective, we feel as if he is saying things to hurt us.

Seeing from a parent's perspective is powerful, sometimes painful. It's also freeing. If you can allow yourself to see how happy your parents are without each other, even if it means admitting your childhood wasn't perfect, then you're allowing your perspective to change. You're opening your eyes to the fact that Mom's and Dad's sole purpose isn't to take care of us. They are people who want a second chance and need to take care of themselves. They didn't think much about how their decisions would impact us, and looking at the situation from their point of view, you can understand why. They were too unhappy, too desperate to consider it. Many had held off divorces from our early childhoods for our sakes.

It's especially important to consider the perspective of an "enemy" parent, or the parent you blame for the divorce. If you sided with Mom, try to see the divorce from Dad's point of view. I made the mistake of always seeing my parents' divorce through Dad. Dad was the victim, so everything Mom did was wrong. If Mom complained that Dad wasn't helping pay the mortgage, I rolled my eyes. I never considered that Mom was really struggling, as she claimed. I only felt sorry for Dad, who lived in a teeny one-room studio apartment. My understanding didn't delve deeper.

When I finally considered all Mom had been through, from her point of view, I was looking at a much different picture. Mom was trying to make it on her own for the first time in twenty-seven years. Life was a struggle—emotionally and financially. But I had ignored her reality because I wasn't ready to see it. Admitting that Mom was struggling meant I'd have to admit that Dad wasn't helping her, which meant Dad was at fault, too. Early on, I needed to believe that Dad was perfect, that I had someone on my side who was going to fight to bring our family back together. To see Mom's point of view would've destroyed that.

Today, I respect my mother more than I ever have. She is an inspiration to me. A role model. Mom showed me that it is OK to demand happiness. Many of us glean similar lessons when we consider our parents' situations. A mother whom we thought gave up had really been trying to save her marriage for years. A father who seemed to be looking out only for himself had actually been protecting assets to ensure they went to his children. One twenty-seven-year-old woman said, "Mom showed me I have to stand up for myself and not take crap in my own relationships."

In a small 1987 study of college students whose parents had divorced, a doctoral student at Harvard University found that 87 percent of college students surveyed believed their parents' split ultimately benefited them in some way. Many of the individuals interviewed for this book felt the same way. Jenna, who barely spoke to her mother after she got engaged, now feels as if her parents' split has made her a more compassionate person. She's come to appreciate all the sacrifices her mother made. "I know how hard Mom tried over the years. She was superwoman," she says. Jenna realizes she was blaming her mother for the divorce even though her father had hardly been the perfect husband. Seeing her mother's point of view helped her heal. Says Jenna, "Recently, I told Mom how proud I was of her. You can tell she's so glad to hear it."

We mature in the years after our parents' divorce. We see our parents at their best and at their worst, during their triumphs and their setbacks. We see ourselves in those circumstances, too, and we are forced to stand on our own two feet. Nothing makes us feel more grown-up. Learning to be independent and self-reliant is a gift. In the months after our parents' divorce, we feel changed. Years later, we're proud of who we've become.

Anger squelches any hope an adult child may have of gaining additional perspective. It is such a powerful emotion that it is often all we can feel when it sets in. We are blinded by anger and sometimes frozen by it. It makes us feel less vulnerable. Rather than collapse against our father and cry, we hold grudges and ignore his calls. Anger makes us feel strong. Instead of allowing ourselves to feel rejected by Mom and Dad, we reject them first. *I don't want to talk to you either,* we think.

Adult children use anger to "cover up" more stinging emotions, such as feelings of abandonment, that may be more difficult to admit. I thought I was always angry with Mom for being selfish, but when I sorted through my emotions, I realized I wasn't angry at all. I was hurt because I didn't think she loved me anymore. I felt ridiculous, like a spoiled child, admitting that. So instead, I got angry at everything Mom did.

In retrospect, I can see that I couldn't really move on until I got beyond how mad I was, which is how it is for all of us. You may accept your parents' separate lives. You may get used to holidays apart. But if you still resent your father for leaving, you will not fully move on and find inner peace until that conflict is resolved.

The single greatest lesson I learned from going through my parents' divorce is this: know what you're angry about. You may think you're angry about the divorce. More often, you're mad about something else, such as the way your parents acted during the falling-out. You're angry that Dad slept with another woman and took secret vacations. You're angry that Mom started putting herself before you. You'll get mad at your parents for something inane, such as not taking out the trash. And you'll have the wrong fight over and over again.

Dealing with my parents' divorce was easy when I was angry. I could roll my eyes at things Mom said. I could make mean jokes at Mom's expense. The more I talked about how stupid Mom was acting, the better I felt. I was running on anger the way cars run on gasoline. After Mom and I cried in each other's arms in her living room, I felt as if I'd been wrung out. Letting go of our anger leaves our limbs slack and our hearts wrenched. At the time, I felt weak. In retrospect, saying good-bye to my anger was glorious.

Even if a parent attempts to make up before you do, you may hold on to your anger as if it were a life raft saving you from the sinking *Titanic*. With loyalties running amok, anger may be all you have connecting you to your parents. Ridding yourself of your anger would make you feel less connected to the unfolding drama. Parents don't have to *explain* things to a child who goes along with their decisions. But if you're against them, they do.

Being mad at a parent brings us closer to them, as twisted as it may sound. "We are desperately tied to that we avoid," writes Finley.

In grade school, remember how the little boys would tease the little girls on whom they had crushes? A boy doesn't know how to act lovey-dovey toward a girl, so he incites her. Then he feels connected to her.

We do the same with our parents. If we don't feel loved by Mom, we get mad at her just so we can feel her get angry back. Then we know we're loved. Her anger proves to us she cares. "It's common for people going through the pain of divorce to maintain their anger stance because it enables them to at least remain connected to the relationship in some way; they'd rather have a horrible relationship . . . than no relationship at all," writes Finley.

Luke, thirty-seven, talks often about how angry he is with his father. Luke was at college when his parents split up. Years later, Luke has only seen his dad a handful of times. He hates his father for leaving and for treating him terribly when Luke was growing up. His father has reached out to him once or twice over the years, asking Luke to dinner. They always end up bickering about things unrelated to the divorce.

Luke may not realize how much his anger has insulated him. He's too mad to feel anything deeper, too angry to ask himself questions such as: Why doesn't Dad call me? Doesn't he care about me? In arguing with his father, he stays connected to his father—without having to deal with the problems between them. Anger has welded an armor around Luke's heart. He doesn't have to feel anything else.

Sorting through your anger is the only way to move on. You don't have to forgive. You don't have to forget. But you do have to stop being mad. Holding on to your anger makes you act as your own oppressor. You are probably so used to your negative feelings that you no longer know how to live without them. Only you know what you're angry about, and only you can choose to confront it. Writes Elizabeth O'Connor in *Cry Pain, Cry Hope*, "Holding even a small grudge takes up space in the soul and captures the energy needed for moving on."

You're going to be OK. I say this to you with confidence because Teresa Cooney, a family sociologist at the University of Wisconsin, said it to me. Cooney studied the impact of divorce on adult children in 1983. Ten years later, she went back and interviewed many of the same individuals to see how they had fared. "The ones who were really struggling when I first interviewed them still are," Cooney says. "But the good news is that their struggles aren't necessarily directly related to the divorce." Adult children who weren't faring well had another obstacle, such as a parent's alcohol problem or attempted suicide, holding them back—problems that existed *before* the divorce. The divorce itself didn't haunt them.

Here's another reason to smile: the majority of individuals in the study were doing well ten years later. Over time, their emotional health improved. They found relationships they felt good about. They moved on.

Talk to anyone whose parents' divorced several years ago, and you'll hear a much different account of their grief. "It feels like such a big deal right at first," said a colleague I'll call Jean. "I felt like my world was ending, too. But I can't tell you how little I think about my parents' divorce now." Jean's parents divorced when she was in her twenties. She turned forty a year ago. "Want to hear something wild?" she says, standing in my office. "My mother is good friends with my stepmother. They get together and talk on the phone. Mom comes over to Dad's during holidays."

People evolve. So do situations. Life. In the first couple of years after a divorce, adult children cannot imagine their parents in the same room together. Ten years from now—even five years—your life will have taken greater shape. You may be living in a different city and working at a different job. You may have bought your own house. Life will have carried on, regardless of what happened during the divorce. Your parents will have moved on as well.

Some parents hold a grudge against their exes for a lifetime, but most don't. Your parents will someday learn to coexist. But ultimately, their lives will no longer include the other. And you'll get used to that, too.

I read once that moving on is the period in which the knot of your grief is untied. So let yourself unfurl. Open yourself up for renewal. You'll soon realize you've been changing all along. You're a different person as a result of the divorce, and so are your parents. You've become strangers to one another in a sense, but as time goes on, you'll grow accustomed to one another's changes. Years from now, you'll feel light-years away from all these transformations. You will just be you, and your parents will just be Mom and Dad.

You will never have closure. Unlike a death, there is no formal ceremony to help you put your parents' loss behind you. There is no organized way to say good-bye. Some of us find creative ways to try. A few individuals have created personal Web pages and dedicated them to their families. They post their thoughts and offer advice. They use the site as a forum for good-bye, holding a virtual funeral, of sorts, via the Internet.

One Web site begins with a gravestone marker: "The Cherepon Family, 1973–1997." The twenty-something woman, Sue, who created the site, searched for some kind of moment to mark her parents' divorce. Many of us are accustomed to the slow unraveling of our families, but Sue was frustrated by it. She wanted one moment to help her say good-bye. Sue decided to lay her family to rest. She gathered items such as her father's old coffee cup, the top piece of her parents' wedding cake, a picture of her family. She wrote a letter and put it, along with the items, in a large tin, and buried it next to a tree behind her parents' house. She said a prayer. She put flowers on the grave. "Something concrete was done to symbolize the end for my family," she writes on her Web site. "It really helped."

Saying good-bye often means leaving childhood homes behind. But soon enough, you'll realize that four walls and a roof aren't what make a home special. It's the furniture and the photographs, the artwork and the knickknacks—and the way they're all put together—that make a house a home. It's the people who greet you when you walk in the front door. And all of this will be replicated, even in a new neighborhood, house, or condo—even if there is a stepparent there to share it with you.

After you move on, you'll be forever drawn to places you once called home. It's why you spontaneously find yourself parked in front of your old college apartment or walking through the halls of your former high school. These places call out to us every so often. Inside, we can hear echoes of who we were and see how different we've become.

Melinda, who has grown close to her stepmother, drove by her childhood home recently. Her parents sold the house when they divorced several years ago. When Melinda pulled up in front of her old house, she noticed a For Sale sign out front. Another sign read, Open House. Melinda watched couples walking in and out. She decided to take a look.

Melinda was touched by all the changes. The house had been built in 1830. Melinda's family had never had a lot of money to refurbish it. Whoever bought the house had restored it. She noticed the kitchen had new wallpaper and new appliances, something her mother used to dream of. It had new windows. The attic and basement had been renovated. Melinda peeked in her bedroom. It was a guest room now.

The couple selling the house approached her. They asked

whether she was interested in the house. "I used to live here," Melinda told them. "I just want to look around." The couple got excited. They had lots of questions. "What did you have in this room?" they asked. Melinda walked through and told the couple how the house was different when she was a child. "It's interesting to see all of the progress," Melinda said. She felt like a part of the house's history.

Then Melinda walked out back and saw the trees. On the day Melinda was born, her grandfather had planted a dogwood tree and a magnolia tree in the backyard. Her sister's birth had inspired a pear tree and a cherry tree. All the trees were thriving.

Melinda used to fantasize about getting married at this house and bringing her own children there. She felt a tinge of sadness, then shook it off. *Remaining bitter about the loss of something gets you nowhere*, she thought. *I need to be happy that a nice family was buying this home and that a nice family once lived here.* "The memories aren't gone," says Melinda.

Besides, Melinda makes new memories every day. She has her own life now: a great job at a New York City publishing house, a guy for whom she has fallen.

We hold on to the past because we're afraid to let go. But somewhere along the way, we'll experience a moment when the present comes into focus . . . and then disappears into time. We watch memories, pain, resentments, even changes . . . fade. We realize we were our pasts. We have been for too long.

Now we must be our futures.

In September 2004, my older sister, Erin, announces she is pregnant. It is surprising news. She and her husband have always hedged if we ask whether they are "trying." We trade rounds of phone calls all day long.

Dad, always the worrier, calls to say he is nervous the baby will cause Erin and her husband financial strain. "There's never a good time to have a baby," I tell him. Dad reluctantly agrees and then admits he'd love it if Erin has a little girl. "Little girls are so cute," Dad says. Then Erin and I speak about the delivery. She fears the pushing and squeezing, and we ponder the wonders of giving a baby its first breath. Then Chelsea calls to say she is going to kiss Erin's belly every time she sees her.

I get Mom when she's in the car on her way home from work. She is thrilled, too. She says the news still hasn't sunk in. "Are you going to let the baby call you grandma?" I tease. "We'll think of something," Mom says. We talk about my old cradle and how Erin should decorate the baby's nursery. We imagine buying the baby itty-bitty sneakers and joke about how we'll all be fighting to babysit.

"I'm just so glad we have something to look forward to now," Mom says. "I mean after all we've been through. We can just move on."

We are all ready to. With the divorce dragging on for three years and ending only two months ago, our family is searching for a new beginning. A baby will give us something else on which to focus our attention. Mom and I feel as if we are being handed a gift: a little bundle of smiles to help us forget all our frowns.

The baby will never know my parents together, which breaks my heart. She'll never know what it was like to watch Dad loop his arms around Mom's waist while she did dishes or see Mom talk hopefully with Dad at our old kitchen table. But the baby won't need to. She'll have her own parents. My sister and her husband can pick up on parenting where Mom and Dad left off. And the baby will get to know us as we are now—people who love one another no matter how we organize ourselves.

These days, I don't cry about my parents' divorce. I don't think about their split much at all. Who my parents have become, and who

I've become to them, feels normal to me. I am best friends with both of them. I require less coddling from them. And my parents and I are as natural in these roles as we were in our former ones. A few weeks ago, Mom and I talked for an hour about why she broke up with her boyfriend. Last year, I would've felt betrayed hearing about her feelings for someone else. Now I'm just so thankful that I have Mom back. That we're close again.

I thought I'd be sad when I walked through my childhood home over the summer. The rooms were empty. Dad had drop cloths and paint cans scattered through each bedroom. A new bathtub was being installed. My things—stuffed animals, books, prom dresses—were packed in boxes in the basement. Several months ago, I would've been in tears.

But the sight of Dad futzing around the yard made everything feel right again. He showed me where he had planted grass seed. In the living room, he pointed to the skylights he had installed and turned on a band of track lighting. We sat on the back deck and talked about his plans for the house and my plans for the future.

Mom got what she wanted in the divorce. Now Dad had, too. For three years, he'd been expelled from my childhood home. Now he could come and go as he pleased. And while he wasn't planning to live there, buying that house was something I think he needed to do to reclaim his place with my sisters and me. "I'm keeping this house for you girls," Dad told me. "I want you to be able to bring your children up here and spend summers."

For too long, I forgot what it was like to feel calm. I was so used to carrying around my anger that I didn't realize how big it had become. I was used to feeling nauseous when I visited home. I was used to beads of sweat forming on my brow every time Mom called to vent about Dad. Moving on from my parents' divorce released me from all the negativity in which I was tangled. I am no longer chained to my anger. Every moment feels as if I were running through a field or floating above the clouds. I've returned to my own life.

I visit my childhood home often. I sit and talk with Dad while he works on the house. I don't feel nostalgic for the past when I'm there. Dad's renovations make it seem like a new space—and the emptiness echoes nothing of family. But I do feel as if something from my childhood has been protected for me in that house. That although I've put my parents' divorce behind me, I don't have to *completely* let go. A piece of me will always be preserved in those walls, in the shadows that dance across my childhood bedroom at dusk.

Select Bibliography

BOOKS

Ahrons, Constance. *The Good Divorce: Keeping Your Family Together When Your Marriage Comes Apart*. New York: HarperCollins, 1994.

Benedict, Ruth. *Patterns of Culture*. Boston: Mariner, 1989.

Conley, Dalton. *The Pecking Order: Which Siblings Succeed and Why*. New York: Pantheon, 2004.

Dychtwald, Ken. *The Power Years: A User's Guide to the Rest of Your Life*. Hoboken, N. J.: Wiley, 2005.

Fielding, Helen. *Bridget Jones's Diary*. New York: Penguin, 1999.

Finley, Guy. *The Secret of Letting Go*. St. Paul, Minn.: Llewellyn, 1990.

Friday, Nancy. *My Mother My Self*. New York: Delta, 1977.

Gabe, Grace, and Jean Lipman-Blumen. *Step Wars*. New York: St. Martin's Press, 2004.

Hetherington, E. Mavis, and John Kelly. *For Better or for Worse: Divorce Reconsidered*. New York: Norton, 2002.

hooks, bell. *Communion: The Female Search for Love*. New York: Perennial, 2002.

LeBey, Barbara. *Family Estrangements: How They Begin, How to Mend Them, How to Cope with Them*. New York: Bantam, 2001.

Lerner, Harriet. *The Dance of Intimacy*. New York: Perennial, 1990.

Paul, Pamela. *The Starter Marriage and the Future of Matrimony*. New York: Villard Books, 2002.

Pittman, Frank. *Private Lies: Infidelity and the Betrayal of Intimacy*. Reprint ed. New York: Norton, 1990.

Trafford, Abigail. *My Time: Making the Most of the Rest of Your Life*. New York: Basic Books, 2004.

Trollope, Joanna. *Marrying the Mistress*. New York: Berkley, 2000.

Vaughn, Peggy. *The Monogamy Myth*. 3rd ed. New York: Newmarket Press, 2003.

ARTICLES

Beach, Patrick. "Are the Bride and Groom Doomed?" *Baltimore Sun*, October 26, 2003, 4N.

Bulcroft, Kris A., and Richard A. Bulcroft. "The Timing of Divorce: Effects on Parent-Child Relationships in Later Life." *Research on Aging* 13, no. 2 (1991): 226–243.

Cantley-Falk, Rebeccah. "Adult Children Find Ways to Deal with Parents' Divorces." *Herald-Dispatch*, October 30, 2003.

Clarke, Sally C. "Advance Report of Final Divorce Statistics, 1989 and 1990." *Monthly Vital Statistics Report* 43, no. 9 (March 1995). National Center for Health Statistics, Hyattsville, Md.

Cooney, Teresa M. "Leaving Home and Coming Back: The Impact of Recent Parental Divorce and Family Dynamics on Young Adults' Residential Transitions." *Sociological Studies of Children* 6 (1994): 159–179.

———. "Young Adults and Parental Divorce: Exploring Important Issues." *Human Relations* 41, no. 11 (1988): 805–822.

———. "Young Adults' Relations with Parents: The Influence of Recent Parental Divorce." *Journal of Marriage and Family* 56 (February 1994): 45–56.

Cooney, Teresa M., M. K. Hutchinson, and D. M. Leather. "Surviving the Breakup? Predictors of Parent–Adult Child Relations after Parental Divorce." *Family Relations* 44 (April 1995): 153–161.

Cooney, Teresa M., and Jane Kurz. "Mental Health Outcomes Following Recent Parental Divorce: The Case of Young Adult Offspring." *Journal of Family Issues* 17, no. 4 (1996): 495–513.

Cooney, Teresa M., and Lori Ann Smith. "Young Adults' Relations with Grandparents Following Recent Parental Divorce." *Journal of Gerontology* 51B, no. 2 (1996): S91–S95.

Cooney, Teresa M., M. A. Smyer, G. O. Hagestad, and R. Klock. "Parental

Divorce in Young Adulthood: Some Preliminary Findings." *American Journal of Orthopsychiatry* 56, no. 3 (July 1986): 470–477.

Enright, Elizabeth. "A House Divided." *AARP: The Magazine.* July–August 2004.

Fabricius, William V., Sanford L. Braver, Kindra Deneau, et al. "Divorced Parents' Financial Support of Their Children's College Expenses." *Children of Divorced, Separated, and Never-Married Families* (Spring 2004): 10–16.

Hiedemann, Bridget, Olga Suhomlinova, and Angela M. O'Rand. "Economic Independence, Economic Status, and Empty Nest in Midlife Marital Disruption." *Journal of Marriage and Family* 60 (1998): 219–231.

Konigsberg, Ruth Davis. "A More Perfect Union?" *Elle*, 2002.

Mahoney, Sarah. "Seeking Love." *AARP: The Magazine.* November–December 2003.

Montenegro, Xenia P. "The Divorce Experience: A Study of Divorce at Midlife and Beyond," May 2004. www.aarp.org.

Peterson, Karen S. "Families Split but Kids Survive." *USA Today*, June 6, 2004, 8D.

Pett, Marjorie A., Nancy Long, and Anita Gander. "Late-Life Divorce: Its Impact on Family Rituals." *Journal of Family Issues* 13, no. 4 (December 1992): 526–552.

Shapiro, Adam. "Later-Life Divorce and Parent–Adult Child Proximity." *Journal of Family Issues* 24, no. 2 (2003): 264–285.

Sweeney, Jennifer. "What's the Secret to Marital Success? It's in the Numbers." *Health*, October 2004, 97–100.

Webster, Pamela S., and A. Regula Herzog. "Effects of Parental Divorce and Memories of Family Problems on Relationships between Adult Children and Their Parents." *Journal of Gerontology* 50B, no. 1 (1995): S24–S34.

White, Lynn. "The Effect of Parental Divorce and Remarriage on Parental Support for Adult Children." *Journal of Family Issues* 13, no. 2 (1992): 234–250.

Whitehead, Barbara Defoe, and David Popenoe. "The State of Our Unions," 1999, 2001. The National Marriage Project. http://marriage.rutgers.edu/.

Index

AARP: The Magazine, 197

Abandonment issues, 25, 27, 53, 59, 166, 245

Alcestis (Euripides), 175

Alcohol use, 7, 29, 41

Allegiances, shifting, 93–97

American Association of Retired Persons (AARP), 8, 197

American Beauty (film), 202

Anger, 26, 28, 33, 36, 37, 146, 213, 216–217, 224, 234, 273, 275, 280–281, 289 (*see also* Parental divorce)

Arguments (*see* Fighting and arguments)

Bargaining stage of grief, 36

Belonging, loss of sense of, 4

Benedict, Ruth, 277–278

Benning, Annette, 202

Birky, Ian, 204, 207, 211, 224, 227

Boundary setting, 75–79, 82

Bridge affair, 199

Bridget Jones's Diary (Fielding), 11, 242

Brothers and Sisters (Leder), 141

Caregiver roles, 5

Caught in the middle, 2–3, 5–6, 83–117

Centers for Disease Control and Prevention, 251

Cheating (*see* Infidelity)

Childhood homes, sale of, 11, 26, 45, 46, 249, 285–286

Childhood memories, 6, 23–24, 34–35, 43, 169, 204, 208, 230, 275–276, 285–286

Christmas, 38, 52, 74, 133–135

Cinderella, 175

Cohabitation, 249–250

Communion: The Female Search for Love (hooks), 9

Confessions of an Ugly Stepsister (Maguire), 76

Confidants, 65, 81

Conley, Dalton, 114

Cooney, Teresa, 12, 21, 60, 112, 116, 137–138, 283

Cry Pain, Cry Hope (O'Connor), 282–283

Custody decisions, 6, 137, 146

Dance of Intimacy, The (Lerner), 147

Dating, 155–164, 170–172

Death of a Salesman (Miller), 269

Denial, 32, 36, 207

Depression and anxiety, 5, 39–40, 43, 90

Despair stage of grief, 36

"Destabilizer" adult child, 167–168

Dickey, Christopher, 193

Disney films, 242

"Distancer" adult child, 167–168

Divorce (*see also* Parental divorce)
adversarial, 57, 81, 91, 105–107, 124–125
age at, 8
increase in, 8
lawyers, 57
rates, 248–249

"Divorce Education" (Walton), 29

Drug use, 39–40

Dychtwald, Ken, 9

Emery, Robert, 21, 23, 76, 260–261

Estrangements, 79, 97, 148–154, 213, 224

Euripides, 175

Extended family members, 121–128

Family Estrangements: How They Begin, How to Mend Them, How to Cope with Them (LeBey), 147, 149–150, 152

Fay, Laurel, 204, 207, 214, 215, 227, 230, 232, 243

Fielding, Helen, 11, 45

Fighting and arguments, 7, 29, 32, 45–46, 88–89, 104, 111, 241, 253, 257, 259

Financial issues, 62, 64, 93–94, 105–112, 114–116, 148, 166, 169, 177–178, 251

Finley, Guy, 277, 281

First Wives Club, The (film), 202

Forgiveness, 37, 38, 231

Frost, Robert, 6

Gabe, Grace, 166–168, 176

Girls' Guide to Hunting and Fishing, The (Banks), 242

"Gods and Fathers" (Gusumano), 119

Gottman, John, 197, 259

Graduate, The (film), 49

Greece, ancient, 23

Grief, 3–4, 9–12, 20–22, 25, 273–277, 28, 36–43 (*see also* Parental divorce)

Grimm brothers, 175

Gusumano, Camille, 119

Harvard University, 279

Hawn, Goldie, 202

Headaches, 39

Health magazine, 259

Helplessness, sense of, 39

Holidays, 6, 38, 52, 74, 119–123, 133–135, 144, 145, 149, 171, 184–186, 191

Honeymoon period, 170

hooks, bell, 9

Household responsibilities, 60–63

How to Make an American Quilt (Otto), 1

Human Relations journal, 112

Idealization, 29, 30

Identity, loss of, 19

Infidelity, 19, 35, 38, 56, 66, 67, 77, 95–96, 102, 108, 172, 193–236
Information swapping, 100–101, 117
Inheritances, 4, 108, 166, 169
Irritability, 39

Jane magazine, 244
Jealousy, 70, 101, 140
"Joiner" adult child, 167–168
Journal of Divorce and Remarriage, 253
Journal of Family Issues, 39, 197
Journal of Marriage and Family, 137

Keaton, Diane, 11, 202
Kincaid, Jamaica, 83
Kin keepers, 142
Kipling, Rudyard, 206–207

Lahiri, Jhumpa, 15
Lane, Diane, 202
"Leaving and returning" phase, 13, 27, 32–33, 56
"Leaving story," 25–27
LeBey, Barbara, 147, 149–150, 152
Leder, Jane Mersky, 141
Lehigh University, 204
Lerner, Harriet, 147
Lipman-Blumen, Jean, 166–168, 176
Loneliness and isolation, 40
Longevity, 9
Loss, sense of, 20–21
Lost-nest generation, 8, 11
Love, lasting, 238–246, 254–255, 263–267
Lucy (Kincaid), 83

Magical reconciliation fantasy, 90–93, 117

Maguire, Gregory, 76
Markman, Howard, 259
Marriage, (*see also* Divorce; Parental divorce)
    cultural views of, 9
    fighting and arguments, 7, 29, 32, 45–46, 88–89, 104, 111, 241, 253, 257, 259
    image of marital perfection, 28–31
    longevity of, 28–29
    therapists, 11–12
Marrying the Mistress (Trollope), 11, 202–203
Midler, Bette, 202
Midlife crisis, 56, 160
Miller, Arthur, 269
Mimic Men, The (Naipaul), 55
Monogamy Myth, The (Vaughan), 197
Mythology, 23
My Time: Making the Most of the Rest of Your Life (Trafford), 9

Naipaul, V. S., 55
National Center for Health Statistics, 8
National Marriage Project (NMP), Rutgers University, 8, 9, 252
Nerburn, Kent, 237
Newsweek magazine, 197
New York magazine, 8
Nicholson, Jack, 11
Nietzsche, Friedrich, 145

O'Connor, Elizabeth, 282–283
Oral history, 24
Otto, Whitney, 1

Paltrow, Gwyneth, 202

Parental divorce
    boundary setting and, 75–79, 82
    caught in the middle and, 2–3, 5–6,
        83–117
    estrangements and, 79, 97, 148–154,
        213, 224
    extended family members and,
        121–128
    financial issues and, 4, 62, 64,
        93–94, 105–112, 114–116, 148,
        166, 169, 177–178, 251
    holidays and, 6, 19, 38, 52, 74,
        119–123, 133–135, 144, 145, 149,
        171, 184–186, 191
    impact on marriages of adult
        children and, 247–261, 267
    lack of information on, 10–12
    "leaving and returning" phase and,
        13, 32–33, 56
    "leaving story" and, 25–27
    news of, 15–19
    reconciliation fantasy and, 90–93,
        117
    relations within subfamilies and,
        136–143, 153
    renegotiation period and, 59–60
    role reversal and, 48, 50–80, 123,
        163–164
    shifting allegiances and, 93–97
    sibling relationships and, 140–147,
        153
    special events (celebrations) and,
        128–133
    staying together for the kids and,
        3–4, 7–8, 34–35, 43
    vesions of the truth and, 103–105,
        117
Patterns of Culture (Benedict), 277–278

Paul, Pamela, 251
Pecking Order, The: Which Siblings
        Succeed and Why (Conley), 114
Pennsylvania State University, 71
"Perfect" family, 28–31, 33–34, 43
Perfect Murder, A (film), 202
Pittman, Frank, 225, 227
Porter, Katherine Anne, 214
Poverty, 62
Power Years, The: A User's Guide to the
        Rest of Your Life (Dychtwald), 9
Prenuptial agreements, 251
Private Lives: Infidelity and the Betrayal
        of Intimacy (Pittman), 225

Reconciliation fantasy, 90–93, 117
Regressive behavior, 56, 81
Relationship Research Institute, Seattle,
        197
Remarriage, 6, 41, 166–167, 171, 189,
        220–222 (see also Stepfamilies)
Renegotiation period, 59–60
Role reversal, 48, 50–80, 123, 163–164
Romantic mythology, 242–246
Rutgers University, National Marriage
        Project (NMP), 8, 9, 252
Ryan, Meg, 244–245

Secret of Letting Go, The (Finley), 277
Secrets, 35, 65, 140, 196, 209–212,
        236
Sibling relationships, 140–147, 153
Signs, 138
Simple Truths (Nerburn), 237
Sleepless in Seattle (film), 244
Sleep problems, 39
Something's Gotta Give (film), 111
Special events (celebrations), 128–133

Starter Marriage and the Future of Matrimony, The (Paul), 251
Steamroller effect, 172, 191–192
Steinem, Gloria, 137
Stepfamilies, 155–192
Step Wars (Gabe and Lumen), 166–168, 176
Stone, Julia, 242, 246, 250, 252, 253, 255
Stress, regressive behavior and, 56, 81
Subfamilies, relationships within, 136–143, 153, 169–170
Suicidal thoughts, 41, 73–74
Summer of Deliverance (Dickey), 193
Support groups, 68, 69

"Temporary Matter, A" (Lahiri), 15
Tessina, Tina, 210
Thanksgiving, 119–123, 133, 144, 145
Time Traveler's Wife, The (Niffenegger), 265

Trafford, Abigail, 9
Trollope, Joanna, 11, 202–203
Truth, versions of, 103–105, 117

Under the Tuscan Sun (film), 23
Unfaithful (film), 202
University of Chicago, 197
University of Missouri, 12, 21
University of North Carolina–Chapel Hill, 7, 112
University of Virginia, 260
University of Washington, 259

Vaughan, Peggy, 197
Viagra, 9

Walton, Anthony, 29
Washingtonian, 10
Wizard of Oz, The (Baum), 277

Years Between, The (Kipling), 206–207
You've Got Mail (film), 244

About the Author

BROOKE LEA FOSTER is a graduate of the University of Maryland and a staff writer for the *Washingtonian*. She has contributed to *Good Housekeeping*, *Parents*, *Reader's Digest*, *Psychology Today*, and the *Baltimore Sun*, among other publications. In 2005, she was a finalist for the Livingston Award, the premier award for journalists under the age of thirty-five. She lives in Washington, D.C.